D1091042

modern greece

modern greece

Profile of a Nation

D. George Kousoulas

CHARLES SCRIBNER'S SONS, New York

Map by Robert Sugar

Photographs on pp. 139–43, 176–85, 252–57
by David O. Johnson

Library of Congress Cataloging in Publication Data
Kousoulas, Dimitrios George, 1923–
Modern Greece.
Bibliography: p.
1. Greece, Modern—History—1821–   I. Title.
DF802.K69   949.5'06   73-1319
ISBN 0-684-13731-3 (pbk.)
ISBN 0-684-13732-1

1 3 5 7 9 11 13 15 17 19 c/c 20 18 16 14 12 10 8 6 4 2
1 3 5 7 9 11 13 15 17 19 c/p 20 18 16 14 12 10 8 6 4 2

Printed in the United States of America

To my son George

contents

preface

This book is intended to be a fairly impartial, informative, yet lively history of modern Greece. My own familiarity with the subject is, I think, in many ways unique. In addition to extensive research in written sources I was able to gain information and insight through talks with major political leaders and other key personalities in Greece—former Prime Ministers C. Karamanlis, P. Kanellopoulos, S. Stefanopoulos, leading political personalities such as S. Markezinis, G. Mavros, C. Mitsotakis, A. Papandreou, P. Vardinoyiannis, as well as top leaders of the 1967–73 military regime, G. Papadopoulos, O. Angelis, S. Pattakos, N. Makarezos, and many others including former members of the legislature, journalists, educators, economists, businessmen, labor leaders, and plain citizens. Several aspects of the story, especially those which refer to the last fifty years, include information that appears in English for the first time. I hope the reader will enjoy this unfolding of a nation's record, from its heroic reemergence in 1821 to the present.

I wish to express my appreciation to Professor Goldwin Smith, who suggested me as the author of this book; Elsie Kearns, history editor of Scribners, who accepted the suggestion; Barbara Wood, who skillfully guided the text through the editorial processing; and my wife Mary who suffered through the writing of still another book.

My thanks also go to all those valuable friends who shared their knowledge and insights with me, the other authors who have ploughed the field before, and Howard University, which lightened the financial burden.

introduction

The Origins . . .

To write a history of modern Greece, one can start conveniently with the War of Independence in 1821 and then move on through the years, using geography and ethnic identity as reliable guidelines. But the historian who aspires to trace the unfolding of Greek history through the centuries will find that he has set for himself an almost impossible task. Not geography, nor religion, nor ethnic purity can guide his steps. In fact, to cope with the mercurial quality of Greek history, he may find that instead of starting with the "beginning" he has to go backwards in time and like the archaeologist unearth one layer and then another, probing further and further into the past until he reaches a point where the historical record begins to blur with legend—and then he must leave open the possibility that others in the future may uncover still another layer hidden below the surface and thus transform legend into history.

Far in the past, almost four thousand years ago, are the uncertain shadows of the Pelasgians, the early inhabitants of the rugged mountains and enchanting seashores that later would take the name

of Hellas from Hellen, the son of mythical Deucalion, who like
Noah survived the flood and with his wife Pyrrha—so the legend
goes—gave a new start to the human race. But these are the
centuries of myth and conjecture. History really begins with the
great invaders from the north, the Achaeans and later the Dorians
who began pouring into the peninsula almost two thousand years
before the birth of Christ. For the next thousand years, the strains of
several cultures came together and there, under the clear sky, they
were given a new force and direction. With the Mycenaeans, the
most famous of the Achaeans immortalized in Homer's epics, and
the Minoan Cretans before them—legends until the spade of the
archaeologist in Troy and Knossos made myth a part of history—we
can begin to trace the proven record carved in stone and marble.

Out of the mixture of blood and spirit, a new form of civilization
was born unlike any that existed before. It valued open inquiry and
had respect for the individual, a passion for beauty, and a devotion
to intellectual excellence. In gestation for several centuries, it came
to full bloom in the fifth century B.C., the period usually associated
with "the glory that was Greece"—the time of Marathon and
Salamis, the time of Socrates, Plato, and Aristotle, the time of the
great dramatists, a miracle of the mind that was finally consumed by
the fires of the Peloponnesian war. But out of the ashes of that futile
struggle, the Hellenic race rose again to new heights with Alexander's
dazzling sweep through history. Until his time, daring colonists had
carried the Greek culture to the far corners of the Mediterranean,
but it was only since Alexander that the territorial boundaries of
Greek history were no longer confined to the traditional peninsula.
For more than two thousand years—between the third century B.C.
and the eighteenth century A.D.—Greece was above all a cultural
entity, a state of mind, not a clearly definable territory or even a
distinguishable ethnic group.

When the Romans spread their rule from Italy to the borders of
Persia and the banks of the Nile, they found a world of "Greekness,"
a Hellenistic world, with classical culture and the Greek language
dominant among the educated elites throughout the Orient. Rome's
political dominion did not dislodge or submerge this Greek civilization; if anything, the Romans preserved and strengthened it as the
unifying element of their eastern empire. But with the advent of
Christianity, especially in the early centuries after the birth of Christ,
classical "Greekness" was already in competition with Christian

"Greekness." During those centuries of transition from paganism to Christianity, the use of the Greek language by the Eastern church gave a new dimension to Greek culture.

When Constantine the Great moved his capital from Rome to the site of ancient Byzantium in 325 A.D., the church in the Orient already had a Greek identity. It took three centuries, from the fourth to the seventh, for the preeminence of Greek culture to become a source of political power; but in the end the impact of Greekness proved irresistible. For the next seven centuries, until the fall of Constantinople in 1453, the Greek language and culture, refashioned by Christianity, formed the sinews of the multi-ethnic Byzantine Empire. During those seven centuries, Byzantine and Greek history were virtually inseparable, and one can keep his search in focus only by thinking in terms of cultural rather than ethnic identity. In fact, ever since the days of Alexander, being "Greek" was more a question of culture than a matter of biology. For centuries, the uninhibited mixing with other groups, the easy acceptance of those who chose to be "Greek" through the infusion of culture, and the incursions of foreign tribes from the Slavic north had altered any biological purity the Greeks might have had in classical times—although enough must have been preserved in the genes to account for the startling similarities to classical features so many Greek men and women possess today.

With the dismantling of the Byzantine Empire, the faith of Islam spread over the old citadels of Christianity and a new culture pushed Hellenism back to its earlier confines. Only scattered elements remained in the Orient. For the next four centuries, the fifteenth to the eighteenth, the Greeks, reduced under the Ottoman domination to a vassal race of mostly ignorant peasants, kept only a dim awareness of their glorious past through the memories passed from generation to generation. Slowly, they began to recover their sense of destiny and in 1821 they resumed their march through history.

Few of today's nations can boast such a long, continuous existence. Unlike the Chinese who have race and culture or the Jews who have religion to bind them together, the Greeks have had no single, unchanging element of identity that a historian might use as his connecting theme. What then? How can one speak of continuity? There is one element that seems to transcend all other aspects of identity. It is the belief in being "Greek." In the nineteenth century and the early part of the twentieth, the Greek government tried to extend its sovereignty over all adjacent lands inhabited by those who believed themselves to be Greek. The effort had its moments of triumph and fulfillment, but it finally ended in 1922 with the Asia Minor catastrophe. Since that time the Greek nation-state has taken in the main its present form. Today Greece is one of the most homogeneous states in the world. Still another version of a Greek diaspora has appeared. Greeks can now be found in many parts of the world; whatever their formal citizenship, they share in this feeling of Greekness.

However undefinable, elusive, or in constant movement and change it may be, this feeling is real. It makes all those thousands of years appear to a Greek as near and contemporary as today. Classical Greece, Byzantium, the War of Independence, are placed side by side on a single visual plane without receding shades of color. The battle of Marathon, thus, is not a long-forgotten incident that took place twenty-three centuries ago, but rather a living moment of national glory that can inspire pride and lead to heroic deeds as though the heroes of Marathon were still alive and watching the performance of their sons.

These ties with the past, an inseparable part of being Greek, continue to shape the thinking of today's Greeks; and their story which unfolds in the pages of this book can be better understood when seen as a sequel to that long record sketched ever so briefly in this introductory note.

modern greece

chapter 1
The Legacies of the Past

The rebirth of a nation

Throughout the year 1820 the air over the Greek peninsula was heavy with anticipation. In the mountain villages and the small towns in the valleys below, landowners and bishops, peasants, shepherds, and artisans, brigands, sailors, and monks traded rumors of things to come. Visitors from the prospering communities of the Greek diaspora as far away as Paris, Vienna, and Odessa were bringing tidings of hope. The day of delivery from Turkish rule, they claimed, was near. Almost four centuries had passed since May 29, 1453, the day the conquering armies of Sultan Mohammed had breached the walls of Constantinople and thus ended more than a thousand years of Byzantine history. In the following centuries, Turkish hegemony spread over the lands where Byzantium once ruled. The Greeks, who previously held the levers of power in the empire, became a vassal people, most of whom were ignorant and reduced to poverty. The more fortunate among them fled to Europe and Russia, where they planted the communities of Greek diaspora. For four hundred years after that, while Europe was experiencing the exhilarating awakening of the Renaissance, the Greeks went through their own belated version of the Dark Ages. During this period of adversity they almost lost their sense of identity; to the Turk, they were part of the faceless mass of infidels, and to themselves, *Romioi* (a corrupted pronunciation of the Greek word for Roman). For three centuries, little of significance occurred to record in the annals of history. Then, during the closing decades of the eighteenth century the Greeks reemerged in history with a strong awareness of their national heritage and uniqueness.

This revival of national spirit was not a sudden flash of inspiration. Many forces had long been at work—some fostered unintentionally by the Turks themselves. The Orthodox church, probably the most important among these forces, owed the Greek character it had maintained under the Turks to a fortuitous action by Sultan Mohammed. Soon after entering Constantinople, he had appointed a Greek by the name of Georgios Scholarios as the new patriarch of all Orthodox Christians in the conquered lands. What the sultan wanted was to set up a convenient channel of control over his new subjects; at the same time, considering the deep hatred between Orthodoxy and the Vatican, he was cleverly thinking of erecting a barrier between his Christian subjects and the Catholic West. Yet, his gesture was to have unintended and far-reaching consequences. It reinforced the notion long maintained by Greeks that they were the heirs of Byzantium, and it vested the church with administrative and judicial authority over the Christians that was to prove critical for the future. The church became a focus of identity and a barrier to assimilation with the Turks, while the Orthodox faith and the Greek language—both of which were taught by the clergy—were to serve in the course of time as the sinews of national identity.

Several other seemingly unrelated factors paved the way toward a resurgence of national spirit. Trade was one of these. The Turkish conquerors regarded trade as being too humble an occupation for proud soldiers. Before long, Greeks in the occupied lands, working closely with their compatriots in Europe and Russia, had taken over most commercial activities, amassing fortunes in the process and building a tradition of independence and self-assertion that would later play a pivotal role. Trade went hand in hand with transport. In 1803 Greek shipping was estimated at 131,000 tons with more than 16,000 sailors aboard. Shipowning families in the islands became wealthy during the Napoleonic wars when their boats braved the British blockade for a high price. Moreover, most of the sultan's navy was manned with crews from the islands since the Turks generally disliked the sea. When later, at the time of the War of Independence, these sailors deserted their posts, control of sea communications in the Aegean passed to the Greek insurgents. On land, the warlike spirit was kept alive by the *klephts*—the celebrated brigands who harassed the wealthy Turks in Robin Hood style—and the *armatoles*—local Greeks commissioned by the Ottoman authorities to keep order in their areas but who often took to the mountains and joined the klephts against the Turkish overlords.

Even fate seemed to take a hand. In 1699 the Venetians seized from the Turks most of southern Greece. The Turks returned sixteen years later but by then the feudal system that they had initially set up was gone, destroyed in the upheaval of the Venetian conquest. Their efforts to revive it failed. A law, which in the past had blocked the transfer of Moslem lands to infidels, was conveniently ignored by corrupt administrators who, for a price, turned feudal fiefs into private estates. In the eighteenth century, Greek landowners made their appearance in the Peloponnisos and in Central Greece. Land ownership became a source of power. Strong ties of dependence were forged between the landlord and the poor peasants who tilled his lands as sharecroppers. Moreover, the need for safety, and the craggy, mountainous terrain, forced rich and poor alike to live side by side in villages. There were no manorial houses overlooking sprawling fields as in Western Europe; life centered in the villages and the small towns, where religious ritual dominated social life.

This provincial, rustic life in the Greek peninsula was worlds apart from that of the sophisticated *Phanariots*—named after Constantinople's quarter where most of them lived. These Greeks, through one of those curious accidents of history, had come to hold many exalted positions in the administration of the Ottoman Empire by the middle of the eighteenth century. To deal with the European rulers, the early sultans had turned to these worldly and experienced Greeks whose families had occupied important posts even in the days of the Byzantine emperors. In the course of time, the

Phanariots entrenched themselves in the inner circles of the administration and became in their own way indispensable to their Ottoman masters.

In terms of life style, wealth, education, interests, and aspirations these various groups had little in common. Yet, shared emotions, appealing myths, and practical considerations would combine in time to forge a nation. The most overpowering emotional elements were their hostility against the Turk and their mystical faith in the revival of the Byzantine Empire. Later, as they approached the moment of insurrection against foreign domination, they visualized a large state embracing all the different peoples living in the Balkan peninsula with the Greeks being the leading element, just as they had been in the days of Byzantium. This expectation was to prove nothing more than an illusion, but in the formative years it nourished their pride and sense of destiny. As time went on, the memories of Byzantium began to merge in the imagination of the most sophisticated with the distant echoes of classical Greece. The humble Romioi peasants were told by the intellectuals that they were the proud descendants of godlike heroes—a notion later encouraged by European humanists and liberals in search of a cause. Thus, history became, after religion, the second major force for building a national identity. Language was the third contributing factor in terms of importance. Religion and history posed no serious problems, but this was not the case with language. The vernacular in the eighteenth century had travelled a long way from its classical origins. But in an effort to prove the nation's unbroken continuity with the past, some scholars—with Adamantios Korais the most prominent among them—invented an artificial linguistic form, the *katharevousa*. In so doing, they created a division between the spoken tongue and an artificial version of so-called purist Greek. This split remains a curse to the present day. Nevertheless, the language remained a key element of identification, although it would be inaccurate to say that only those who spoke Greek felt themselves to be a part of the nation. For example, some prominent families that gained fame in the War of Independence spoke Albanian at home. In such cases, it appears that geography was an important factor; practically all Orthodox Christians who lived in the traditionally Greek lands came to regard themselves as Greek whatever their linguistic expression.

By the end of the eighteenth century, the tide of nationalism had

Ties with the Past

Bronze of Athena, fourth century B.C., found in Piraeus in 1959. Courtesy, Greek Embassy, Press Office, Washington, D.C.

(above) The Academy of Athens, in the classic style. Courtesy, Greek Embassy, Press Office, Washington, D.C.

(below) Classical drama performed in Athens. Courtesy, Greek Embassy, Press Office, Washington, D.C.

gathered momentum. Not surprisingly, poets and men of letters were the first to embrace the vision of national liberation. But there was no unity of purpose at the outset. The Phanariots advocated caution; they favored a strategy of increasing infiltration into the Ottoman power structure, confident that in time they would bring the empire under their—and thus Greek—control. Many wealthy landowners on the mainland were reluctant to act in any way that might jeopardize the modest improvements that they had achieved in their relations with the Turkish authorities. Even the patriarchate in Constantinople and many prominent bishops saw with misgivings the mounting revolutionary agitation.

Those who opposed a violent uprising could point to the disaster of 1770 when the Russians had instigated a revolt in the Peloponnisos only to abandon the Greeks at the critical moment to the tender mercies of the sultan's Albanian soldiers. They could also argue that after the fall of Napoleon conservative forces dominated European politics. The Holy Alliance regarded any revolutionary activity as a criminal plot. Britain, on her part, favored the preservation of the Ottoman Empire as a barrier to Russia's expansion into the Mediterranean.

Yet, the arguments of cold logic were in the end swept away by the forces of revolution. With the opening of the nineteenth century the visionary intellectuals were joined by more practical merchants and sea captains, dedicated monks and proud klephts, patriotic bishops and landowners. The proponents of revolution united in a secret organization known as the *Philiki Eteria* (Society of Friends), which was formed in 1814 by three Greek merchants of obscure origins in Odessa. To conceal their uninspiring identity the founders of the organization invented a supreme authority, which many Greeks assumed to be the czar himself. The society's activists, of course, made no effort to dispel this useful misapprehension. With an elaborate system of ranks, secret rites of initiation, a fearsome oath, and the allusion to supreme backing, this secret society spread far and wide within five years. By 1820 the revolutionary agitation had reached the point where no patriotic Greek could stand aloof, let alone be openly hostile.

In the summer months of 1820 the advocates of revolution increased their pressure for action. Sultan Mahmud II, they argued, was about to lock horns with Ali Pasha, the wily and cruel Albanian who had carved a virtual satrapy out of the sultan's possessions in

Greece. For years the sultan had chosen to ignore Ali's challenge, content with his verbal expressions of allegiance. But in 1820, on the pretext that Ali's agents had committed murder within sight of the Imperial Palace—a colossal affront—Mahmud gave the signal for a showdown. The Greeks saw in the brewing clash the long-awaited opening for their war of liberation.

Some of the activists in the Society of Friends spoke of another reason for moving against the Turks. The Serbs had already forced the sultan to grant them a degree of autonomy, and this seemed to suggest that other than Greeks might lead a Christian uprising in the Balkans. Seeing themselves as the rightful heirs of the Byzantine Empire, the Greek revolutionaries felt that they should be the ones at the forefront of any such undertaking.

In their search for a prominent and experienced leader, the activists of the society turned to Ioannis Kapodistrias, a Greek from Corfu, who had risen in the czar's service to the post of associate foreign minister. However, he could hardly have accepted the leadership of a secret, revolutionary society while still remaining in his post, and so he turned down the offer. It was not an easy decision for a Greek to pass up the opportunity to lead his nation's struggle for freedom. As he later confessed, he actually became ill at the end of his talk with the society's emissaries.

Rebuffed, the society turned to another prominent Greek in the czar's service, Alexandros Ypsilantis, a Phanariot who was serving at the time as aide-de-camp to the czar. Fifteen years earlier, the Turks had executed his grandfather and had forced the family into self-exile in Russia. Ypsilantis accepted the society's invitation to leadership, seeing the struggle as a historic mission to restore the Byzantine Empire. The fact that his family traced its origins to the Komninos dynasty must have sparked a personal ambition. He resigned his commission and joined the secret society as its supreme leader.

Ypsilantis' plan for revolution called for the eruption of simultaneous uprisings in southern Greece and in Serbia. In this way he hoped to split the sultan's forces between two distant theaters of war. In addition, he figured that the fight between the Porte (the government of the Ottoman Empire) and Ali Pasha would further fragment the Turkish armies. To set off the revolt, he decided that he himself would lead an army of volunteers into Rumania, where he was already in contact with Tudor Vladimirescu, a fiery Rumanian revolutionary whose support came mostly from peasants opposing their local landowners (the boyars).

On the surface, Ypsilantis' strategy appeared eminently sound. In reality, however, it was riddled with weaknesses and contradictions, not the least of which was the conflicting goals of the various political leaders and factions involved in the scheme. Milos Obreno-vich, the Serbian leader who had wrested autonomy from the sultan in 1815, had no reason to risk his newly-gained position in a foolhardy operation. Vladimirescu had little in common with the aristocratic Ypsilantis, whose ancestors had actually ruled over the Rumanians in the name of the sultan. Moreover, Ali Pasha was to be eliminated much sooner than Ypsilantis anticipated.

In January 1821 events began to move swiftly. The Turkish armies, sent to eliminate Ali Pasha, advanced with unexpected ease toward his stronghold in Epirus. Ypsilantis became impatient. Realizing that if Ali Pasha were defeated, a crucial diversion would disappear, he called on Vladimirescu to start his rebellion. The Rumanian leader responded and within a few weeks his peasant rebels put to the flames the properties of the Rumanian landowners. The czar received the news of Vladimirescu's uprising with utter indignation. Clearly, Ypsilantis could no longer count on Russian benevolence, but it was too late for him to pull back. In early February he crossed the river Prut and entered Moldavia. He hoped that its *hospodar* (Phanariot ruler) would join the fight and declare his independence from the sultan. With a secure sanctuary on the borders of Russia, Ypsilantis could move into Serbia, where he would unite with Obrenovic and then move south to join forces with Ali Pasha. With the Balkan peninsula in flames, Ypsilantis believed, the end of Ottoman rule would no longer be simply a dream.

He was in for a rude awakening. At the very time he was setting the fuse for the revolution, Russia and her partners in the Holy Alliance were conferring at Laibach, making plans to extinguish the revolutionary fires in Latin America, Spain, and Italy, and to preserve the post-Napoleonic status quo. The czar could not but disown publicly Ypsilantis' venture. Then, the alliance with Vladi-mirescu fell apart. The Rumanian uprising was above all a social rebellion of the poor peasants against the rich landowners; but as the insurrection gained strength, its thrust changed direction. A strong nationalist spirit took hold, and Vladimirescu joined forces with some of the more enlightened Rumanian boyars and proclaimed a struggle for Rumanian independence. Confused by this unexpected turn of events, Ypsilantis tried to give his movement a social content in the hope of thus being able to keep Vladimirescu and his followers in line. It was already too late. In March, Ypsilantis and Vladimirescu clashed openly. Within days, Ypsilantis had Vladimirescu executed on charges of trying to strike a bargain with the Turks. The czar, incensed by the excesses of the Rumanian peasants against the landed gentry, and bound by his commitments at Laibach, had already agreed to let Turkish troops enter Rumania and crush the rebellion. With this, Ypsilantis' situation became hopeless. Deserted by Vladimirescu's peasant rebels, he was left with only a small force of Greek volunteers in a foreign, inhospitable land. On June 18 his small detachment was surrounded by the Turks at Dragasani. Few survived. Ypsilantis escaped in the darkness of night after the battle was over. He managed to reach Austria, only to be thrown into prison there by the authorities.

When the tragic epilogue of Ypsilantis' rebellion became known in Greece, the time for turning back had long passed; the rebellion in the Peloponnisos and Central Greece was already in its third month. Greek legend has it that on March 25, 1821, the feast day of the Annunciation, the metropolitan of Old Patras, Germanos, raised the standard of revolution at the monastery of Aghia Lavra, near Kalavrita in the Peloponnisos. An appealing legend, but a legend no less. Actually, the revolution started with minor, isolated incidents which in less volatile times would have been little more than insignificant and rather inept acts of banditry. But in March 1821, with the news that Ypsilantis had already crossed the Prut a month earlier, these incidents acted as the spark that sets off the powder keg. Already, at the beginning of the month, the vezier (governor) of the Peloponnisos had summoned to a conference the bishops and *proestes* (prominent Greeks) of the area. His real purpose was to hold them hostages in case of serious trouble. Given assurances for their safety by the Turks, several of them went to Tripolis, the area's capital. Others, including Metropolitan Germanos, decided to ignore the summons. After that act of defiance there was no turning back. The word was out that the uprising would start any day, and both sides were nervous and apprehensive. In the middle of March, small bands of young peasants, encouraged by their landlords and proestes, attacked some Turks whom they found travelling alone in the open country, and the first blood was spilled. The Turks moved to their strongholds and began to prepare for the upcoming fight.

On April 3 (March 22)* Theodoros Kolokotronis† launched the first major operation and captured Kalamai, eliminating its weak Turkish garrison. The following day he moved toward Karitaina, another Turkish stronghold. In the northern Peloponnisos, other groups seized Kalavrita and surrounded the Turkish garrison in the fortress of Patrai. The revolt was on. The small, isolated Turkish garrisons were soon cut off as the armed bands scored one success after another, gaining experience—and valuable weapons—in the process. Sentiments were inflamed when news came that, in retaliation, the Turks had strangled Patriarch Gregorios in Constantinople and had vilified his body. In a terrible act of revenge a few months later, in October, Kolokotronis stormed Tripolis and put all Moslems there to the sword.

For the first three years of the fighting, the Greeks were able to hold their own against Turkish efforts to put down the rebellion. The trouble came from the rivalries that broke out among the revolutionaries. The proestes saw in the rising power of the armed fighters a threat to their long-established position; consequently, they insisted that the guerrilla bands should come under civilian control. There were also fierce disputes over the use of two foreign loans received from European sources in 1824. And, of course, there were the inevitable local jealousies and personal ambitions. No commanding personality emerged who was capable of taking over and assuming leadership of the struggle. In the early days, Ypsilantis' younger brother, Dimitrios, had sought to become commander in chief, trading on his name. But he was "short, bald, speaking through his nose, timid and awkward in his manners, looking forty-years-old at twenty-five, requiring much sleep, [with] neither eloquence nor the art of dealing with men." Without a central focus of leadership, the revolution nevertheless persisted as a fragmented effort. As a contemporary noted, "Anyone could get together an armed band.

* Until 1923 the Greeks used the Julian calendar, which in the nineteenth century differed by twelve days from the Gregorian calendar used in Europe. The dates in this text are those of the Gregorian calendar.

† Theodoros Kolokotronis was born in 1770. His father was chief of the armatoles in the area of Corinth, but during the 1770 rebellion he fought against the Turks and was later killed in battle. The family then moved to the island of Zakinthos to avoid persecution. Theodoros Kolokotronis served as a young man in the British military forces that were occupying the Ionian Islands at the time. During the War of Independence he emerged as the major military figure in the Peloponnisos. Politically, he identified with the Russians.

The only unifying element was hatred against the Turk and the determination to cast off the foreign yoke." Efforts to write a constitution and set up some form of central government proved only partly successful. A constitution was enacted in January 1822 in Epidaurus, but the government it set up was a weak, faction-ridden executive. In 1824 civil war broke out and in the heat of internal strife even Kolokotronis was thrown into prison. By the next year, the struggle for independence seemed to have reached its final gasps. A strong Turkish army had laid seige to the strategic town of Mesolongion while another Moslem force under the command of Ibrahim Pasha—the capable son of Egypt's satrap Mehemet Ali—had sailed from Alexandria and had landed in the Peloponnisos.

Before long, Ibrahim captured Tripolis, and from this stronghold he lashed out in all directions, devastating the countryside. Kolokotronis was hastily set free but there was little he could do against the disciplined and well-trained Egyptian force. In the fall, Ibrahim crossed over to Central Greece and reinforced the siege of Mesolongion. One by one the outlying ramparts fell to the enemy, while behind the walls pestilence and famine took a heavy toll. One of those who died at Mesolongion was Lord Byron, the romantic and adventurous British poet who had come to Greece to join the struggle. In April 1826 those who were still alive decided to fight their way out through the enemy lines. They were cut to pieces, but the long siege and the heroic exodus revived pro-Greek sentiments abroad.

During the onslaught of Ibrahim and the siege of Mesolongion, the Greeks made an effort to write a new constitution, which they hoped would at long last set the foundation for a strong, effective government. By the time the constitutional assembly came together at Troezina, the revolutionary effort had reached its nadir. Spiliades, secretary of the Troezina Assembly later recalled that "the government did not exist except in name . . . dissension devoured the motherland . . . and at every moment civil war threatened to break out again . . ." In spite of these chaotic conditions the assembly produced a remarkable document that sought to strike a happy balance between democratic freedom and effective government. The delegates discarded their former fascination with the spirit of the French Revolution and turned to the guidelines offered by the United States Constitution. Their document provided for a *kyverni-*

Massacre of Chios, by Delacroix: the Greek War of Independence.   Louvre. Photographie Giraudon

Refugees from Athens, nineteenth century.   Picture Collection, The New York Public Library

tis (governor), who was to serve in a capacity similar to that of the American president, that is, as both head of state and head of government. He was to be elected by male voters for a seven-year term. The enactment of laws was entrusted to a single-chamber legislature called *Vouli*, elected for a three-year term, with one-third of its seats renewable every year.

The Troezina Assembly elected to the position of governor, Ioannes Kapodistrias, who had by then left the Russian service and lived in semiretirement in Switzerland. With Ibrahim holding sway over most of the land, the selection may have appeared to Kapodistrias as a supercilious exercise in futility since Greece was not yet a sovereign state. But at this very moment, fate took a different turn. The death of Byron, romanticized by the European press beyond proportion, had fired public sentiment in favor of the suffering Greeks; European liberals found in the Greek revolution a cause they could make their own. Even conservative statesmen, schooled in the classical tradition, felt duty-bound to give a helping hand to this "ancient race fighting to recover its long-lost freedom." The atrocities committed by Ibrahim's troops made indifference appear almost as a betrayal to all the principles of civilized humanity. Even the new czar, who had come to the throne of Russia in 1825, was more liberal and more sensitive to the fate of his Orthodox brethren than his predecessor had been. These emotional motivations were strengthened by very practical considerations. The statesmen in London and Paris were afraid that Ibrahim and his efficient Egyptian forces would take over southern Greece for good and replace the less troublesome rule of the sultan, thus bringing Mediterranean trade under Egyptian control. With Britain and France in favor of intervention, Russia could not remain aloof. On July 6, 1827, the three powers signed a treaty in London and decided to press for an armistice and for the withdrawal of Ibrahim's troops. The Egyptian general refused to comply with the demand. In October the combined fleets of Britain, France, and Russia entered the bay of Navarino, where the Egyptian fleet was at anchor. The powers were planning nothing more than a show of strength; but someone in the Moslem camp opened fire. In a fierce exhange, most of the Egyptian ships were destroyed. After what turned out to be a momentous encounter, the victory of the revolution was no longer a dream, although sporadic fighting continued for another year, especially in Central Greece, where the Greeks made every effort to keep the revolution alive while the powers were debating which lands to include in a new Greek state.

The rule of Kapodistrias

As the turbulence of war gradually began to give way to a calmer atmosphere of peace, new problems rose to the surface. The peasants who had traded the plow for the guerrilla's sword now found it difficult to return to the humble occupation of tilling the land or tending their flocks; many turned to brigandage. The economy was in shambles; the treasury virtually empty. Economic and social problems were aggravated by the demands of the powerful. As is inevitably the case, there was a scramble for the distribution of the meager spoils freedom had brought in its wake, with each faction seeking to wrest a lion's share. Some groups sought to grab power from others who hoped to preserve traditional prerogatives. The landowning proestes, who had held the reins of local power even under the Turks, were not about to accept the authority of a centrally-controlled bureaucracy. Those who had moved to the center of the political stage during the War of Independence wanted to preserve their prominence and expand their power. Kapodistrias, who came to Greece in February 1828 to take over as kyvernitis, decided that the situation called for drastic action. Within days he pressed the Vouli to suspend the Troezina constitution temporarily. With his prestige he probably could have governed just as effectively without eliminating the democratic constitution. Be that as it may, the Vouli buckled under his pressure and voted itself out of existence, declaring that "the dire conditions of the Motherland and the duration of the War have not justified and do not justify the full implementation of the Constitution." The ordinary people in the villages and the small towns shrugged off the suspension of their nascent democracy. Hoping for a period of peace and stability after so many years of war and internal strife, the people hailed Kapodistrias as a savior. The cycle was to be repeated several times in the future; a period of instability and strife would lead to a restrictive regime, which in turn would lead again to a period of instability and strife.

Kapodistrias was not a reactionary autocrat by conviction, but he was convinced that the democratic provisions of the constitution were much too liberal for a country that had just come through seven years of savage fighting. "I cannot close my eyes," he often said, "to Greece's ills caused by four centuries of slavery and seven years of anarchy." He regarded the people as politically unprepared for the responsibilities of self-government. "It is dangerous to entrust a child with a razor," he once told a British visitor. "If I were governor," the visitor replied, "I would give a razor to the child and then, holding his right hand, I would show him how to shave without cutting himself." Kapodistrias remained unconvinced.

Conditions seemed to support his reluctance. The small town of Nauplia, which became Greece's first capital, was a far cry from the splendid court of St. Petersburg or the sophisticated European cities where Kapodistrias had spent most of his adult life. The traces of four centuries of Turkish rule were much too evident in everyday life, especially in the people's ambivalent attitude toward authority. A somewhat apocryphal anecdote from those early days is very revealing. It appears that Kapodistrias wanted to introduce the potato as another staple in the Greek diet. At first he tried to distribute the potatoes free, but he found little public interest. Then someone suggested that the potato loads be placed in the square under guard but that the soldiers be instructed to turn the other way if anyone tried to steal the potatoes in the darkness. The stratagem worked perfectly—anything worth guarding must be worth stealing. The next morning most of the potatoes were gone. The anecdote may indeed reflect the low cultural level the people had reached under foreign domination; but it also shows the popular view of the state as a virtually hostile institution that cannot be trusted. Kapodistrias apparently expected to overcome and eventually eradicate the people's political shortcomings through a restrictive regime, not realizing that in the area of politics experience can best be gained through participation. In any event, his autocratic rule did not avert the emergence of an opposition force which, having no regular outlets for reasoned interaction with the government, turned into sullen rejection of the regime and eventually into rebellion. In late 1829, the representatives of the central government were expelled from the island of Idhra, where pro-British sentiment prevailed and where the leading families regarded Kapodistrias as Russia's man in Greece. A constitutional committee made up of prominent islanders took over the administration, and Kapodistrias could do little to restore his authority.

Local opposition to Kapodistrias was encouraged—and skillfully exploited—by Britain and France, the two European powers that, together with Russia, had become Greece's so-called protector powers. Britain, in particular, always concerned with the possibility of Russia's expansion into the Mediterranean, saw Kapodistrias as being merely a Russian puppet. To undermine his position, she pressed for a protocol stipulating that "Greece shall form an independent State . . . with a monarchical and hereditary government according to the order of primogeniture." The protocol was signed by the three protector powers on February 3, 1830. In effect, this document created for the first time an independent and sovereign Greek state. In the process, the Troezina constitution and its form of republican government were discarded.

This interference of the foreign powers in the affairs of the new state was to remain a constant feature of Greek history for a long time. Throughout the nineteenth century, the protector powers saw Greece always through the prism of their own vested interests in the future of a weakening Ottoman Empire. The czar had overcome his dislike of revolutionaries when he saw the possibilities of gaining a foothold in the Mediterranean by establishing an Orthodox state in the Aegean. Britain, for her part, agreed to an independent Greece mostly to counterbalance Russia's growing influence. France acted as a stabilizing force while she looked after the expansion of her own interests in this vital area. Even without homegrown forces of disruption, these foreign influences and antagonisms would have been bad enough. As it were, these two sources of turbulence, domestic and foreign, reinforced each other. Even the political parties, which had made their appearance in the last four years of the revolution, openly identified themselves with one or the other of these three foreign powers. The Russian party found its popular base mostly in the Peloponnisos, the British in the islands, and the French in Central Greece.

For the next two years, the search for a monarch to place on the newly-carved throne of Greece found no eager candidates. One possibility was Leopold of Saxe-Coburg—who later became the first king of Belgium—but he rejected the offer, pointing out that the decision of the powers to limit the new state to a small area, leaving under Ottoman control Greek-populated Thessalia, Epirus, and Crete, "will augur no good . . . [because] it will cripple the Greek state both morally and physically, will make it weak and poor, expose it to constant danger from the Turks and create from the beginning innumerable difficulties for him who is to be the head of that Government." He was right. The decision of the protector powers to establish a small state of less than a million people, with twice as many of their countrymen left under foreign rule, was to remain a major cause of conflict for three generations.

With Greece now officially a monarchy, Kapodistrias' position became increasingly weak. His opponents were heartened by the action of the protector powers to establish a monarchy and intensified their defiance. To hold the opposition forces down, Kapodistrias was forced to resort to police measures, which only resulted in even greater discontent. On a Sunday morning, October 9, 1831, he was assassinated on his way to church. Suspicions that "Britain's hand had armed the assassins" were never verified. Most likely, his violent death was the tragic climax of a personal feud with the powerful Mavromikhalis family in Mani. Perched on the rocky slopes of the Taigetos Range, Mani had wrested from the Turks virtual autonomy long before the revolution. Kapodistrias' attempts to collect taxes and bring the authority of his government to Mani, together with a downturn in the area's economic fortunes, had kindled a deadly feud between the Kyvernitis and Mani's most prominent family. On that fateful Sunday morning, Konstantinos and Georgios Mavromikhalis came upon Kapodistrias as he was entering the church. Georgios stabbed him in the abdomen while Konstantinos shot him in the back of the head. Kapodistrias died instantly. Konstantinos Mavromikhalis was lynched by the enraged crowd, while Georgios was court-martialled and shot a few days later.

The death of Kapodistrias opened once again the floodgates of anarchy and partisan contention. The pendulum swung to the opposite extreme. A governing committee of key personalities from the various factions took over, but internal rivalries brought the government to a standstill while the country was virtually torn apart. Brigandage was rampant in the countryside, the threat of renewed civil war was hovering over the unfortunate land, and "the poison of dissension had spread into the provinces of the state."

Otho, the first king

The chaotic conditions following Kapodistrias' assassination forced the protector powers to take action. In May 1832, they selected a seventeen-year-old Bavarian prince to become Greece's first king. His name was Otho, the second son of Bavaria's King Ludwig. The governing committee, rightly suspecting that the powers were planning to set up an absolute monarchy, called a National Assembly to draft a new constitution that would set limits to the royal authority. A vain effort. In July, the envoys of the protector powers told the governing committee that "the discussion on establishing a permanent Constitution or on any fundamental laws cannot take place without the participation of the royal authority." In other words, no constitution. Again, the ordinary people, sickened by the pettiness of their political leaders, voiced no objection to the interference of the foreign powers and rather looked forward to the arrival of another savior. When Otho arrived on board a British frigate and stepped on Greek soil on February 2, 1833, he received a glorious welcome from the people of Nauplia and the surrounding countryside.

In the days of Kapodistrias, most of the agitation for a constitution had come from the political factions normally under British influence. Not surprisingly, these fervent advocates of constitutionalism suddenly lost their voice when the British took the lead in blocking the effort to enact a constitution for Otho's monarchy. The British had a very good reason for their turnabout. When Otho came to Greece he was a minor, and the royal authority was entrusted to a three-member regency council of Bavarian notables, with Count Armansperg as its chairman. For all practical purposes, Armansperg was Britain's man in Greece.

The absolute monarchy stunned and further distorted the growth of democratic institutions in the country. The most effective politicians were eased out of the country into ambassadorial posts abroad, while those who remained had to resort to sterile criticism, petty intrigues, and demeaning attempts to gain the favor of the throne. The reins of state power were in the hands of Bavarians, with Armansperg acting as the actual prime minister. Greek politicians who were appointed to cabinet posts were often treated as lowly civil servants. At the same time, the ambitious policies of the new rulers gave the protector powers more opportunities to manipulate the system, turning Greece into a client state by expanding their intervention into Greek politics. This foreign penetration into the affairs of state was to remain a constant feature of the political system for generations.

In those formative years, the throne became the·center of political action. Still, it was not an easy matter for the Bavarians to govern effectively a people so different from themselves in culture and temperament. Behind the facade of absolute monarchy, Otho found himself continuously trying to balance the influence of rival political factions. Nearly all his efforts were directed at averting civil war, preventing the formation of a common front against the throne, and just keeping the administration going. To broaden his popular base, he embraced the national yearning to liberate all Greeks under Ottoman rule and restore the Byzantine Empire with Constantinople as its capital.

This ambitious objective—the Great Idea (Megali Idea)—remained for three generations the dominant theme of Greek foreign policy. Yet, from the outset, it was an impossible dream. The other nationalities in the Balkans had no interest in the revival of a Greek-dominated Byzantine Empire, while the major European powers had quite different designs of their own in this part of the world. Britain, in particular, had come to consider the preservation of the Ottoman Empire the pillar of her foreign policy in the eastern Mediterranean. Otho closed his eyes to these formidable barriers and tried to push forward the Great Idea by naively playing one protector power against another. In the process, he gave them new opportunities to penetrate even more deeply into the political system of Greece. In the end, he only succeeded in uniting all three powers against himself.

A coup for a constitution

Armansperg remained the prime mover of Greek political life even after Otho's twentieth birthday and ascension to the throne. But with the passing of time, his relations with the young monarch became increasingly strained and in 1837 he left the country. His departure from the political stage visibly cooled British support for Otho's monarchy. Eleven years later, Lord Palmerston, in a long memorandum to Queen Victoria, revealed that British influence in Greek affairs had waned "since the end of the Regency of Count Armansperg." Not surprisingly, the agitation for constitutional government, dormant for some years, flared up again with Armansperg's departure. To be sure, the issue had no wide support at first. Apparently, to many ordinary citizens the idea of a constitution was synonymous with anarchy and strife. It is said that Greek mothers in those years often threatened unruly children that "the constitution will come and eat you up." But for the politically active, especially those associated with the British, the constitution promised new avenues for influence and personal power.

The opposition to Otho's absolutism gained momentum in 1841, when the island of Crete rose in revolt against Turkish rule and Otho found it difficult to take a strong, nationalist stand because of the country's meager resources. Throughout the nineteenth century, this island remained at the center of irredentist passion. Given the high emotions generated by the agitation to free all Greeks under Ottoman rule, it was inevitable that the major powers would exploit and even instigate conflicts in Ottoman-held territories in order to promote their own interests and manipulate Greek politics to their own advantage. In 1841 the Cretan uprising had received the subtle encouragement of the British. Not that they were interested in the island's union with Greece; far from it. What the British apparently expected was that a critical confrontation would enable them to take over the island on a temporary basis, as a kind of compromise solution. In the end, however, Britain did not take over the island, but neither did the uprising achieve Cretan union with Greece.

Otho's opponents, always ready to exploit his failures, put the blame on his shoulders, arguing that his ineffective and procrastinating leadership had resulted in the country's weakness and humiliation. Few had the integrity to face up to the implications of the Great Idea and ask openly the crucial question: Was Greece in a position to go to war with the Ottoman Empire in support of the Cretans or other "unredeemed brethren"? Instead, the constitution was offered as a panacea, "a magic word exciting the imagination of the young, pleasing the intellectuals, and inspiring the people, a word equated in the public mind since 1830 with unrestrained freedom," to quote the contemporary historian N. Dragoumis. By coincidence, the anti-Otho agitation was fueled with exciting news from abroad; in nearby Serbia, Alexander Karadjordjevic had ousted King Mikhail Obrenovic in 1842. Many of Otho's opponents saw in this an enticing example.

To sidestep the pressure for a constitution, Otho called Alexandros Mavrokordatos to the premiership. Mavrokordatos, a Phanariot who had gained prominence in the War of Independence and had since become one of the leading figures of the English party, posed certain conditions that had to be agreed to before he would accept the post. In themselves the conditions give us a revealing picture of the realities of power in Otho's absolute monarchy. Mavrokordatos asked the king: (1) to give decisive authority over financial and taxation matters to the State Council, a twenty-seven-member body of distinguished Greeks, which had been used by Otho as an advisory board with hardly any decision-making powers; (2) to dismiss the *camarilla* (the palace officialdom surrounding Otho); (3) to give the cabinet members freedom to carry out their responsibilities without constant dictation from the palace; (4) to give formal recognition to the office of the prime minister; (5) to entrust the ministry of military affairs to a Greek national; and (6) to initiate the gradual withdrawal of the Bavarians from Greece. These six conditions formed a modest but realistic attempt to transfer some power to the Greeks, to limit the throne's involvement in politics, and to give the country a healthier mix of stable government with the rudiments of representation and diffusion of power. Mavrokordatos hoped to achieve this without going through the complex and difficult operation of drafting a constitution in a free-for-all arena of an assembly. Otho failed to see the opportunity. In the face of domestic and foreign pressure he promised to carry out the proposed reforms, but as soon as the crisis had passed its peak he went back on his word. Mavrokordatos resigned in protest. Time was running out for Otho's absolute monarchy. The British envoy now openly encouraged the agitation for a constitution. He found in this movement an unexpected ally, the Russian envoy, who had his own ulterior motives. The Russian diplomat hoped that the agitation would eventually turn into a popular demand for Otho's abdication, thus opening up fresh opportunities for placing an Orthodox prince— under Russian tutelage, of course—on the throne. After all, with Otho's Catholicism, the religious question remained a constant irritant and an emotional instrument in the hands of Russian diplomacy. The British, however, had no intention of letting a Russian puppet replace Otho. They encouraged the outcry for a constitution because they believed that in a more open and competitive political system they would be able to find many new channels in which to exert influence.

The agitation against Otho's absolutism received additional impetus from the country's severely debilitated economic condition.

The country was indeed on the verge of bankruptcy. In the spring and summer of 1843 representatives of the three protector powers met in London to discuss the Greek financial situation. Their recommendation: cut down on military expenditures. The army, with 892 officers and 9,060 noncommissioned officers and enlisted men was not large, but it was obviously top-heavy. Besides, it absorbed 43 percent of the state's revenues. Otho, hard-pressed by the powers, agreed to remove approximately 1,200 officers and men from the rolls, including all remaining Bavarians.

Even without foreign pressure, the quest for a democratic form of government would have found easy support, at least among the politically active. After all, democracy alone could open the gates to the citadels of power for most of them. On the night of September 14 to 15, a bloodless military coup forced Otho to agree to an election for a Constituent Assembly. The conspiracy had not been initiated by the military. Col. Dimitrios Kalerghis, who led the coup, had been brought into the plan only a few weeks earlier. The opening moves for the coup came from the leaders of the so-called Russian and English parties. Mavrokordatos—the foremost personality in the English party—knew of the conspiracy but took no active part in it.

To allay any suspicions that drastic action was afoot, Kalerghis went to the theater the night of the coup. Then, shortly after midnight he surrounded the palace with his cavalry. A small but boisterous crowd joined in with cries for a constitution. There was no violence, no great outpouring of people surging through the night to overwhelm the king with the enormity of their numbers. Still, what Otho saw proved sufficient. He made a feeble attempt from a ground window to address the troops and draw them to his side, but his voice was drowned under the general clamor and Kalerghis' own military commands. By dawn, Otho, isolated and dispirited, signed a royal decree stating that "within thirty days, a National Assembly shall be convoked so that We may compose with them the Constitution of the State." In memory of this victory, the area in front of the palace was later named Constitution Square, a familiar site to tourists visiting Greece today.

The National Assembly that came out of the election was composed mostly of lawyers, professional men, old revolutionary heroes, many proestes and landowners from the provinces, and a few wealthy merchants and sea captains. This largely conservative body enacted a charter in March 1844 which was patterned after the French constitution of 1830. Otho, who had by then recovered from his initial shock, played a key role in the making of the constitution. In his exchanges with the assembly he argued successfully that this was a charter granted by him, a constitution contract based on the monarchical principle. Nevertheless, he accepted several provisions for the protection of civil rights. In reality, most power remained in his hands. The constitution provided for a Vouli elected by direct and universal ballot (excluding only servants, apprentices, and women) but legislation required the agreement of an upper chamber, *Gerousia* (Senate), with its members appointed by the king for life. Moreover, laws needed the king's signature. Executive power was also lodged effectively in the palace since the king had the authority to appoint and dismiss the cabinet ministers at his discretion. On balance, however, the 1844 constitution did reopen the way to popular participation in the political process.

Mavrokordatos and Kolettis

At this turning point in the nation's modern history, two personalities came to embody not merely different political viewpoints but, more important, different cultural orientations, different political mores, different action styles, and different ideas of the nation's destiny. Alexandros Mavrokordatos was one, Ioannis Kolettis the other. Both men had gained prominence in the War of Independence, but by temperament and background they were worlds apart. Mavrokordatos, a Phanariot born in Constantinople in 1791, had come to the Peloponnisos at the outbreak of the fighting in 1821. Throughout his political career he remained a friend and admirer of the British. By 1840 age had mellowed the ambition of his revolutionary days and he was now a man of moderate and realistic temperament. Mavrokordatos had a healthy appreciation of the country's need for stability and internal development combined with a modicum of responsible freedom. A nineteenth century democrat, he was very much at home with the European political currents and personalities of his time. Even his attire reflected his Western culture and political style. He never donned the Greek *fustanella;* a short, corpulent man, wearing eyeglasses, he would have looked rather ridiculous in the national costume. He preferred the dark,

Lincolnian frock coat, which was popular in the West during the mid-nineteenth century. In his Western appearance and mentality, Mavrokordatos differed markedly from Ioannis Kolettis, who was for almost three decades the leading personality in the French party. Born in Epirus in 1774, Kolettis was, in the words of a contemporary foreign observer, "the genuine personification of contemporary Greece." A physician by profession, he had served in his early years as personal physician to one of Ali Pasha's sons. His apprenticeship at the court of Ali Pasha had taught him to be not only amoral and unscrupulous, but also cautious, cunning, and devious. He combined the arrogance, harshness, craftiness, and suspiciousness of the guerrilla with the diplomatic versatility, amiability, and demagoguery of the consummate politician. Sporting a heavy, drooping moustache, he always wore the national fustanella as a visible demonstration of his Greekness.

While Mavrokordatos wanted to remove with dispatch the residue of customs and habits encrusted on the nation's soul by centuries of foreign domination, Kolettis maintained that "these customs imposed by the Tyrant will take a long time to disappear." "The Greeks," Kolettis would add in a transparent jibe at Mavrokordatos, "do not wear black frock coats; nor do they speak French or English. They wear the fustanella . . ." To the extent that one can speak of the existence of a coherent, deliberate political philosophy in those days of intense partisanship and self-centered ambitions, Mavrokordatos appears to have favored domestic development and a foreign policy of restraint and peaceful coexistence with the Turks, at least until the nation's resources would allow a more assertive foreign policy. In contrast, Kolettis became the foremost advocate of the Great Idea, calling for an ambitious policy that far exceeded the nation's resources and capabilities at that time. Speaking at the Constituent Assembly of 1844, he articulated the essence of the Great Idea.

The kingdom of Greece is not coterminous with the free country of today. This is only one section, the smallest and poorest part of Greece. Greeks are not only those who inhabit the present kingdom, but they are also those who live in Ioannina, in Salonika, in Adrianoupolis or Constantinople, in Trapezous or Crete or Samos or any other land of Greek history or Greek race . . . There are two great centers of Hellenism today. Athens is the capital of the kingdom. Constantinople is the grand capital, the polis, the dream and hope of all Greeks.

Kolettis' eloquent, passionately nationalistic, and extravagant message was bound to arouse the national pride and fire the people's imagination. It was also in keeping with Otho's own aspiration to play a heroic role, culminating with his own crowning in Greek Christendom's most sacred temple, Constantinople's fabled Aghia Sophia. Given the country's meager resources and the opposition of the major powers, the Great Idea was a patently unrealistic and adventurist policy. But with millions of Greeks under Turkish rule, every other policy appeared unworthy of the nation's history. In retrospect, it could be argued that Mavrokordatos' policy of restraint and domestic development was better suited for the small, impoverished kingdom of the 1840s. But such a policy was no match for the heady emotional wine of the Great Idea. Besides, Mavrokordatos was an *heterochthon* (a Greek from abroad), and as such he was too Western for the Greek mentality of that period. This conflict between heterochthons and *autochthons* (Greeks living in the Peloponnisos and Central Greece) had remained an ever-present irritant since the days of the War of Independence. Being much better educated than most native Greeks, the heterochthons had taken over the bureaucracy, thus cutting into the traditional lines of local influence and patronage. The rivalry continued until the latter part of the century, when a new elite of native-born intellectuals came to the fore.

In the spring of 1844, upon the enactment of the constitution, Otho asked Mavrokordatos and Kolettis to form a government together and conduct the first election. He wanted these leading figures of the English and the French parties to join forces and thus dramatize the support of the two protector powers to his regime. But who was to become the prime minister in this government? Kolettis half-seriously suggested that they flip a coin since both of them "could not possibly fit in the same cabinet." Mavrokordatos rejected the suggestion as being an insult to the office, whereupon Kolettis offered to support a Mavrokordatos cabinet in which he himself would take no part. This proved to be a shrewd move in that it would allow Kolettis complete freedom of action in the electoral campaign. He exploited this tactical advantage to the hilt. In an almost classic display of dirty politics he used every conceivable smear tactic and destructive political maneuver. One particularly damaging device was a whispering campaign that claimed that even Otho wanted the defeat of Mavrokordatos, who was portrayed as a traitor to the nation's aspirations. By injecting the views of the palace into the electoral campaign, Kolettis unwittingly introduced a feature that was to become a lasting one in the Greek political process.

In the election no party won a clear majority in the Vouli. As soon as the indecisive results became known, Kolettis in collusion with the palace instigated a popular demonstration in Athens and Mavrokordatos was forced to resign. Writing later to a friend, Mavrokordatos blamed Otho for this sorry beginning of constitutional government.

The king and the country, having taken the oath to the constitution, ought to have worked for its implementation. I never had any illusions as to the difficulties which would inevitably appear. But I hoped that I would be able to overcome them if those who had given me promises of support would have supported me sincerely. Again they did the opposite. They thought of nothing else than to overthrow me with false accusations, by cultivating passions, by promoting disorder and anarchy. Such methods may be good to bring disaster but to build, one needs different tools.

As the leader of the majority in the Vouli, Kolettis became prime minister. He remained in that post until his death in September 1847. His was not an overly long tenure, but he was the first elected prime minister in the history of modern Greece and he stamped on the Greek political ethos a lasting reflection of his personal style. He raised the art of political corruption and patronage to remarkable heights of intricacy and boldness. The state resources, whether in the form of money, positions, or favors (rousfeti) were used almost without restraint for political advantage. The public servants became part of this ingenious system. They would not perform the simplest service for a citizen until he came with a party representative. In this fashion, the civil servant obliged the politician, the politician the citizen. The komatarkhis (the local political boss) took over the traditional function of the proestes, dispensing favors to those willing to toe the line; in many cases the proestes moved into the new role themselves with little change in the identity of the local power-holders.

It appears that to Kolettis all methods were permissible to keep power or assure electoral victory. A few years later, in 1853, an official who had received instructions to keep that year's election honest and fair commented dryly that "at the time of Kolettis . . . even murders and forgeries and all other crimes were ordered, the only requirement being that they achieve an electoral victory . . ." In the words of historian Spyros Markezinis, the rise of Kolettis to power "was an unfortunate occurrence" for the country. At the very time constitutional government was coming into being, the first person called to set it in operation was "the man who had often fought under the slogan of the constitution but who had never believed in it or in the principles of true liberalism." In the election of 1847 Kolettis won a resounding victory but he died a few weeks later in August. He was the first Greek politician to enrich himself in office. Upon his death he left a sizable fortune of 630,000 gold drachmas.

With the death of Kolettis, the British pressed Otho to call Mavrokordatos to the premiership. Otho reluctantly agreed but Mavrokordatos again posed a number of conditions. He insisted that the king should reign within the constitutional limits, that the palace should not meddle in politics, and that an honest election be held to bring a new Vouli into existence that would truly reflect the public sentiment. Otho refused to go along and resorted to the appointment of palace-made cabinets. Behind the facade of democratic institutions the politicization of the throne reached new heights. At the same time, Otho's relations with the British became increasingly strained.

The Don Pacifico affair

In spite of all the grandiose rhetoric of the Great Idea, the small kingdom remained weak and vulnerable to outside pressures. One minor incident, blown out of proportion by the British, tells much about conditions in Greece around the middle of the nineteenth century. During Holy Week in 1849 a member of the Rothschild family was visiting Athens and the government decided, as a matter of courtesy to the prominent Jewish visitor, to ban the popular custom of burning Judas in effigy. The people ignored the ban, the police resorted to force, and in the melee that followed the house of a Portuguese Jew known as Don Pacifico was ransacked. Britain seized on the opportunity to intervene. Palmerston, the British prime minister, claimed that Pacifico, who was born in Gibraltar, was a British subject and therefore entitled to "her Majesty's protection." He disregarded Queen Victoria's advice for moderation and "in a display of gunboat diplomacy at its most blatant," to quote his biographer, imposed a blockade on Greece. He expected to teach Otho a lesson and turn the people against their king; predictably, Palmerston's high-handed intervention had the opposite effect. The king's defiant resistance to Palmerston's demands raised his prestige in Europe and rallied the Greek people to his side.

In London a compromise on Don Pacifico's claim was reached with the French, who had entered the case in the role of a mediator. But Palmerston kept the agreement secret even from the British envoy in Athens, who continued to press the authorities there with demands on behalf of Pacifico. The Greek government, unaware of the British-French compromise, buckled under the pressure and accepted Palmerston's initial demands. When the facts of this deliberate deception became known, Queen Victoria was outraged. The French went so far as to withdraw temporarily their ambassador from London. Palmerston weathered the storm with a brilliant five-hour oration in Parliament, which ended with the words "Civis Romanus sum," implying the right of all British subjects to rely on the government for protection abroad. Eventually the matter was settled at a small fraction of Pacifico's initial demand and the blockade was lifted forty-two days after it had started.

Miscalculations during the Crimean War

Still, the humiliating experience showed how exposed Greece remained to the pressures of the major powers. The advocates of the Great Idea turned to their familiar argument that as long as the kingdom remained small and impotent there would be no hope for genuine independence. Eager to compensate for the frustrations of the recent past they convinced themselves that the big power politics of the moment held a promise for the realization of the Great Idea. The political sky in Europe was indeed darkening in the early 1850s. Napoleon III, determined to strengthen French influence in the Near East, had embarked on an assertive foreign policy, much to the annoyance of Russia. Especially irksome was his demand that Turkey grant privileges to the Catholics in the Holy Land at the expense of the Orthodox churches there. This had infuriated Czar Nicholas, who considered himself protector of all Christians in the Ottoman Empire under the broadly interpreted terms of the 1774 Treaty of Kuchuk-Kainardji. When the sultan accepted the French demand, Russia declared war on Turkey, and in August 1853 Russian troops entered the principalities of Moldavia and Wallachia (today's Rumania). This was the opening scene of what was to become known as the Crimean War.

In this emotional climate, even an illiterate monk such as Papoulakos could move the multitudes in the Peloponnisos with his prophesy that the nation's dreams would soon be realized with the aid of that great Orthodox power, Russia. Not only the ordinary people, but even Otho and the key political leaders saw in the Russo-Turkish conflict the long awaited opportunity for territorial expansion. In their enthusiasm, they woefully misread the realities of the moment. The czar's policy had found little favor in the various European capitals. Austria, in particular, was fearful of increasing Russian influence in the Balkans and thus demanded that the Russian troops withdraw immediately from Moldavia and Wallachia. France and Britain, both of whom also wanted to keep Russia bottled up behind the Straits, joined in the fray. Greece, exposed as she was to the pressures of Britain and France—the two powers who controlled the Mediterranean with their fleets—had nothing to gain from an alignment with Russia. The British blockade of just two years earlier should have been a telling warning to Greece. Yet, the Great Idea had such an overpowering grip that no Greek leader— and certainly not King Otho—was willing to recognize the geopolitical realities. With official encouragement, Greek irregulars entered Thessalia and Macedonia, inciting the Orthodox inhabitants to rise against Ottoman rule. Turkey, preoccupied with the main theater of war, did not react very vigorously at first; she only responded by severing diplomatic relations with Athens. Otho, emboldened by this failure of Turkey to take direct military action, ordered the army to deploy along the northern borders and be ready to move into Thessalia under his personal command. He even toyed with the idea of crossing the frontiers alone in secrecy and, once inside Thessalia, calling the Greeks there to rise in revolt. These ambitious and somewhat romantic designs might have worked if Turkey had not enjoyed the considerable support of Britain and France. In April 1854 a combined force of British and French troops landed in Piraeus. Faced with an ultimatum, Otho moved his troops away from the frontier and recalled his irregulars from Thessalia and Macedonia. For a moment, the British considered that the time had come to get rid of Otho altogether. Palmerston, commenting on the idea of ousting Otho, said: "The very idea of such a change does one's heart good." To Palmerston, Otho was always "the spoilt child of absolutism."

Once again, as in other moments of national crisis, Otho called Mavrokordatos to the helm. Without illusions, he served as a dutiful soldier for a little over a year, earning for his government the unflattering sobriquet "occupation cabinet." In September 1855 he retired from politics. Despite his long involvement in Greek political affairs, Mavrokordatos' impact on the country's institutions and political ethos remained marginal. Too proud or too inept to stoop to the low levels of intrigue, patronage, rousfeti, and infighting, all of which had become an integral part of Greek politics at the time, he never stayed in office long enough to imprint the seal of his personality and convictions on the Greek political system.*

Otho was only too happy to see the difficult Phanariot retire and move out of the political arena. In the hope of finding a more pliable prime minister, he turned to Dimitrios Voulgaris—a wealthy sea captain from Idhra who was already sixty years old. An intelligent but willful and calculating man, Voulgaris was to play a central role in Greek politics for the next fifteen years. His view of politics was not much different from that of Kolettis, and his impact on the political ethos only reinforced the habits of pettiness, corruption, and partisan infighting. An autocrat by nature, he soon came into conflict with Otho and the palace officials, all of whom found him much less accommodating than they had anticipated. Two years after coming to power he asked the king to call a new election so that he could get more of his personal friends elected to the Vouli. Otho, in response to the growing friction with his prime minister, played a mean trick on him. He accepted his resignation but instead of calling an election, Otho appointed a palace cabinet, thus turning Voulgaris into an implacable enemy of his throne.

* Mavrokordatos died on August 5, 1865.

King Otho.   Picture Collection, The New York Public Library

The new prime minister was Athanasios Miaoulis, son of a major revolutionary hero. His venerated name was his only political asset, but with the king's support and the ample use of patronage Miaoulis lasted three years as Otho's prime minister. In the absence of cohesive party organizations, the Vouli deputies were in all but name independent political activists ready to shift their support to the highest bidder—usually the palace or the man in the post of the prime minister. The electorate, made up largely of illiterate and poor peasants, were readily subject to pressures and petty enticements. Consequently, they could only supply a shifting and uncertain foundation for the political system. Constituencies resembled feudal fiefs controlled by local political bosses, the komatarkhis. Many deputies held personal, undisputed control over a constituency and this made them independent of any partisan ties and loyalties. This fragmentation of the political forces made corruption easier and the throne's involvement in politics all the more pervasive.

The ouster of Otho

In 1858 Otho celebrated his twenty-fifth anniversary on the throne. The foreign occupation had ended the year before, the Miaoulis government was stable and obedient, and the economy was doing fairly well. The warmth of public sentiment seemed to augur many more anniversaries for his reign. Yet, within four years, Otho would be an exile, a victim of his own ineptitude and of foreign machinations. Nationalist aspirations were rekindled in Greece during the closing of the decade, which was crowded with momentous events: the emergence of an independent Rumania; the war over the unification of Italy, which pitted Austria and France against each other; the exploits of Garibaldi and the popular expectation that this Italian hero would come to the Balkans to lead the Christians against their Turkish masters; and finally, the insurrection in Herzegovina. All these caused great excitement among the Greeks, who saw in the conflicts new opportunities for the realization of the Great Idea. Ironically, Otho, the foremost proponent of this nationalistic policy, was to become its most prominent victim. Many Greeks suspected that with his monarchical convictions he sympathized with the Austrians in their effort to prevent Italian independence and unification. They were wrong; in fact, Otho had made secret contacts with Garibaldi and had even discussed with the Serbs the possibility of joint action. But these diplomatic intrigues had to remain secret, and so the popular suspicions persisted. Otho's opponents charged that the realization of the Great Idea had always been frustrated because of his incompetence and poor judgement. In truth, the failures could be traced to forces that were beyond Otho's control. No matter, for as it often happens in history, the people were looking for a convenient scapegoat. In the face of growing criticism, Otho became nervous. In a clumsy effort to stamp out opposition, he dissolved the Vouli in 1860 and held rigged elections; he even packed the Senate with new and more pliable senators, but all to no avail. His detractors persisted in their attacks on him and cleverly exploited popular fears that the childless king might be succeeded by one of his Catholic brothers. This would be in violation of the constitution, which clearly stated that the next occupant of the Greek throne should belong to the Orthodox faith.

Otho had faced opposition in the past, but this time the situation was decidedly different. The generation of the War of Independence was receding into history. For the first thirty years, almost all the members of the political elite came from three groups: those who had distinguished themselves during the struggle for independence and their close relatives; the prominent proestes families; and the educated Greeks from abroad. None of these groups was ideologically radical. But as the nineteenth century entered its second half, new personalities and new ideas moved to the forefront. The University of Athens and especially its law school became the spawning ground for the country's emerging political elite. The gates of the university were open to any person who had the formal qualifications and who was capable of passing the entrance examinations. Students came from the small, budding middle class, the peasantry, and to some extent from the more affluent minority at the top although the scions of this latter group usually went to Europe for their studies. Higher education and particularly a law degree often led to a career in politics. Needless to say, the varied background of the university graduates was reflected in their political views although a strong nationalist spirit seemed to be a common trait shared by all. It also appears that personal ambition often took precedence over ideological, economic, or social ties.

Gradually, but with increasing intensity as time went on, the forces for change focused on Otho as their main target. By 1861 even some of those who had served Otho through the years in high positions were turning against him. Early in the year, the police arrested several university students on charges of conspiracy but the courts refused to convict for lack of evidence, thus setting a good precedent for the independence and integrity of the judiciary. In March, during the festivities on Independence Day, Otho was booed by the crowd; then, in September, someone tried to assassinate Queen Amalie; before the end of the year, most of the ministers in the Miaoulis cabinet indicated their desire to resign.

In desperation, Otho turned to Constantinos Kanaris, the old naval hero of the revolution, in the hope that his national prestige would silence the opposition. But Kanaris was no longer devoted to Otho; in fact, he had secretly joined the ranks of Otho's enemies. Responding to the king's offer of the premiership, he posed almost the same conditions Mavrokordatos had made in 1841. Within exactly twenty years, history seemed to repeat itself. Kanaris asked that the ministers be selected and replaced by the prime minister; that the king abide by the policies of the cabinet, otherwise the cabinet should resign; that the camarilla be abolished and that the palace officials be approved by the cabinet.* Kanaris asked further for a new election, more liberal rules on the press, the reorganization of the national guard, and certain new fiscal measures for servicing the public debt. The first three conditions amounted to nothing less than a demand that Otho change in one fell swoop habits and processes that had emerged in the course of thirty years and which were encrusted in the very foundation of Otho's monarchy.

In an effort not to embarrass the king by a premature disclosure of his terms, Kanaris did not give his memorandum to the newspapers. This proved to be a mistake. Otho, realizing that Kanaris was no longer a willing servant, ignored the memorandum and tried instead to make it impossible for Kanaris to form a suitable cabinet. In the end, the Miaoulis government was kept in office. With public discontent turning into open defiance, the government resorted to police measures, further alienating the population and fueling the fires of opposition.

In Britain and elsewhere the eventuality of Otho's ouster had

---

* In his memorandum Kanaris said: "This is especially necessary with regard to military officers serving at the Palace . . ." It is interesting to note here that the 1968 constitution limited, for the first time, such service to only one year.

already been talked about confidentially at the highest levels. In January 1862 Queen Victoria discussed in a letter to her daughter, the crown princess of Prussia, the removal of Otho and the choice of a successor as though she were talking about some family affair or the change of cooks at Buckingham Palace. The queen wrote:

Uncle Ferdinand [prince of Saxe-Coburg, first cousin to Queen Victoria, and the former king of Portugal] refuses to go to G [Greece]. The G-s [Greeks] will have a near relation of ours, and the English Government most earnestly advise that Uncle E [Ernst II, duke of Saxe-Coburg, the brother of the prince consort] should go, and Alfie [Alfred, Queen Victoria's second son] become at once Duke. Dear Uncle Leopold [the king of Belgium, who in 1830 had turned down the Greek crown] originally suggested this and now it is most earnestly pressed. You can imagine how this agitates me, how in my state of desolation [following the death of her husband Albert], I feel the importance of this event. What Uncle E will say and do I know not. Uncle L [Leopold] is sounding him . . .

A military revolt broke out in Nauplia in February. The government reacted vigorously and within two months the revolt had fizzled out. The episode revealed a basic feature of power realities in Greece; that is, a military revolt that originated outside of Athens had practically no chance of succeeding because whoever controlled Athens had the odds in his favor.

With most of the agitation centered in the Peloponnisos, which was the traditional stronghold of Russian influence, the British government assumed that Russia was trying to take advantage of anti-Otho sentiment and replace the childless Otho with an Orthodox prince. In a final twist in the long story of Britain's ambivalent attitude toward Otho, London decided to shore up his tottering regime. In March 1862 Britain offered Greece the Ionian Islands. There were, of course, certain conditions attached to the offer: free elections, no involvement of the crown in politics, and peaceful relations with Turkey. In effect, Otho was being asked to abandon the Great Idea and become a constitutional monarch, leaving government and politics to the politicians. The terms were constructive and had they been accepted Otho might have saved his throne. But it was too late for him to change the course of a lifetime. He passed up the British offer and went on with his plans to prepare for military action in Thessalia and Macedonia in cooperation with the Serbs. It is possible that Otho clung to the vain hope that public discontent would be swept away by the wave of patriotic enthusiasm that a war might produce. He only succeeded in angering the British. In a personal letter to the British envoy in Athens, foreign minister Lord Russell ominously wrote: "Tell the King of Greece that a war against Turkey will shortly lead to his overthrow and abdication."

Otho's foreign policy, inspired as it was by the Great Idea, was in basic conflict with Britain's objectives in the area. The British had correctly resolved that to keep the Russians away from the Mediterranean, the two land masses flanking the Straits should be controlled by a single power friendly to Britain. This meant either Turkish control over Asia Minor and the major part of the Balkans, or a Greater Greece extending into Macedonia and Thrace, including Constantinople, as well as into the Asia Minor litoral and all the Aegean islands, including Crete. The latter could have been possible only if Britain had embraced the Great Idea and had become Greece's exclusive patron and champion. But from the outset Greece had three protectors with conflicting interests in the eastern Mediterranean. This was a fate suffered by none of the other countries in the Balkans during this period. In addition, the British were far from being convinced at the time that the Greeks had the ability to replace the Ottoman Empire as the guardians of the Straits. A British diplomat summed up London's point of view in 1859 with these words: "The Greeks even at the time of their apogee proved splendid citizens of small free states . . . but they were never able to establish and rule large states like the Romans . . . To suggest then that the dynasty of Osman could be replaced by the dynasty of Otho is a plain utopia." A reply to this might have been that the Byzantine Empire was dominated by Greeks for most of its history and that even the Ottoman Empire had relied heavily for centuries on the skills of the Phanariots. But that was past history. For the present, the internal squabbles of the small kingdom, the volatile temperament of the population, and the low caliber of the country's political leadership, were bound to dampen any zeal the British might have had in making the Great Idea their own policy in the area.

To complicate matters further, the Greeks themselves were divided in their sympathies and allegiances. Many were drawn to the side of Russia because of the Orthodox faith. For others, the French cultural influence, aided by an affinity of temperament among the people of the two nations, remained very strong. The British influence, emotionally nurtured by the memory of Lord Byron, was above all political, based on a healthy appreciation of Britian's commanding role in the Mediterranean. All these currents of sentiment and thought revolved around the Eastern Question—that is, what to do with the decaying Ottoman Empire.

In the summer of 1862 Otho's position weakened even further. His rejection of Britain's suggestions in March acted as the proverbial last straw. In June the Miaoulis government resigned. Otho, unable to find a single leader among the established politicians who was willing to shoulder the responsibilities of government, asked Geneos Kolokotronis, the son of the revolutionary hero, to form a cabinet. Kolokotronis was a decent man, but he was also a high official in the palace. Thus it appeared that Otho was again resorting to a palace cabinet, this time acting in effect as his own prime minister.

Dimitrios Voulgaris and many other disgruntled politicians began to think seriously of getting rid of Otho altogether. To their guarded inquiries, the envoys of the protector powers replied with encouraging gestures. In a last desperate effort, Otho sought to recapture popular support by going directly to the simple folk in the provinces, for in the past they had always reassured him with their unassuming and spontaneous loyalty. Accompanied by Queen Amalie he left Piraeus in early October for a royal tour. Within days revolts broke out in Central Greece and in the Peloponnisos. A temporary government was proclaimed in Patrai. Otho decided to return to Athens and take steps to restore his authority. It was too late. On the night of October 22 the military—now thoroughly disenchanted with Otho's failure to promote the Great Idea—sided with his political opponents and seized power in Athens. At first, the politicians seemed uncertain as to what course to follow. It was at this crucial moment that one of the younger political activists, Epameinondas Deliyiorgis, pushed decisively for Otho's abdication. Deliyiorgis' sudden prominence was a symbolic harbinger of the new realities. This eloquent firebrand represented the new educated elite who had been nourished with the intoxicating wine of the Great Idea but who rejected Otho as an incompetent standard-bearer.

As soon as the boat carrying the royal couple set anchor off Piraeus, the envoys of the protector powers came aboard and were immediately led to Otho's cabin. Their advice was simple and to the point. The revolt was successful and there was nothing left for Otho to do but accept the verdict and leave the country. Queen Amalie, her face flushed with anger and her eyes moist with tears, called on Otho to strike back, go to Messini, summon the people who had cheered the royal couple only a few days earlier, rally their loyal troops and "march back to Athens against those ingrate traitors." But Otho, so often in the past swayed by his queen, did not accept her advice this time. He realized that with Athens in the hands of the rebels, there was little hope for his return to the throne. He had no stomach for bloodshed. "As long as I remain on Greek soil," he said, "the Greek people will not be able to see that I am not to blame for all that has happened." Before the day was over, he informed the British envoy that he was ready to accept the offer and leave the country on the British frigate *Scylla*. In his farewell message to the Greek people, Otho wrote:

Convinced that after the recent events which have occurred in various parts of the kingdom and especially in the capital, my further stay in Greece at this time might cause bloody clashes among its inhabitants, which may be hard to contain, I have decided to leave the country I have loved and still love so much, and to whose well-being I have spared no effort and no toil for almost thirty years. Avoiding every ostentation, I have kept before my eyes only Greece's true interests, and with all my strength I have tried to promote her material and moral development, giving my special attention to the impartial dispensation of justice. Whenever there was a case of a political crime against my person I always showed the greatest leniency and let the deeds be forgotten. As I return to the land of my birth, I am aggrieved thinking of the misfortunes threatening my beloved Greece because of this new entanglement, and I pray to the benevolent God to grant His grace upon Greece.

This was Otho's last official communication to the Greek people.

Otho never formally abdicated. He simply left the country, a beaten, brokenhearted man. For almost three decades, he had sought to *govern* Greece, not merely *reign* over his adopted country, but he was a procrastinating and hopelessly inefficient administrator. In the words of a contemporary writer, Otho

spent half his life planning and the other half wondering . . . Blind to the clouds and storms of the sky, he searched through a microscope for the water's invisible amoebas . . . He had the best of intentions, he was most sincere in his love for Greece, a Greek at heart as few native Greeks ever were, he often harmed Greece out of his deep affection, like those inexperienced mothers who render their children feeble because of their excessive pampering and protection.

Once, in an almost classic exchange with one of his ministers—Alexandros Rangavis—Otho argued that he had an obligation to guide the electorate "as others do." When Rangavis countered that the "others" were party leaders while the king was supposed to stay above partisan politics, Queen Amalie interrupted angrily: "What do you mean? Shall we remain indifferent to the election of evil men, embezzlers, incompetents—and not guide and enlighten the people?" "Do you really think, Your Majesty," Rangavis querried wryly, "that you are in a position to distinguish the good from the bad people among your subjects? . . . This you can do less effectively than anyone else because those who enter the Palace do so under a guise, and often the most adroit in flattery appear to be the best. . . . Why undertake a responsibility which is not really yours?"

As the *Scylla* sailed, taking Otho on his way to exile, the ousted king could find some consolation in the thought that the land he had come to love so much had made remarkable progress in the three decades of his reign. Of course, to a foreign visitor, Greece still appeared as a semioriental, backward little kingdom, where conditions remained primitive by European standards. But progress in this case could be measured properly only by contrasting the present to what Otho had found when he came to Greece as a young man of seventeen. Still, Otho could not rightly take credit for all the advances; much of the country's progress could be traced to the efforts of enterprising Greeks who were engaged in commerce and shipping, as well as to the activities of Greeks who had amassed fortunes abroad and had brought their riches to the free corner of their native land. In spite of the improvements wrought by these men, the country remained largely a land of poor peasants. There was practically no industry. Most of the money was in commerce, mining, and shipping. The merchant marine, which had suffered great losses in the War of Independence, bounced back from 88,000 tons in 1832 to 320,000 tons in 1862, but most of the vessels were sailing ships that had to face stiff competition from foreign steamers.

Athens, where the capital moved in 1834, was a small village around the slopes of the Acropolis when Otho came to Greece. By the time he left, Athens had grown into a small city of twenty thousand people, dotted with several imposing buildings which stand prominently to this day. For example, the old royal palace today houses the legislature and the prime minister's office. Education had also moved forward during Otho's reign. In 1862 the University of Athens had a faculty of 34 and a student body of 250; nearly 6,000 students were enrolled in 58 junior and 7 senior high schools; approximately 30,000 youngsters were receiving some education in 321 primary schools. The church in Greece, for centuries under the jurisdiction of the patriarchate in Constantinople, had declared its independence in 1833 and, after much controversy, this *autocephalous* status was eventually recognized by the patriarchate in its *tomos* of 1850. This separation was not a display of defiance but a political expedient to free the Greek clergy as an advocate of nationalism and relieve the patriarchate of any responsibility or involvement in the frequent disputes between the Greek government and the sultan.

There was also some progress made in other areas. Some 250 miles of hard-surfaced roads connected Athens with major towns in the kingdom. Piraeus, a fishing village in 1832, had developed into the country's fastest growing port.

Otho's passing from the scene* marked the end of infancy for the small kingdom as new forces in the Balkans and in the country itself moved to the foreground. The Great Idea in particular was soon to clash with new and more complex aspirations and designs as Russia shifted her focus from Orthodoxy to Pan-Slavism and sought to advance her interests through the Slavic nationalities in the Balkans and especially through the emerging Bulgarians. In Europe, too, greater changes were in the offing. In less than ten years, France would be defeated while a new power, Germany, would enter the stage of European politics.

In search of a new monarch

With Otho's departure, the new government gained complete control throughout the country without any bloodshed.

---

* Otho died near Munich on July 26, 1867, at the age of fifty-two. To this day no monument commemorating Greece's first monarch stands on Greek soil.

Furthermore, no reprisals were taken against those who had been close to Otho through the years, probably because so many of those now in power had themselves served Otho in the past. Those who had remained in his service to the end made no effort to show their loyalty once he was gone. Within days it seemed that a whole era had faded as though it had never existed. Otho Square in the center of the capital was renamed Omonia Square, the Otho University in Athens became the National University, and Otho's bust in Piraeus was replaced by that of Themistocles, the ancient naval hero.

Voulgaris, a guiding spirit of the uprising, assumed the post of prime minister. The old fox had repaid Otho in full measure for his perfidy in not proclaiming elections for Voulgaris' benefit in 1857. Expectations that radical improvements would immediately be achieved once Otho was gone were soon frustrated. The country's economic, social, and political problems remained as acute as ever. Before the end of November 1862, the government was shopping around for a loan of 200,000 pounds sterling.

More crucial for the country's future was the search for a new monarch. Hardly anyone at the time thought of establishing a republic. With the exception of Switzerland, there was no other significant republic in Europe to serve as a model or example. Even France had an emperor at the time. Besides, the royal institution appeared to be more in tune with the heroic undertones of the Great Idea—the crowning of the Greek monarch in Constantinople being the dream's unchanging ending. If these reasons were not convincing enough, Palmerston's warning that the establishment of a republic in Greece "would be incompatible with the European interests" certainly carried a great deal of weight. Painful past experiences had brought home the point that Britain, with her mastery of the Mediterranean, held the key to Greece's destiny. With this in mind, the National Assembly, which convened in November, opted for a member of the British royal house, Victoria's second son, Alfred, to be the country's future king. Even the Turks, knowing the British views on the Eastern Question, saw with favor the selection of Alfred. The Turkish envoy to Athens even suggested—but, as it was later revealed, without explicit authorization from his government— that the selection of Alfred might induce Turkey to transfer Epirus and Thessalia to Greece. Apparently Queen Victoria was at the time also in favor of such a territorial rearrangement. In a letter to Palmerston she wrote that with the transfer of Epirus and Thessalia, the Greeks "will be less likely to throw themselves into the arms of Russia when Prince Alfred refuses, besides checking their desire to attack Turkey in the hopes of enlarging their territory."

The hint "when Prince Alfred refuses" was pregnant with meaning. Strange though it may seem, Queen Victoria did not want her son to accept the Greek crown. She had already written to Palmerston that "upon no earthly account and under no circumstances would I consent" to Alfred's going to Greece. Whatever the official explanations, the real reason was that Victoria did not want her favorite son to go off to what she regarded as a backward Balkan country, where bandits roamed the countryside and seamy politicians fanned the passions of a volatile people. The picture was overdrawn to some extent, but it was Victoria's image of Greece nonetheless. In addition, Victoria considered Alfred much too young for such a hazardous task, and much too near the succession to the British throne to be spared for another country. Above all, she disliked the thought of her grandchildren being brought up in the Orthodox faith.

The Queen's veto on this matter was a serious setback for Palmerston's plans. But the British prime minister was a very resourceful man, and so he needed to be for now the Russians were pressing hard for their own candidate, the czar's son-in-law, Prince Nicholas. Keeping Victoria's objections a well-guarded secret, Palmerston played his cards with mastery. Speaking to the Russian ambassador, he indicated that if Russia were to remove her candidate from the running, Britain would also agree to remove Alfred. The Russians, unaware of Victoria's views, happily agreed.

While Palmerston was secretly striking this clever bargain, the Greeks were getting ready to go to the polls and vote on their choice for a future king. On the morning of the balloting, some Athenian newspapers came out with "reliable but unconfirmed reports" that two days earlier the protector powers had exchanged notes ruling out the candidacy "of all princes related by close family ties to their reigning houses." The reports were entirely accurate, but the British envoy denied any knowledge of such an agreement among the powers. The plebiscite went on as scheduled. Alfred received 230,016 votes against 2,400 cast for all other candidates, including Prince

Nicholas. The near unanimity in favor of Alfred showed that the Greek voters, led by an almost totally united political leadership, were embracing Britain as the country's chief patron.

The British were afraid that when the Greeks learned of Alfred's refusal, they might turn to extreme solutions. Fearing that they might even go to the point of proclaiming a republic(!), the British quickly informed the Greek government that their offer to transfer the Ionian Islands to Greece, which was initially made to Otho, was still valid provided the National Assembly remained "loyal to constitutional monarchy, prevented any aggression against neighboring states, and elected a King against whom no valid objection could be raised." The delegates, unaware of the British-Russian bargain, joyfully ratified the results of the referendum and declared Otho's reign officially at an end. They were about to send a formal delegation to London to present Alfred with the Greek crown when the charade was abruptly ended. On February 12 a stunned National Assembly heard the official announcement that "Her Majesty was forced because of diplomatic obligations and other considerations to decline this distinguished honour."

With this, the search for a monarch was on again. For another two months the Greek crown was peddled through Europe's royal houses but there were no takers. In the words of a Greek newspaper at that time, "many are astonished and cannot fathom why the sons of kings do not rush to the Kingdom of Greece, soon to become the Kingdom of the East, which is waiting for them." These were words of honest indignation and surprise, not irony or self-derision.

Fate was soon to come to the aid of the hard-pressed and frustrated searchers. In March, the prince of Wales married Princess Alexandra, daughter of Denmark's future King Christian IX. Her younger brother, William George, was one of the royal guests. Palmerston met the young prince at the wedding and the thought must have flashed immediately through his mind: the Danish prince was almost perfect for the role. His older sister was the bride of the prince of Wales and his younger sister was engaged to Russia's czarevitch. The only drawback was that the prince was only seventeen years old. When Victoria was told of Palmerston's choice, she wrote to the king of Belgium with cutting humor: "The Government has kidnapped unfortunate Willie, Alix's second brother, a good but not overbright and very plain youth—to become king of Greece, and are very proud of it!"

In their talks with Denmark's king, the British posed the same old conditions: the young king's mission would be above all to prevent Greece from disturbing the status quo in the Balkans and the eastern Mediterranean. The Danish monarch could not care less about Greek aspirations. The terms were accepted. Needless to say, with more than two-thirds of the nation still under Turkish rule pledges made by the king of Denmark could hardly stand in the way once the Greek forces were ready for the confrontation.

On June 18 a delegation headed by Kanaris, the old hero of the War of Independence, handed the king of Denmark the official document of the National Assembly declaring Prince William to be George I, king of the Hellenes. Kanaris in a brief, emotional address welcomed Greece's new sovereign and asked that he devote himself "to the development of the nation's free institutions." The young monarch in his reply pledged "to inscribe on [his] heart with indelible letters the motto of the King of Denmark: 'My power is the love of my people'."

The new king, after visits to Russia, Britain, and France, came to Greece on October 18—almost a year to the day since Otho, standing on the deck of a British frigate had cast a final, nostalgic gaze at the receding coastline of the Peloponnisos as he sailed on his way to Europe and exile. With the arrival of King George I, a new chapter was opening in the nation's modern history.

The interregnum

The Athenians had good reason for giving their new sovereign a glorious welcome. During the preceding months, intense partisan strife and violent rivalry had once again engulfed the country. The leading politicians and their factions had thrown themselves into the arena with a vengeance as they jockeyed for position in anticipation of the young king's arrival. Brigandage, never totally extinct, had flared up again, and it was difficult at times to tell who were the bandits and who were the soldiers, or where brigandage ended and the partisan factions and their political machines began. In the National Assembly, the fragmentation of political forces bordered on the ludicrous; it was a vain search to identify political ideologies, loyalties, or programs. The familiar egocentrism was showing a new flash of vigor. Each faction was led by a dominant personality and concentrated solely on enhancing its own power position. Certain radical elements, including many university students, called for violence, arguing that "revolution without blood is a battle without dead, music without melody."

In June 1863, the hot-tempered advocates of violence had their wish fulfilled—although in characteristic fashion the incidents had their tragicomic overtones. The June crisis started when a band of brigands was captured near Athens. As they were being escorted to the capital, they managed to break loose from their captors and barricade themselves in a monastery. The government sent a battalion to dislodge and recapture them, but the soldiers started instead to fraternize with the bandits. It appears that the battalion commander was a friend of Voulgaris, who was at the time a member of the opposition. He seized this opportunity to embarrass the government and force its downfall. The government responded by sending another detachment, which immediately placed the disloyal commander under arrest; whereupon, the arrested leader's men captured two cabinet ministers who had come to the scene hoping to inspire awe with their presence. With Voulgaris' sly prodding, the mutiny spread into other military units and the shooting started. In the end, the envoys of the protector powers had to intervene. They threatened that unless the fighting stopped immediately they would be forced to sever all relations "with a country where bravery is being so misused and true patriotism appears to have been for ever lost." The landing of small units of foreign soldiers from the frigates that were usually anchored in Piraeus added the necessary punch to the warning. The fighting stopped. In the process, the familiar complaints about the pettiness of the politicians received fresh fuel—although the political leaders were not really an alien breed, but rather a reflection of the nation's own political ethos. Nonetheless, most of the newspapers expressing the prevailing views among ordinary people turned their hopes to the young king, who appeared in the public imagination as a living promise of stability and progress.

As though to give a visible testimony to this anticipated new beginning, the assembly that was elected after Otho's ouster started work on a new, more democratic constitution. In a resolution approved a few days before King George's arrival, the assembly pointedly stipulated that the king had no constitutional powers, all of which were reserved exclusively for the people. King George acknowledged this declaration of popular sovereignty when during his swearing-in ceremony he said: "I ascend the throne to which your vote has invited me." This was a simple phrase filled with meaning.

The constitutional work in the assembly moved at a snail's pace for almost a year. At length, King George told the delegates that unless they moved with dispatch he would be forced to renounce the crown and leave. "My bags are always packed . . ." he told a friend. The royal intervention had its desired effect; within ten days, the assembly completed its task. On October 21 the text of the constitution was forwarded to the king for promulgation.

The new document embodied a very liberal form of constitutional monarchy, which became known as *vasilevomeni dimokratia* (crowned democracy). This was not the term used in the text, but it flowed from its declaration that "all powers belong to the nation, and are implemented in the manner specified by the constitution." This statement, incidentally, was taken from the Troezina charter. The notion of popular sovereignty was further accented by the stipulation that "the king has no other powers than those expressly granted him by the constitution and the appropriate laws."

King George's first decade

The young monarch came to a country that was vastly different from his native land. True, Greece had moved away from the conditions that had prevailed in the days of Kapodistrias and in the early years of Otho, but the improvement loomed large only when compared to what existed when the new state first came into being. At George's ascendancy almost eight in every ten people still lived in villages, farming their small, craggy plots, or tending their flocks of sheep and goats. Most families had only a few acres of land, which often were scattered in separate parcels. Peasant families continued to produce primarily for their own needs, with currants being the only product exported in quantity at that time. Few roads fit for wheeled traffic crossed the dusty plains; the mountain villages could be reached only by donkey or mule. To transport olive oil or wine, the peasants used goatskins that were essentially not much different from those used in the days of Homer. Most of the family clothing was spun or woven at home. Very little money was used in the villages, as the peasant usually paid with produce the ironsmith

who fixed his plow, the priest who baptized his children, the owner
of the mules he used to thresh his grain. It was a simple and frugal
life. The tithe, a primitive form of tax levied on the gross harvest,
was the state's principal source of revenue. This form of taxation,
inherited from the days of Ottoman rule, did not disappear until
1880, and in some parts of the country it remained in effect until
much later. It completely disappeared only during the Metaxas
dictatorship in 1940.

Most towns were hardly more than enlarged villages, with narrow,
unpaved streets, small, unimposing rowhouses, a bazaar-like cluster
of tiny stores, and hardly any municipal services at all. In a land
where there are few rivers, most of which are actually dry riverbeds
that turn into wild torrents during the rainy season, water has always
been a problem. A spring well in the backyard was a coveted
convenience even in Athens. Most of the townspeople had to rely on
a central water fountain, where people and pack animals shared the
precious supply in placid equanimity.

Athens, already spreading over the empty Attica plain without
much design, was inhabited by a heterogeneous assortment of
people—Phanariot families who had come to Greece in search of
high positions; rich merchants from abroad; shipowners from the
islands; aging men who had fought in the War of Independence;
university students; civil servants and others aspiring to find a job in
the growing bureaucracy; intellectuals who were rich in the treasures
of the mind but typically poor in financial resources; politicians and
their cohorts; and, as you would expect, an increasing number of
artisans, shopkeepers, lawyers, and tradesmen serving this disparate
society. There was no titled aristocracy, and what passed for the
city's upper class relied for distinction either on the family's record
during the War of Independence, or on wealth, or on political
prominence, or on connections with the palace. The distance
between the few wealthy and the mass of low-income families was
great, with no broad middle class yet providing a reliable foundation
for stability and cohesion. These social disparities, however, were
usually obscured by the overpowering impact of nationalism, which
was forceful enough to forge bonds that transcended economic or
social differences.

This spirit of nationalism cemented the people into a cohesive
union, especially in moments of crisis, but it also tended to sweep
away prudence and moderation, often with disastrous consequences.

With over 2.5 million Greeks living under Ottoman rule, compared to less than 1 million within the borders of the kingdom, the Great Idea remained for almost every Greek the only honorable policy. This was a reality that King George could not easily ignore in spite of his uncle's pledge to the British.

Before long the young king faced his first major test. The British, keeping their promise, had transferred the Ionian Islands to Greece. But this gesture, instead of satisfying at least for a while the nation's aspirations, merely rekindled hopes of Greeks elsewhere under foreign domination. Within a year, the island of Crete was again on the verge of revolt. Not surprisingly, the agitation had been secretly encouraged by the British, who hoped to push the situation to a point where they could step in and take over the island temporarily as a compromise solution—exactly as they had tried to do in 1841. Unlike the Ionian Islands, which were of little strategic importance, Crete was considered vital to the control of the eastern Mediterranean and the sea lanes to the Orient. The Cretan revolt broke out in the summer of 1866. Within months, superior Moslem forces brought in from Asia Minor and Egypt forced the revolutionaries to retreat to their mountain hideouts. By November, their headquarters in the monastery of Arkadi came under siege. Hard pressed, the defenders set fire to the powder magazines stored in the monastery's vaults, blowing up themselves, their families, and a good number of the enemy troops.

The incident, reported in banner headlines throughout Europe, stunned public opinion. In France Napoleon III, who was busy playing big power politics on a worldwide scale* shifted temporarily in favor of the island's union with Greece. He even toyed with the idea of pressing Turkey to transfer Epirus and Thessalia to Greece provided that this would mark the end of her expansion. The Russians, on their part, agreed to the union of Crete, but they would not go along with the transfer of Epirus and Thessalia because they were already moving toward the new policy of Pan-Slavism and a future Bulgarian state. The British, of course, doggedly rejected any thought of letting Crete become part of the Greek kingdom; but, expectedly, they began to speak of autonomy as a possible compromise. Greek diplomacy failed to take advantage of this more or less

---

* At this time Napoleon III was involved in the ill-fated venture of imposing Maximilian as the emperor of Mexico.

favorable climate, and before very long several events changed the whole picture. In the summer of 1867 King George, without even informing the government in advance, became engaged to the czar's niece, Grand Duchess Olga. In the eyes of Britain and France this seemed to give Russia a secure foothold at last in Greece. Napoleon, in a characteristic reaction, said with pique: "France is not about to give Crete to a Russian princess as part of her dowry." With this, French support for Crete's union with Greece vanished.

At about the same time, Athens approached Belgrade and proposed joint action in the Balkans. This move was bound to infuriate both the British and the Russians, albeit for different reasons: the British were enraged because such an alliance would have no other purpose than to dismember the Ottoman Empire; the Russians were enraged because it would upset their designs for a future Bulgarian state. Disregarding these repercussions, Greece and Serbia signed a secret treaty in August 1867. The two countries, having no basic conflicts of interest in the area, agreed to work together for the liberation of the Christian populations in the Balkans. The Great Idea of the Serbs was primarily aimed against the Austro-Hungarian Empire, which controlled Slavic populations in the north and along the Dalmatian coast. The Great Idea of the Greeks, by contrast, was primarily directed against Ottoman control in the southern part of the peninsula and in the islands. A possible area of contention, Macedonia, was left for future discussions. The secret treaty, half-heartedly approved by King George, was never implemented because Mikhail Obrenovic, the Serbian king who earnestly favored such cooperation, was mysteriously murdered in June 1868. Turkish diplomacy took advantage of these developments and of the vacillations and disagreements that they caused among the major powers. In 1868 the sultan, in an unprecedent move, visited Paris and London. In return for support in preserving the territorial integrity of his empire, he promised to take several steps to improve the lot of the Christians in Crete and elsewhere.

Greece, diplomatically isolated and without sufficient resources, could not risk a military confrontation with Turkey over Crete. By necessity she remained officially an anxious bystander, contributing some funds collected privately and allowing a few volunteers to join the Cretan revolutionaries. Greece also permitted her newspapers to vent public frustration in reams of patriotic but harmless rhetoric. When the European statesmen met in Paris in 1869 to take up the

Cretan issue, Greece could not gain at the conference table what she was unable to claim on the battlefield. Crete remained under Turkish control. Still, the revolt had not been entirely in vain. The sultan issued an imperial decree, the *Hatti Humayum*, which helped improve conditions on the island for the next ten years—at least when the decree was not violated or ignored by the Turkish authorities.

During the Cretan revolt, political instability had only added to Greece's already severe internal problems. The 1864 constitution, which had ushered in the system of vasilevomeni dimokratia, was quite liberal and progressive for its day, but politics continued to suffer from the traditional practices of paternalism, corruption, and narrow-minded partisanship. A remark made by King George in 1870 in the wake of an unfortunate episode having international repercussions is quite revealing. In the spring of that year, a band of brigands operating less than fifteen miles from Athens had captured for ransom a group of prominent foreign visitors as they were returning from an excursion to Marathon. When government troops tried to free the captives by force, the brigands killed their defenseless hostages. This caused an uproar in Greece and abroad, especially since the victims included foreign diplomats and members of British high society. King George, apologizing in a letter to his brother-in-law, the prince of Wales, remarked that "many say that the opposition organized the coup only to discredit the Government, and this because the internal situation was improving (of course, they never thought for a moment that this calamity would be the outcome). I consider this possible . . ." This was certainly a serious charge against the politicians of the period, but one which was made plausible by the close ties that existed between some of them and the bands of brigands.

The partisan rivalries within the country were, of course, exploited by the foreign envoys with no less vigor than had been displayed in the days of Otho. In 1866, after five cabinet crises within a year, King George complained that the British envoy was responsible for at least two of these.

The interventions by foreign governments and the frequent cabinet changes—between 1867 and 1870 the country had five different prime ministers—were only symptoms. When the 1864 constitution scuttled Otho's handpicked Gerousia, the authority of the elected Vouli increased accordingly but its fragmentation into several kaleidoscopic factions remained. A practice to use lead ballots, which had been introduced in 1864, succeeded only in reinforcing this tendency to move away from consolidation and unity. Each candidate was assigned a separate, personal ballot box with his name printed on the outside. Each box was divided into two compartments, a black one for no votes and a white one for yes votes. The voter dropped one lead ballot for each candidate in either of the two compartments. The candidate with the largest number of lead ballots in his white compartment was elected. There was no reference to a political party and each candidate had to rely mostly on his own means of appeal, patronage, or even intimidation. Under the circumstances, friendship with a brigand or the local police chief could be at times decisive. Patronage and kinship ties were equally important. By officiating as a best man at a wedding or as godfather at a baptism, a politician could reasonably hope to forge insoluble ties of loyalty. The effect of all these practices on the political system was predictable. The Vouli deputies acted mostly as free agents— just as they had done in the days of Otho.

In the absence of a commanding political figure, the Vouli was split into five or six factions led by an equal number of political leaders who succeeded each other in the premiership by forming short-lived alliances. Even within the factions there was little cohesion, as deputies moved easily from one group to another—usually because of personal grudges or enticing offers. No clear-cut differences in ideology or policy existed, except possibly on the issue of the country's relations with Turkey. The division on this question was largely between those who advocated caution and those who played without restraint the patriotic theme of the Great Idea for political gain. King George, more by instinct than deliberate judgement, chose to go along with these political practices, giving the opportunity to one faction after another to taste the fruits of power. This, probably more than anything else, helped the young monarch win wide popular acceptance for his reign. Nonetheless, the frequent cabinet changes resulted in governmental weaknesses and a climate of uncertainty, which, as the Cretan revolt had revealed, showed more clearly on matters of foreign policy. The king was the only constant factor in the formulation of foreign policy, and this inevitably made his personal influence all the more considerable.

With more than 75 percent of the population relying on subsistence farming, the frequent cabinet changes had little direct effect on the economy, which continued to inch upward during the first decade of vasilevomeni dimokratia. Most of the progress could be traced to the efforts of individual businessmen, many of whom were former expatriates with fortunes that had already been made in Constantinople, Alexandria, Odessa, Vienna, or London. Significantly, most of the major public buildings in Athens and elsewhere were constructed with sizable gifts and bequests from wealthy Greek merchants who had prospered abroad. By 1874 the urban population had gone over the 25 percent mark but many of the former peasants who had come to the cities and towns in search of a better life found few job opportunities there. Consequently, they had to become pushcart vendors and handimen in order to make even a meager living. Only seven thousand people in the entire country were employed in small industrial enterprises, most of which were engaged in olive oil processing, pottery, handicrafts, tanneries, flour mills, and small-scale shipbuilding. Hardly any of these enterprises employed more than a dozen workers.

chapter 2
New Forces, Greater Challenges

The Bulgarians move to the foreground

Before the Greeks had time to recover from the failure of the Cretan uprising, they received another piece of bad news. In February 1870, Sultan Abdul-Aziz accepted a Russian suggestion and decreed that the Bulgarian dioceses were no longer under the patriarchate. The Greeks correctly interpreted this Turkish move as an action directed against their aspirations in the Balkans. To an outsider the Greek protestations might have appeared totally unreasonable since the church in Athens had declared its own autonomy in 1834. But to the Greeks, the separation of their church from the partriarchate in no way implied a break of relations with the mother church. As far as the Greeks were concerned, the separation from the patriarchate was to be only temporary, to last until the day when Constantinople would again become a Greek city. By contrast, they saw in the Bulgarian autonomy not only a serious blow to the prestige of the patriarchate but also the recognition of a new force in the Balkans that was destined to become their major rival in the future. As time was to show, they were right in this assessment.

Strange though it may seem, the sultan's decree had been largely the work of the Russian ambassador to Constantinople. He had succeeded in convincing the Turks that a separation of the Bulgarian dioceses would cut down the stature of the patriarchate and reduce Greek influence in Turkish-held Macedonia and Thrace. Behind this seeming concern for the welfare of the Ottoman Empire, the hand of the Pan-Slavists, who had already gained a great deal of influence among the governing circles in Russia, could readily be seen. The key argument of the Pan-Slavists was that Russia, in pursuing her traditional objective to reach the Mediterranean, should rely more on her affinity with the Slavic populations in the Balkans than on her common faith with the Orthodox Christians in the area. In his efforts to promote an independent Bulgarian church, the Russian ambassador found an unexpected ally in the French. They were quick to recognize that any blow to the Orthodox patriarchate was bound to please the Vatican and Catholics everywhere. The British, who had no illusions about the Russian motives, tried at first to block this separation but then they decided to go along with it because they did not want to let the Russians monopolize the friendship of this emerging national force in the Balkans. Besides, the argument that the Bulgarians should have a clergy speaking their own tongue was a hard one to refute. Until that time, most of the clergy and especially the bishops in the Ottoman-held territories were Greeks appointed by the patriarchate, which since 1453 had been recognized by the sultan as the authority responsible for all Orthodox Christians in the occupied territories. For four centuries those clerics had made no effort to assimilate the largely illiterate peasants who had little awareness of their national identity. Instead, the clerics had often treated them with the rapaciousness and insensitivity of colonial masters. Now the time of reckoning had come.

In 1870 few people in Europe knew that a Bulgarian nationality even existed. The Bulgars, a tribe of wild horsemen, had originally come to the Balkans from central Asia in the seventh century. Following the Huns through the Russian plains into eastern Europe,

A view of Athens in 1870.   Picture Collection, the New York Public Library

they eventually settled in the area between the Danube and the Balkan mountain range. Relatively few in numbers, they intermingled with the Slavic tribes already living there and adopted their language and customs. No trace of the original Bulgarian tongue is found in the language spoken today in Bulgaria. In 870 their king, Boris, decided to accept the Christian faith from the patriarchate in Constantinople instead of from the Vatican. He did so mainly because the pope refused to grant independence to the Bulgarian church. For the next six centuries the fortunes—and the borders—of the Bulgarian state went through many changes as a result of armed conflicts with the Byzantines to the south, the Serbs to the west, and other groups pressing from the north. In the late fourteenth century, the Bulgarian empire was destroyed by the invading Turkish forces, and for the next five centuries all the areas formerly ruled by the Bulgarian czars became an Ottoman province. Together with all the other Christians in the Balkans, the Bulgars were placed under the patriarchate in Constantinople and Greek bishops and priests moved into the area. Although Greek became the language of the upper classes in the Bulgarian towns, the Slavic vernacular survived in the countryside.

In the nineteenth century, a sense of national identity was revived under the influence of Russian scholars and agents. The Russians had discovered that the Bulgarians spoke a language very similar to their own. Disregarding the fact that the original Bulgars were not Slavs at all, they embraced the modern Bulgarians as a dynamic offshoot of the great Slavic family. The Bulgarian nationalists, realizing that the Greekness of the clergy—who also controlled whatever educational instruction was locally available—stood as a barrier to national awareness, decided that before they could take any other steps for their national liberation, the church organization first had to be freed from the patriarchate's hold. In 1870, exactly one thousand years since Boris had accepted Christianity, the sultan's decree created an autonomous Bulgarian exarchate. The patriarch refused to recognize the separation, and when the first exarch was elected in February 1872 he excommunicated the Bulgarian church as schismatic.

The controversy suddenly thrust upon the Greeks the awareness of another rival force in the Balkans. Until then they had assumed that they alone had a legitimate claim on Epirus, Macedonia, and Thrace. Now another potential heir had appeared on the scene.

That the first major move of this new force was to defy the authority of the patriarchate—a Greek institution—inevitably raised the Greek ire. This was only the opening act. Before the end of the decade, the Bulgarians would move with strong Russian backing to the center of the arena.

Kharilaos Trikoupis

The emergence of the Bulgarian exarchate, following hard upon the heels of the Cretan failure, cast a heavy shadow of frustration and anger over Athens. Those who understood the realities standing in the way of Greece's territorial expansion blamed the advocates of war for the country's setbacks; those who were guided by their nationalist feelings blamed the moderates for leaving the country militarily unprepared. Through the years the king had appointed prime ministers representing both policies, and therefore the throne could not escape criticism. In June 1874 one of the younger politicians, Kharilaos Trikoupis, wrote a newspaper article with the title "Who is to blame?" He held the crown responsible and charged that "Greece is governed as an absolute monarchy." A few days later he followed up with a second, even more critical article in which he made the provocative point that "the responsibility for revolutions does not fall on those who carry them out but on those who make them inevitable." The articles were published anonymously, but when the authorities arrested the newspaper publisher, Trikoupis came forward and admitted that he was the author. He was promptly arrested. Although he was released four days later and all charges were eventually dropped, Trikoupis had become in the meantime the hero of the liberal forces in the country. What his previous public record had failed to achieve, his prosecution produced overnight.

Trikoupis, of course, was already a well-known personality. Born in Nauplia in 1832, he was the scion of a prominent family. His father, Spyridon, was a former prime minister, a renowned historian, a respected figure in the War of Independence, and a brother-in-law of Alexandros Mavrokordatos. Kharilaos Trikoupis received the best education and was appointed early to a most respectable diplomatic post in London. As a young diplomat he played a key role in the transfer of the Ionian Islands to Greece. As foreign minister during the Cretan revolt, he had negotiated the secret treaty with Serbia. Multilingual, urbane, a frugal and meticulous man with a tendency to appear aloof, Trikoupis was an accomplished orator with a cutting wit and a striking dislike for the practices of patronage and empty verbosity, which were so much a part of the politics of his time. A man of liberal views, he favored strongly the parliamentary form of government as practiced in Britain. A hardheaded realist, he was not easily swayed by extravagant nationalist aspirations. However, because he was also an eminently practical politician, he would, at critical moments in his career, use the kind of rhetoric that seldom failed to fire the emotions of his countrymen. His relations with King George had been correct, but not cordial, because he never liked to play on the king's favor. A bachelor throughout his life, he had only one passion, politics. His two controversial articles in the summer of 1874 reflected this passion.

Public reaction indicated that Trikoupis' articles had indeed given expression to a general feeling of dissatisfaction and to a growing desire for change. Voulgaris—by now a synonym for corrupt politics—had in February again been appointed prime minister; this time he had found the going rougher than ever before. A majority of the Vouli deputies had even refused to take part in legislative work, and Voulgaris had thought for a moment of changing the constitution to make it more monarchical. Rumors of such plans served only to foment public uneasiness. In March, university students launched a series of protest demonstrations calling for the government's resignation. Then, the opposition newspapers published veiled charges against two cabinet members who were suspected of accepting bribes to influence the election of three bishops.

At this critical moment, King George acted with the flexibility and moderation that were his greatest assets. His first move was to dismiss Voulgaris. The old man who had dominated political life for the king's first decade retired in sullen resentment. He died two years later, "an autocrat with no love for order, a rebel with no love for freedom," in the words of a contemporary writer. The king's second move was even more unexpected. Disregarding the offending articles, he asked Trikoupis to form a cabinet and take the country to elections. Apparently, he was influenced in his choice by the British, who held Trikoupis in high esteem. In later years, King George would often bring a critic to power, reasoning that if he succeeded in office the country would benefit by having some problems solved, if he failed his criticism would be silenced by the embarrassment of failure.

Trikoupis accepted the mandate but in the electoral campaign that followed he deliberately avoided the familiar practices of patronage and corruption. He barely managed to have himself and a handful of his political friends elected to the Vouli. At this point, he took a step that in itself reveals the man's character. In the traditional Speech of the Throne—delivered by the king but written by the prime minister—he added a significant paragraph stipulating that henceforth the king would call to the premiership only those "who enjoy the declared confidence" of the majority in the legislature. This was in keeping with the basic feature of a parliamentary system which Trikoupis strongly favored. In the past, the king had often resorted to minority cabinets, and on at least one occasion he had dismissed a prime minister who enjoyed at the time majority support in the Vouli. This happened in 1868 at the height of the Cretan revolt, when the king dismissed Koumoundouros, who favored an assertive policy in Crete in contrast to the king's more cautious approach.

The requirement for majority support was fine in principle; the trouble was that with the fragmentation of political forces, there was seldom a cohesive and durable majority to rely on. Be that as it may, Trikoupis was the first to suffer from the application of this principle, as well he knew when he proposed it. Having no majority support in the Vouli, he resigned and was replaced by Koumoundouros, who received 136 of 153 votes cast. In spite of this setback, Trikoupis had gained one important asset for the future: he had become prime minister and had thereby reached the top level of the political hierarchy. He could look forward to new and greater opportunities in the future.

The Russo-Turkish war of 1878

While the politicians in Greece were spending much of their energy and intelligence on internal squabbles, the Balkan volcano, never totally quiescent, was again rumbling with threats of impending eruption. In the summer of 1875 the mountaineers of Bosnia and Herzegovina along the Adriatic rose up in arms against their Turkish overlords. The sultan sought to dampen the forces of revolt by promising reforms, but to no avail. The uprising, initially encouraged by the Serbs, soon found support in other quarters as well. Austria, somewhat embarrassed by Prussia's success in beating France and establishing a German state five years earlier, had turned its gaze toward the Orient in an ambitious policy labeled *Drang nach Osten* (Drive to the East). This policy of expanding Germanic influence to the Middle East was also favored by Germany, which, under the forceful leadership of Bismarck, had moved to the center of international politics. France was still licking her wounds while the Russians, with their Pan-Slavist designs now fully conceived, were anxious to force another showdown with Turkey. Britain could do little by herself to stem the rising tide.

The failure of the Turkish forces to put down the rebellion in Bosnia and Herzegovina fired the aspirations of Christians throughout the occupied territories. The Bulgarians, with all the vigor of a people with a newly-discovered identity, were especially troublesome. They formed armed bands that turned against Moslem civilians as well as Christian rivals in Macedonia and Thrace. In April 1876, with tempers rising on all sides, a Turkish mob attacked the Christians in Salonika. During the violent clashes, the consuls of France and Germany were both killed. Foreign naval units—including two Greek gunboats—rushed to the scene to protect the Christians. Other units moved to Smyrna and Constantinople, where similar incidents were threatened. One week later, the Bulgarians launched a general uprising. Within days, Sultan Abdul-Aziz was overthrown by his thirty-six-year-old nephew, Murad, a man of liberal and progressive ideas. Murad, in fact, proved much too liberal for the Turkish establishment and three months later he was forced to resign in favor of his younger brother, Abdul-Hamid. These internal upheavals did not prevent the Turks from turning with savage fury against the Bulgarians. Some fifteen thousand were massacred and dozens of villages razed to the ground. European public opinion suddenly became keenly aware of the Bulgarian nation. A pamphlet decrying those atrocities was published in Britain by no lesser a figure than Gladstone himself, generating a wave of sympathy for the victims.

Russia took full advantage of the situation. In April the czar demanded that two principalities be established for the Bulgarians, one with Sofia as its capital and the other with Plovdiv. Apparently, the czar hoped to achieve a quick settlement without war. To his surprise, the sultan refused to bow. The Russian military establishment, determined to recover the prestige lost in the Crimea, forced the issue and within days Russia declared war on Turkey.

The Russian troops, commanded by the czar's brother Nicholas, were allowed by the Rumanian government to pass through that country, and in June they crossed the Danube. The czar had been led to believe that his troops would march all the way to Constantinople with hardly any resistance. He was in for another surprise; the Turks reacted quickly and vigorously. By reinforcing the garrison in the town of Pleven they cut off the Russian lines of communication, while with other forces they hit the advancing Russians at the Shipki pass. For a moment the entire Russian operation seemed on the verge of collapse. But the Turkish generals failed to follow up their early successes. This gave the Russians time to regroup, bring fresh forces from Russia, and lay a successful siege on Pleven, where the garrison was forced to surrender. By January the Russian troops had reached Adrianople in Thrace and were moving toward Constantinople almost unopposed. At this critical point in the conflict, the Serbs declared war on Turkey, while in Greece a coalition government continued to wonder as to what course to follow.

With the Russian troops marching through Eastern Thrace, the hard-pressed Turks turned to the other powers, asking for their help in arranging an armistice. The British, anxious to prevent a Russian takeover of Constantinople, sent a squadron of their naval units into the Marmara. The Russians, who were only a few miles away from the city, threatened to move in if the British units entered the Golden Horn. For a moment it appeared that a war between the two powers was imminent. But the British had no interest in war; their move was merely a stratagem aimed at preventing the Russians from entering the city. To the Russian threat they offered a compromise: the British would stay away from the harbor if the Russians would agree to stay away from the city. The armistice was signed on January 31. Still, the Russians could not easily be denied the fruits of their spectacular victory against the Turks. Turkey was forced to sign a wide-ranging treaty (see p. 64) in the small village of San Stefano, which thereby gained a distinct place in European history.

With the Turks prepared to make any sacrifice to save their empire, the British cleverly offered a helping hand in exchange for the island of Cyprus. In a separate agreement, Cyprus was transferred to British control although the sultan retained nominal sovereignty over the island. The Greek inhabitants hailed the changeover, confident that before long the British would give Cyprus to Greece, just as they had done with the Ionian Islands a little over a decade earlier. This expectation was never to be realized.

Indecision in Athens

During the hostilities, the Greeks had found themselves caught in the vise of an excruciating dilemma. Should they come out in favor of Russia, thus helping the Pan-Slavist designs? Or, should they stay out of the conflict and discourage any rebellious thoughts among the Greeks in Epirus, Thessalia, or Macedonia, thus helping the Turks? In the early stages of the war, when the Russian armies were having a difficult time, the czar wrote to King George and asked for a diversionary operation by the Greeks to relieve the pressure on his troops. Trikoupis, who was then foreign minister, insisted that before Greece could take such a serious step Russia would have to give specific pledges on the transfer of territories inhabited by Greeks. The Russians, having their own plans for a large Bulgarian state, demurred. They would promise only to give appropriate weight to the Greek claims once victory had been achieved. In response, Trikoupis rejected the Russian request for assistance and Greece opted for neutrality—a move which, incidentally, was in keeping with British admonitions. Before long the czar was to pay Greece in full measure for her refusal to come to his aid at the moment of need.

Strange as it may seem, Greece was without a prime minister during this most crucial period. A coalition government with all former prime ministers participating under the premiership of Kanaris, who was approaching ninety at the time, had been formed in May 1877. In September Kanaris died and none of the participating leaders would accept another for the prime minister's post. For the next four months, the headless coalition government remained in office uncertain as to what to do although popular feeling was strongly in favor of military action. Such action, however, was hardly possible since the Vouli had rejected an earlier proposal by Koumoundouros to approve funds for strengthening the country's military forces. He had a majority at the time but when the Vouli deputies were told that they should also vote for more taxes, his support evaporated and he was forced to resign the premiership. In January 1878, as the Russians were moving toward Constantinople, public impatience reached the point of explosion. Demonstrations in Athens forced the king to dismiss the coalition government and recall Koumoundouros to the premiership. As prime minister, Koumoundouros responded to the public pressure for military action by sending troops into Thessalia—not knowing, due to the slow communications of the time, that Russia and Turkey had already signed an armistice and that the war was over. Embarrassed, the government tried to explain to the powers that its action had no other objective than to protect the Christians in the area. Turkey, facing other more serious problems, accepted the explanation and the Greek troops returned to their bases.

The Congress of Berlin

The victorious Russians may have failed to take Constantinople, but they made up for this by forcing the Treaty of San Stefano on the sultan. Under this agreement, Turkey formally recognized the complete independence and sovereignty of Serbia, Montenegro, and Rumania. But more significantly, she was forced to give up most of her remaining possessions in the Balkans for the creation of a large Bulgarian state covering almost three-fifths of the peninsula south of the Danube, extending from the Black Sea to the Aegean and on to the Adriatic, and having a population of 4 million. Within the short span of less than a decade, the Bulgarian nation had moved from obscurity to preeminence in the area. The Russians had chosen the cohesive, strong-willed Bulgarians as the standard-bearers of their Pan-Slavist policy.

The Greeks and the Serbs saw with alarm and dismay the emergence of this large state over territories they considered their own. But they could do little to counter this major challenge. Fortunately for them the other major powers in Europe, especially Britain, were not willing to let this Russian client-state take roots. Within weeks they were pressing Russia to agree to an international conference to discuss a different settlement that would be acceptable to all concerned. The Russians agreed. Delegates from the major European states met in Berlin, and in July the Congress of Berlin signed a treaty establishing a much smaller Bulgarian principality located between the Danube and the Balkan mountain range. To the south of this principality, in the area reaching to the Rhodope range in Thrace, the treaty set up an autonomous province, subject to the sultan but having a Christian governor. The province was christened Eastern Rumelia. Ironically, the new arrangement was almost identical with that initially proposed by the czar and rejected by the sultan.

A Greek memorandum asking for the liberation of Crete, Thessalia, and Epirus received scant notice by the powers. The Russians showed no interest and the British retorted that the objective of the congress was not to dismember the Ottoman Empire. Only the French took a sympathetic view and suggested that Greece's northern frontiers be redrawn at a later date through direct negotiations between Turkey and Greece. The French suggestion was eventually incorporated into the treaty in the form of a protocol. In reality, a thorny issue had temporarily been swept under the rug.

At the time of the Russo-Turkish War the Cretans had again taken up arms, but once again they had failed to realize their cherished goal of union with Greece. Nevertheless, they succeeded in gaining several important concessions from the Porte. The Khalepa Pact provided for an elected assembly of forty-nine Christians and thirty-one Turks, an independent judiciary, some freedom of expression, and a governor general appointed by the sultan for a five-year term. Ironically, this greater freedom only prepared the ground for future confrontations because the demand for union, temporarily shelved, remained the Cretans' unalterable goal.

Looking back at the Congress of Berlin, the Greeks could find modest comfort in the thought that the worst—represented by the large Bulgarian state of the Treaty of San Stefano—had been averted. Of course, there were no positive gains; Greek territory had not advanced one inch. The only ray of hope was in the protocol initiated by the French at the congress. Koumoundouros, who was prime minister at the time, asked Turkey for direct negotiations to redraw the frontiers in Thessalia and Epirus, as the protocol suggested. At first, the sultan ignored the subject. It was only after the intervention of the French government, supported in this by Austria and Russia, that the sultan agreed to send his representatives to a conference. To create a diversion, he cleverly incited the Albanians to demand Epirus. The ploy did not succeed in the end, but for almost two years the talks went on with little progress.

Several cabinet changes in Athens did little to help the Greek cause. Finally, in February 1881 the British government headed by Gladstone offered a compromise solution: the transfer of Thessalia and of only a small corner of Epirus on a take-it-or-leave-it basis. Koumoundouros had little choice but to accept. Nonetheless, he was vilified by a public outcry as though he had given up territory instead of gaining new lands for the kingdom. In characteristic fashion, the public had been led to believe by the newspapers and the political orators that, under the protocol, Greece was "entitled" to receive much more. Koumoundouros, who knew full well that the country was too weak to press for a confrontation, had no alternative but to accept the offer. Nevertheless, in the elections that followed the annexation of Thessalia, Koumoundouros' party was roundly defeated. Even the new deputies from Thessalia belonged to the opposition. Brokenhearted, Koumoundouros resigned. His death followed a year later. His passing from the scene marked the beginning of a new period, which was to be dominated by the forceful personality of Kharilaos Trikoupis.

Progress in spite of instability

In the twenty years since the arrival of King George, Greece had moved ahead in spite of innumerable cabinet changes, international entanglements, the frustration of national aspirations, and the paucity of its resources. Education in particular had made remarkable progress. The number of youngsters enrolled in primary schools had reached almost 75,000 by 1882 compared to 6,700 in 1833. Less spectacular, but not entirely insignificant, was the expansion in secondary education, where the number of students had gone up from 2,528 in 1833 to 9,106 by 1882. The University of Athens, in forty years of operation, had granted diplomas to 1,258 lawyers, 1,118 physicians, 286 pharmacists, 152 literature and language teachers, and 22 theologians. The Polytechnic School, a makeshift operation in 1837, had developed by 1863 into an impressive institution for the teaching of engineering and the fine arts. By 1878 its enrollment reached 214 in engineering and 189 in fine arts.

This positive record had its dark spots. In the absence of industry, most of those who graduated from the secondary schools or even

from the university had to seek employment with the state bureaucracy. Moreover, most of them tended to leave their hometowns and
villages and move to Athens, which continued to grow and prosper.
By 1882 Athens had become a city of more than 65,000 people. Its
broad avenues were dotted with imposing buildings, many of which
were constructed with funds donated by wealthy Greeks. The
donors, born in areas still under Ottoman control, were unable to do
much for their places of birth and lavished their largesse on Athens.
In fact, the capital was rapidly outdistancing the rest of the country.
Its population had grown sixfold in less than fifty years, while that of
other urban centers in the country had scored only modest increases.

In the villages and small towns life had changed hardly at all since
the days of Turkish rule. The peasant, who typically still used a
primitive wooden plow, continued to produce little more than what
he needed to feed himself and his family. To meet the demand for
foodstuffs and other consumer goods, the country had to import a
great deal and it was always difficult to find the foreign exchange to
pay for those products. Greek exports consisted mostly of currants
and some unprocessed minerals. The government relied heavily on
the tithe, some import duties, and indirect taxes on key consumer
items. The intake was usually inadequate to pay for anything beyond
the servicing of the public debt (for foreign and domestic loans), the
salaries of state employees, and the pensions of war victims, retired
employees, and their widows and children; the budget also included
some modest outlays for education and for military preparedness.
Secondary and higher education received approximately $200,000
annually from the national treasury. The cost of primary education,
amounting to another $300,000 was borne mostly by the municipali-
ties. The small armed forces with a strength totalling twelve
thousand men cost annually the equivalent of $1.15 million. Almost
40 percent of the national revenue went to servicing the national
debt.

Below a thin layer of wealthy merchants, shipowners, high-ranking
officials, a scattering of absentee landowners, and some senior clergy,
two major social groupings could be identified in the 1880s. With
increasing urbanization, a petty-bourgeoisie developed, which was
made up mostly of shopkeepers, medium-level bureaucrats, teachers,
lawyers, physicians, military officers; the second and larger group
consisted of the low-income strata of subsistence peasants, sharecroppers, artisans, handymen, servants, and a handful of workers. In spite

of rather sharp contrasts of wealth and income, political alignments did not follow clearly defined social divisions. Personal ties, emotional orientations, patriotic feelings, and expectations of patronage and rousfeti continued to be much more relevant determinants of political allegiance than income or social group.

Trikoupis at the helm

Such was the country's profile as Trikoupis moved center stage in 1882. He found no major rivals in his path; most of the political leaders who had occupied the premiership during the past twenty years were either dead or in retirement. Their so-called parties had faded away and new political alignments were being formed. Without competitors of comparable stature, Trikoupis retained a stable majority in the Vouli and remained in office for three years, a significant achievement in itself considering that the average life-span of the cabinets in four decades of constitutional government (1843–1883) was approximately nine months.

The British, especially the economic circles in London, watched the rise of Trikoupis with genuine satisfaction. His personality and his views promised a period of stability and moderation. After three decades of almost constant turmoil in the Balkans, the British now hoped for an era of peace to avert further erosion of the Ottoman Empire. With a fine sense of history and geography, they held to the view that to keep the Russian bear away from the Mediterranean shores, a single power—friendly to Britain—should control both sides of the Straits. The Greeks aspired to replace the decaying Ottoman Empire in this role. But in their eagerness to reach their goal, they vacillated from one patron to another, all the while allowing their emotions and illusions of past grandeur to becloud their judgement. Foreign friends had tried for years to convince the Greek leaders that their best policy was to focus on domestic development while at the same time strengthening their cultural ties with the Greek communities under Ottoman rule throughout the Balkans. They were repeatedly urged to wait for the day when, in the natural course of events, these Greeks would be freed of foreign rule. The trouble was that Greece could not develop and become a viable country until the fertile plains of Thessalia, Macedonia, and Thrace became part of the free kingdom. These economic imperatives together with the emotional issue of having so many thousands of unredeemed brethren under Turkish rule, formed the horns of a dilemma that dominated Greek politics throughout the nineteenth century.

The British, who could have assigned to the Greeks the role of guardian to the approaches to eastern Mediterranean, regarded most of the Greek leaders as petty, quarrelsome, and unrealistic men who were incapable of handling with competence even the minor problems of their small country. The objection might have been raised that it was precisely the smallness of the kingdom that caused the pettiness, the impatience, the anxious haste, the unsteadiness, and the deep sense of frustration. Be that as it may, it was difficult for the Greeks to accept Disraeli's gratuitous advice that "Greece, like individuals with a future, can afford to wait." Yet, because of the realities of the time, the Greeks could do little to realize their national dreams as long as Britain stood in the way.

Trikoupis had a clear understanding of these harsh truths. In the three years of his stewardship, he shifted the emphasis to domestic development. He took steps to suppress such endemic crimes as brigandage and goat-snatching; he moved against the usurers, who extracted exorbitant rates of interest from poor peasants; he reorganized the urban and rural police; he made certain that embezzlers of public funds could no longer rely on the protection of powerful friends, who often shared in the bounty; and he tried to end the traditional spoils system, which had made the staffing of the civil service a game of musical chairs, by establishing for the first time a permanent status for certain categories of civil servants. But the most important area of his concern was the construction of public works. When he came to office in 1882 there were only seven miles of rail tracks connecting Athens with the Piraeus harbor. Within two years, work had begun on the construction of railways connecting Athens with the major urban centers in the Peloponnisos, in Central Greece, and in Thessalia. Trikoupis also initiated the draining of Kopais, a large swamp in Boeotia, which had been since the days of antiquity a perennial nesting ground for malaria-carrying mosquitoes.

The most spectacular and ambitious project was the opening of the Corinth Canal at the narrow neck connecting the Peloponnisos with the rest of Greece. The dream to open a shortcut between the Ionian and the Aegean seas was a very old one indeed; Nero, in fact, had once started the opening of such a canal, but the project was soon abandoned. The opening of the Suez Canal in 1869 revived interest in the project, and in 1881 the Koumoundouros government signed a contract with a German engineer named Stephan Tuerr. Work on the project, however, did not actually start until a year later, when Trikoupis was in office. In a picturesque ceremony, the royal family sailed from Piraeus to the site of the proposed canal, accompanied by units of the navy, hundreds of small caiques in festive bunting, and even a few foreign warships. After the religious blessing and the inevitable speeches, King George used a silver spade to dig symbolically the first lump of earth while Queen Olga pressed the lever that set off a chain of dynamite charges in a spectacular display.

Trikoupis did not limit his efforts to the construction of public works. He gave generous financial support to the schools and other cultural institutions of the Greek populations in Ottoman-held territories. Also, a large part of the nation's revenue was channeled into the development of the armed forces, increasing their strength from twelve to over thirty thousand. The navy, in particular, received a great deal of attention and financial support.

To pay for his ambitious projects, Trikoupis imposed additional taxes on such staples as tobacco, kerosene, and other consumer items; in addition, he tried to attract private investment, especially from wealthy Greeks residing abroad. However, by and large his efforts to increase revenues proved only mildly successful. Budget deficits began to pile up as tax receipts fell far below anticipated levels. In 1884 alone, actual revenue was 30 percent less than what the government expected.

In April 1885, when the country went to the polls to elect a new Vouli, Trikoupis' party suffered a serious defeat. Out of a total of 250 seats, his party managed to capture only 85. Theodoros Deliyiannis, a man very much in the tradition of Kolettis and Voulgaris, succeeded with unrestrained demagoguery to exploit public discontent with Trikoupis' taxation policies. He scored an electoral triumph. True, most of the wealthy businessmen in Athens were solidly behind Trikoupis because they could appreciate the advantages of economic development. But the wage earners, the artisans, the pensioners, the peasants, who had been hit hard by inflation and who carried a disproportionate burden, turned a sympathetic ear to Deliyiannis' attacks. Besides, Trikoupis was unwilling to use the nationalist rhetoric that had for decades succeeded in firing up emotions and turning public attention away from economic and social problems. For three years he had deliberately shunned such devices. He had also refused to employ the familiar tactics of patronage and intimidation, which were so easily translatable into votes in those days.

Deliyiannis fails the test

Deliyiannis, in an effort to live up to his electoral promises, embarked on a policy of economic retrenchment. By reversing the gears, he led the country to an economic slowdown that inevitably affected the pocketbook of most wage earners and tradesmen in Athens and the major towns. Public opinion made a sharp aboutface. When Trikoupis returned in the fall of 1885 from his customary trip to Europe, thousands of Athenians came to the railway station to give him a rousing welcome.

This outpouring of public enthusiasm had an additional motivation. A few weeks earlier, the Bulgarian principality had taken over in a successful coup the province of Eastern Rumelia, thereby practically doubling in size and population overnight. To the surprise of those who expected a strong reaction on the part of the powers who had participated in the Congress of Berlin, the coup hardly caused a ripple. Even the Turks remained unusually quiet. The reason for this general equanimity was not hard to find. The British, disappointed with Trikoupis' defeat, had turned to the Bulgarians. Salisbury, speaking in the House of Lords, gave an outline of British thinking on the issue. "Conditions have changed," he said. "Our goal remains the same; to prevent a Russian advance to Constantinople. A Bulgaria tied to Russia with the bonds of gratitude appears dangerous to us, but a Bulgaria united under a prince who accepts European guidance and remains the Sultan's faithful ally is, in our view, a major safeguard against Russian aggression." Since the death of Czar Alexander II, relations between Bulgaria and Russia had cooled off markedly, and in 1882 Prince Alexander of Bulgaria had come into a serious disagreement with his Russian friends over financial matters concerning the construction of railroads. Ironically, the prince's estrangement from Russia found broad appeal among the Bulgarian intellectuals and liberal politicians. With imaginative diplomacy, Bulgaria gained a great deal of support in London and Paris. The move to seize Eastern Rumelia was well-timed.

In spite of his usual bluster, Deliyiannis adopted a cautious, wait-and-see policy, hoping that Turkey would react vigorously and recapture the province. But Turkey, advised by Britain to accept the new situation, limited its reaction to some troop concentrations along the border. In the meantime, the Austrians, seeing in the emergence of a large Bulgarian state a potential barrier to their designs in the Balkans, encouraged the Serbs to move against Bulgaria. In a brief war, the Serbian troops reached the outskirts of Sofia, but then the Bulgarian forces regained the initiative and, with determined fighting, reversed the tide of battle. Within a few weeks they reached Belgrade. At this point, Austria intervened and the fighting ended. During this conflict, Bulgaria solidified her control over Eastern Rumelia and gained much respect in Europe for her military prowess. Greek pride was deeply wounded, especially since popular rhetoric had painted a picture of Bulgarian inferiority and backwardness. Taken in by their own oratory, most Greeks could not understand how it was possible for civilized Europe to look with favor on those "savages." To vent public frustration, the press and most political leaders launched a vitriolic campaign of hatred against the Bulgarians—whose very existence was virtually unknown a few decades earlier—by dusting off the ancient feuds between the Bulgars and the Byzantines. The Bulgarians had started their anti-Greek propaganda much earlier when they turned against the Greek Orthodox bishops in Bulgaria and forced the separation of their church from the patriarchate. Then, after the Treaty of San Stefano, Bulgarian territorial aspirations lost all sense of proportion. In an effort to prepare the ground for later conquest, Bulgarian bands embarked on a bloody campaign of genocide against the Greek populations of Macedonia and Thrace. Since the two nations claimed the same territories, their enmity was inevitable.

Deliyiannis' timid policy incensed Greek public opinion. To mollify his outraged critics, he took steps to ease the tax burden, hoping thereby to win the support of the low-income groups. In vain. With nationalist feelings at fever pitch, social and economic issues were quickly submerged. Faced with demonstrations and a virulent press intoxicated by its own rhetoric, he made an aboutface and mobilized his own oratorical talents in favor of war. To meet the cost, he imposed some taxes on key consumer items. Hostilities broke out along the border in Thessalia, but the powers, especially Britain, had no intention of letting another war erupt in the Balkans. They resorted to their familiar tactic and imposed a blockade on Piraeus in the spring of 1886. Within days Deliyiannis resigned. After two weeks of uncertainty, many of those who had supported Deliyiannis in the past abandoned him in favor of Trikoupis, who took over with the support of a majority of the deputies in the Vouli.

Trikoupis resumes leadership

The new prime minister moved quickly to restore peaceful relations with Turkey. In addition, he pushed through the Vouli a series of measures including a revision of the electoral law. In reducing the number of constituencies from 245 to 150, it was expected that larger electoral districts would tone down the practices of patronage and voter manipulation. Soon after the return of Trikoupis to office, the foreign powers quietly lifted the blockade. As the hot summer months passed in relative tranquility, Deliyiannis' former supporters in the legislature began to have second thoughts. Sensing the danger in this, Trikoupis decided in the fall to take the country to the polls while the mismanagement of the nation's affairs by Deliyiannis was still fresh in the minds of the people. King George, who had come by now to appreciate Trikoupis' moderate and realistic views, agreed. In the election of January 1887 Trikoupis' party scored a resounding victory.

As in the past, Trikoupis assigned first priority to domestic development; but within a year, Crete, this irrepressible bastion of nationalism, appeared to writhe ominously again. Five Christian governors, appointed by the sultan since the Khalepa Pact of 1878, had been replaced one after another in spite of the pact's provision that the governor be appointed for a five-year term. Because of the social and economic conditions on the island, the liberal party, composed of educated, progressive young men, remained in the minority, while local power rested mostly with the conservatives, who had deep roots in the villages. The electoral system itself favored the conservative, traditionalist interests. The deputies to the Cretan legislature were elected indirectly through the *dimogerontes* (village elders) in each community. In 1886, however, the electoral system was drastically changed to follow the Greek practice; henceforth, deputies would be chosen by secret, direct vote, using lead ballots.

The conservatives, sensing that power was about to slip through their fingers, incited the killing of a few Moslems. This resulted in similar acts of violence from the Turkish inhabitants of the island. The Greek government tried, through its consul in Crete, to discourage a new flare-up of revolutionary activity. Trikoupis was adamant in his opposition to another uprising. His grand design called for a strengthening of the armed forces, especially the navy, before Greece could undertake a serious effort to bring Crete into the national fold. He had already contracted for the purchase of three cruisers, but they had yet to be delivered. He admonished the Cretans to "wait," but the situation soon slipped beyond his control. In April 1889 the Cretan liberals won by a landslide. They captured thirty-five of the forty-nine Christian seats in the eighty-seat legislature. One of the liberal deputies, Eleutherios Venizelos, a young man in his middle twenties, was later to dominate Greek politics for almost three decades.

The conservatives refused to accept with grace their fall from power. At first they tried to disrupt the work of the assembly by charging irregularities in the election, accusing the liberals of winning their victory through fraud and violence. Then, five conservative deputies drafted a declaration calling for the island's union with Greece and threatened to bring it formally before the legislature. The Greek consul tried in vain to bring them to their senses. "Don't you realize," he told them, "that you place all other deputies in a terrible dilemma, either to support your declaration— to the detriment of the country's major interests—or to remain silent at the risk of being misunderstood? Because, there will be those who will say: Only ten persons favor union with Greece while the rest remain silent because they oppose it." The conservative leaders, of course, were not so naive as to be unaware of the implications of their move. Apparently, they were acting on the advice of the British consul, who was thinking of once again creating a situation that would enable Britain to take control of the island temporarily in a compromise move. The conservatives also wanted to embarrass the sultan-appointed governor, who had been rather favorable to the liberals. Whatever the motives behind this declaration for union, the move placed the liberal majority in a very delicate position. With notable political skill, they refused to support the move of the five conservative deputies, but at the same time they handed the foreign consuls a statement in which they said: "We consider it our supreme duty to comply with the specific instructions of the Greek government, which is our true and natural sovereign, and preserve order and tranquility on our island. . . . The flaming desire of the Cretan people we are privileged to represent is one and one only: union with mother Greece. We are looking forward to the moment when the Greek government will give us the signal to overthrow the Turkish rule."

Sultan Abdul-Hamid, in an effort to avert another uprising in Crete, sent a personal emissary to the island. Mahmud Pasha was a man of considerable experience and polish, but the mission foundered, nevertheless, in the quagmire of internal Cretan politics. In the middle of June 1889 the conservatives and their followers formed a Revolutionary General Assembly while armed gatherings in various parts of the island caused apprehension in many quarters. The government in Greece, in particular, was still strongly opposed to an armed uprising. Even the Christian population in Crete was ambivalent, but no matter, the advocates of revolt knew that they could always count on the Cretan's natural desire to fight for liberty.

Mahmud Pasha was rather abruptly recalled in July and within days bloody incidents forced many of the Moslem inhabitants to leave their homes in the villages and seek shelter inside the walls of the major towns, where Turkish control was more effective. With tempers rising, armed groups of Moslem civilians began to attack Christian villages in hit-and-run operations. With the regular Turkish troops on the island unable to restore order, the Porte decided to dispatch additional forces. Fearful of massacres, more than two thousand Cretans left the island and sought refuge on the mainland of Greece. Their arrival in Piraeus, and their excited and somewhat exaggerated tales fired nationalist feelings and gave the newspapers ample fuel for patriotic rhetoric. The Trikoupis government found it increasingly difficult to maintain its restrained, moderate posture. In a note delivered to the major powers on August 6, the Greek government stated: "To avert the necessity of our own direct action, [the powers] should act by taking over, through [their] own military forces, the cause of peace and humanity on the island." The powers responded by pointing out that Crete was a Turkish possession and that it was the responsibility of the Turkish forces to restore order. They suggested to the Porte, however, that its regular forces should take every necessary step to curb the attacks of irregular elements against defenseless Christian villages.

The sultan, encouraged by the mild reaction of the powers, moved decisively. By September, more than forty thousand troops were on the island. A new governor, Sakir Pasha, declared martial law, restored order in the major towns, and moved his forces to reestablish Turkish control over the countryside. Within a month all rebellious activities had stopped. Sakir Pasha then turned against the leading personalities among the Christians and forced many of them to seek refuge in Greece. There political refugees tried to pressure Trikoupis to follow a more assertive policy but the prime minister told them bluntly that Greece did not have the means to take direct action against Turkey at that time. Behind the scenes he turned to the British and asked for their help in convincing the sultan to be less harsh with the Cretans. In April 1890 Sakir Pasha lifted the martial law and granted a general amnesty. Nonetheless, the Turks did not return to the liberal reforms of the Khalepa Pact. They continued to govern with a strong hand. The 1889 revolution had ended but the seeds for fresh trouble were already deeply imbedded in the soil of the island. Crete would again resort to armed rebellion before the decade was over.

Trouble in the economy

While public interest in Greece was riveted on the happenings in Crete, Trikoupis' attention continued to focus on domestic development. His interests ranged from such major projects as the opening of the Corinth Canal and the construction of railroads in Thessalia and the Peloponnisos to such less ambitious endeavors as the building of an archaeological museum, the beautification of the capital, and the construction of a new military academy. Moreover, as if to underscore official detachment from the Cretan rebellion, his government celebrated with impressive ceremonies the jubilee of the University of Athens, King George's twenty-fifth anniversary on the throne, and above all the wedding of Prince Constantine, the *diadohos* (crown prince), with Princess Sophie, the sister of Germany's Kaiser Wilhelm II. The wedding, which took place in October 1889, brought to Athens the kaiser, the king and the queen of Denmark, the prince of Wales, Russia's Crown Prince Nicholas, and an array of other luminaries. For a glorious week the Athenian public turned away from the depressing news coming out of Crete to the happy event and the impressive sight of assembled royalty. The image of the handsome, dashing, young diadohos with the legendary name of Constantine standing next to his beautiful bride could not but fill the hearts of the people with a feeling of optimism and hope for the future. The presence of Kaiser Wilhelm, in particular, seemed to symbolize in many eyes the forging of strong ties with Germany, Europe's emerging new power. As so often in the past—and in the future, as we shall see—the Greeks allowed wishful thinking to becloud their view of international realities. The sad truth was that the German emperor had hardly any regard at all for the country his sister was henceforth to call her own. He had already embarked on an ambitious plan to forge strong ties with the sultan and push German influence toward the Middle East and the Persian Gulf. Abdul-Hamid, on his part, disillusioned with the British, was ready to enlist other allies in his desperate effort to save his remaining possessions in the Balkans.

The euphoria generated by the spectacular celebration of happy events did not last long. The harsh realities of the Cretan failure, coupled with the country's increasing financial and trade difficulties, turned public sentiment against Trikoupis. He had been on and off at the helm for almost a decade. His measures for economic development had been costly, financed for the most part by borrowing from foreign sources and by piling up huge deficits in the budget. Many of the projects, though eminently sound, were not of the type that could yield immediate benefits. Inevitably, inflationary pressures had forced prices to climb. Trikoupis' opponents in the Vouli, with Deliyiannis in the forefront, lashed out at the government, drawing ample ammunition for their assault from the country's economic difficulties and the national disappointment over the failure of the uprising in Crete. A volatile electorate listened to the emotional appeal of the opposition. In the election of October 26, 1890, Trikoupis' party was virtually demolished. Two days later, the king gave Deliyiannis the mandate to form a new government.

Trikoupis' defeat came as a serious disappointment to British and French officials and bankers; Greece's heavy borrowing had been made possible largely because of the confidence he had inspired abroad. However commendable his motives might have been, Trikoupis had set his economic policy on dangerously shallow foundations. It rested primarily on his personal prestige and on the willingness of foreign creditors to wait and not press for their claims. With his downfall, these two indispensable props disappeared.

As though to reinforce a pitiful tradition initiated at the time of Koumoundouros by his opponents, Trikoupis was made the target of vicious charges of corruption and "misuse of the proceeds of the foreign loans." For almost a year the Vouli spent much of its time debating the largely unconvincing accusations of wrongdoing. In the end, the matter was dropped but the affair left a bitter aftertaste.

Concern over Macedonia

In spite of his electoral defeat, Trikoupis continued to command considerable respect abroad. In the summer of 1891, while on his customary summer vacation in Europe, he visited Belgrade and Sofia and explored the possibilities for joint action against the Turks. He was already contemplating a course of action that was not to be realized until twenty years later by Eleutherios Venizelos. Common action by Greece, Serbia, and Bulgaria to liberate the Christian populations in the Balkans would appear to a casual observer to be a most reasonable goal. In reality, the successful pursuit of such a policy was almost impossible because of a serious obstacle. The Ottoman Empire jutted out into the Balkans, covering Thrace, Macedonia, Epirus, and Albania, reaching all the way to the Adriatic. The people living in those areas formed a complex mixture of many quite distinct strands. Especially in the geographic region of Macedonia (extending from the city of Salonika on the Aegean to the town of Skopje in the north and from the borders of Eastern Rumelia to Lake Ohrid), the people, mostly peasants and artisans, identified with either one or the other of the major nationalities— Greeks, Serbs, Bulgars—or with no one group in particular. The Bulgarians, with their national aspirations inflated by the never-implemented Treaty of San Stefano, regarded all the Slavophones in Macedonia as Bulgarians. To the Serbs this was a provocative and unsubstantiated claim. The Greeks, knowing that the Greek-speaking element was concentrated mostly in the south, around Salonika and along the Aegean coast, strongly opposed any identification of

Macedonia as a unified region inhabited by a Macedonian national-ity. Trikoupis articulated this point of view while speaking to a foreign journalist in 1889:

When the war breaks out, and it is bound to happen in three, five, or eight years, Macedonia will become Greek or Bulgarian, depending on who is the victor. If it is taken by the Bulgarians, I have no doubt but that within a few years they will be able to turn into Slavs all those living today as far south as the borders of Thessalia. If we take it over, we will turn into Greeks all of those living up to the borders of Eastern Rumelia. The majority of the inhabitants have no declared nationality; they are ready to accept the one that will be attached to them.

In the next few years, Greece and Bulgaria would embark on a bloody struggle to win the allegiance of the inhabitants of Macedonia. The Turks were secretly delighted with this brewing rivalry, which was to keep their potential opponents apart for another twenty years.

The dismal end of the Trikoupis era

When Trikoupis returned to Athens in the fall of 1891, he was again given an enthusiastic welcome by the Athenian public. Already the Deliyiannis government was in deep trouble. Saddled with Trikoupis' heavy financial burdens but without his advantage of friendly relations with the country's foreign creditors, Deliyiannis was unable to overcome the many-sided pressures. Within a year, prices had increased by almost 12 percent, and they continued to rise. In February 1892 the king decided to take a drastic step; he asked for Deliyiannis' resignation and then called on Trikoupis to take over. He declined, pointing out that he could not govern effectively with a hostile majority in the Vouli. At first the king wanted to avoid an election for fear that a Deliyiannis victory might be interpreted as a popular rebuke to the king's action; but when the Vouli rejected his second choice for a prime minister, King George, with his characteristic flexibility and acumen, quickly opted for a new election, setting the date for May 15.

For almost five weeks Athens and the rest of the country went through an unusually contemptible and at times violent campaign. Deliyiannis' political rallies in Athens seemed, with their enormous crowds and enthusiasm, to presage a landslide for his party. But when the votes were counted, Trikoupis had won a resounding victory—to the king's obvious relief. The foreign creditors were elated, but Trikoupis was not a magician. The public works he had financed with the proceeds of the foreign loans were by their nature slow in yielding the kind of revenue needed to pay the foreign creditors. Greek exports at the time, mostly currants, were extremely vulnerable to market fluctuations. Trikoupis sought to ease the economic pressures by taking another loan but this time the foreign bankers demanded guarantees that amounted to virtual control over the Greek economy. In May 1893 Trikoupis resigned—only to return to office again in the fall. By then, there was no escape. In a drastic move, he introduced legislation suspending payment of the principal and reducing interest payments by two-thirds on the foreign loans of 1881, 1884, 1887, 1889, and 1890. Trikoupis' ambitious program for economic development and military preparedness had proved to be beyond the country's capabilities. Financial bankruptcy led to a breakdown of the economy, which, while it hit every group, was especially painful for those with small and uncertain incomes. By the end of 1894 demonstrations against the Trikoupis government could no longer be attributed to purely partisan motives. His efforts to find new sources of financial aid met a stone wall of opposition in foreign banking circles.

On January 23, 1895, Trikoupis resigned the premiership for the last time. He died in Cannes a year later, on April 11, after a short illness. The news marred the happy mood generated by the first Olympic games held in Athens and the victory of a Greek peasant—Spyridon Louis—in the marathon race. The funeral of Trikoupis, attended by the king, the diadohos, and a great multitude seemed to mark the end of an era. For two decades, Trikoupis had dominated the political scene by the very force of his personality. Never truly popular in a country where enchanting demagogues have always had a better chance to enjoy public adulation and acclaim, Trikoupis virtually dragged the people behind his ambitious plans. Cautious in his foreign policy, he moved boldly to push the country's economic development ahead; his grand design was basically sound. He may have failed in the short run, but his audacious financial policies paid off twenty years later when another leader of genius—

Eleutherios Venizelos—carried into being Trikoupis' vision of the national destiny. But before the dreams could turn into reality in the fateful years of 1912–13, the country had to pass through many more years of misery, defeat, and instability.

The war of 1897

For the next two years, Deliyiannis, who had returned to power in the election of April 28, 1895, wrestled unhappily with the demands of the foreign creditors. National pride was deeply wounded, and, as it often happens, the public instinctively turned to an almost mystical revival of the nation's claims and aspirations. In flaming editorials the Athenian newspapers cursed the "heartless foreign bankers" who dared to treat Greece as an ordinary debtor, with no regard for her glorious past and their "eternal debt" to the nation responsible for having given Europe the "light of civilization." The editorials blamed the country's constant humiliations on the inadequate territory imposed by the powers "concerned with their own unholy interests, not with the dictates of justice." The only way out of the morass was a self-assertive policy of national expansion against all odds, even "against the will and the wiles of the foreign potentates." These feelings eventually crystallized in a secret organization called the *Ethniki Etairia* (National Society). In the short span of three years the society managed to bring into its fold many leading personalities and to galvanize the public with its extravagant, proud, and inspiring rhetoric. The Great Idea, never extinct in the public mind, was given fresh impetus. With Trikoupis' sobering influence gone, the field was left wide open to well-intentioned, idealistic advocates of military action for the liberation of their so-called unredeemed brethren. In 1896 the Turkish atrocities against the Armenians aroused strong feelings against the Turks in Europe; now many Greeks thought that the international climate was at last favorable for the taking of bold action.

Not surprisingly, the first signs of approaching unrest appeared on the island of Crete. For six years, the Christian inhabitants had lived under the restrictive regime imposed by the sultan in the wake of the unsuccessful 1889 revolt. Fearful of another explosion, the sultan decided to improve conditions. This time the opposition came from the Moslem inhabitants, who had become accustomed to their new privileges and were now resentful of what they considered a pro-Christian policy. In the summer of 1895 they decided to take out their anger on the Christian villagers. In retaliation, the Christians formed a revolutionary committee. Deliyiannis, beset with the country's economic problems, had no alternative but to abandon his customary bravado and advise the Cretans to show patience and moderation. It was too late. Violence broke out on the island.

Meanwhile, in Greece public outrage and demands for bold action reached dangerously intense levels. Reports that the Bulgarians had launched new guerrilla operations in Macedonia only added to the popular excitement. Even King George, a moderate and cautious man, had to agree to the mobilization of twelve thousand men. Suggestions of foreign friends to end the impasse by accepting autonomy for Crete were rejected indignantly by both Cretans and Greeks. In January 1897 news of massacres in Crete, emblazoned in banner headlines in the Athenian newspapers, rekindled centuries-old resentments and hatreds. A wave of holy anger swept away all sense of caution. "If the government is incapable of leading the ultimate struggle, it must resign before it is crushed by the people" intoned one of the Vouli deputies in fiery rhetoric. Dimitrios Rallis, a key opposition leader, went so far as to threaten "to take the lead and raise the standard of revolution against this regime." On February 10 Deliyiannis informed a jubilant Vouli that a squadron of naval units under the command of Prince George—the king's second son—had already left for Crete. Five days later, a force of fifteen hundred men, including a unit of mountain artillery, landed west of Khania. The commander of the expeditionary force, Col. Timoleon Vassos, issued a proclamation declaring that he was "occupying the island of Crete in the name of George I, King of the Hellenes . . ." The Greek people received the news of the landing with almost hysterical exaltation. Their joy was premature.

The Greek force had been able to land only because the fleets of the great powers had not tried to block the operation. The move was unexpected and the foreign admirals lacked precise instructions. Their stand, however, changed rapidly once their governments were apprised of the situation. To prevent more violence on the island, they landed small detachments, while their envoys in Athens called on the Greek government to withdraw the small expeditionary force from Crete. But the public temper in Athens was beyond reason. Intoxicated by the seeming success of the landing, the National

Society addressed a memorandum to the foreign envoys, bristling with nationalist rhetoric and threatening to unleash offensive operations against other parts of the Ottoman Empire. The National Society was virtually threatening the powers with a general conflagration in the Balkans unless they embraced the Greek claims.

The Great Idea had by now been taken over by romantic enthusiasts who were unable or unwilling to understand that a country's foreign policy must be consistent with her capabilities and with the prevailing international conditions. The Greek army was small, ill-equipped, and poorly-trained, and the major powers were opposed to any major changes in the area. Lord Salisbury, the British prime minister, summed up the reasons with brutal candor in one of his communications to Queen Victoria: "If Greece were to gain now or in the near future by her recent action, then Serbia, Bulgaria, and Montenegro will not long remain quiet. They will be forced to move not only because of the success of the Greek action, but also, even more so, because in this contest of power Greece is their main competition. . . ." Britain again favored some form of autonomy for Crete but she could not force the other powers to accept such a compromise solution. Germany's Kaiser Wilhelm, in particular, who had become the sultan's new friend, was adamant against any step that might appear as a reward for the audacity of the Greeks. That his sister Sophie was married to the Greek diadohos and would one day become queen of Greece seemed to contribute no weight at all to his considerations.

The Greeks were equally opposed to any solution short of *enosis* (union). Autonomy for Crete was certainly one safe path out of the minefield, but Greek public opinion was so inflamed that anyone speaking in favor of autonomy was likely to be branded a traitor. The Deliyiannis government, facing the constant charges of the opposition for its "timid and cowardly demeanor," began to prepare for military action in Macedonia. Although the army was in no position to engage in a serious confrontation with the Turks, the Greek prime minister was solemnly giving assurances to the Vouli that within a few days the army would be "ready to fulfill its historic mission." Dimitrios Rallis, leading the opposition in a display of splendid inconsistency, was deploring the army's poor state on the one hand while on the other he was urging the government to invade Macedonia—and this in the face of unconcealed big power disapproval.

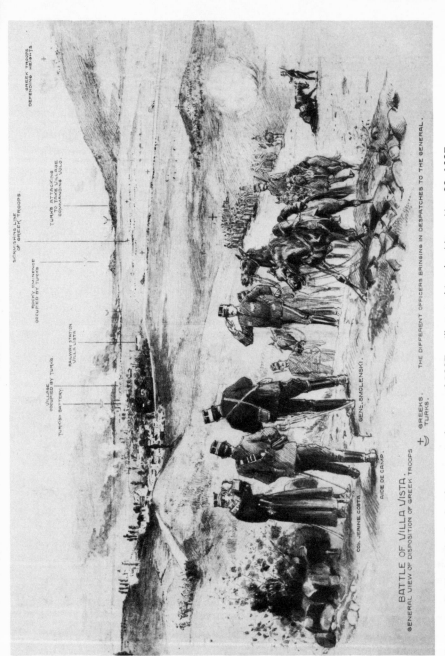

GREEK TROOPS
DEFENDING HEIGHTS.

SKIRMISHING LINE
OF GREEK TROOPS.

TURKS ATTACKING
TO TAKE VILLAGE
COMMANDING ROAD.

ROCKY EMINENCE
OCCUPIED BY TURKS.

RAILWAY STATION
VILLA VISTA.

VILLAGE
OCCUPIED BY TURKS.

TURKISH BATTERY.

BATTLE OF VILLA VISTA.
GENERAL VIEW OF DISPOSITION OF GREEK TROOPS.

COL. JEAINE COSTA.

AIDE DE CAMP.

GENL. SMOLENSKI.

THE DIFFERENT OFFICERS BRINGING IN DESPATCHES TO THE GENERAL.

GREEKS.
TURKS.

Correspondent's sketch of a battle scene in the war of 1897.   *Illustrated London News,* May 22, 1897

In March the diadohos was named commander in chief and moved his headquarters to Larisa in Thessalia. Already guerrilla bands were filtering through the border into Turkish-held Macedonia. Suddenly, on April 18, 1897, the Turkish forces launched a preemptive offensive and crossed into Thessalia. With injured innocence, Deliyiannis protested the Turkish action, conveniently forgetting for the moment that he had publicly declared his determination to take military action against Turkey. The Turks had simply chosen the right moment to make their move. They attacked as soon as the spring weather made the movement of their forces easier. Their objective was to teach the Greeks a lesson, knowing full well that the powers would not allow any territory in the Balkans to revert to Ottoman control once it had been liberated.

Against the superior Turkish forces, the Greeks had to rely mostly on the extravagant rhetoric of their leaders. Deliyiannis, in oratory reminiscent of his younger days, expressed—to the Vouli's enthusiastic response—his confidence in the victory of the Greek people, "the proud descendants of that great race which has taught East and West the meaning of truth and justice." Rallis, as the leader of the opposition, went even further and roared in his rich baritone voice: "This is the blessed moment when the Turks provoked us by embarking on this undeclared war. This is not merely a war between two states, it is a war for the very existence of our nation. . . . Hellenism must revenge the insults of four centuries, and in this struggle the nation must either win or disappear from the face of the earth."

The echo of these proud words had hardly faded when reports of the first major setback reached Athens. Poorly supplied, weak in artillery, and with their forces widely dispersed along the border, the Greeks were forced to fall back. Within days, the retreat turned into an ignominious rout. Larisa fell on April 25. Five days later, King George replaced Deliyiannis with Rallis. By then the Turkish forces were pushing toward Lamia. Salisbury had already ordered the frigate *Nile* to sail to Piraeus and wait there at the disposal of the royal family. In a communication to the British envoy in Athens, he said: "I have no doubt that [the Greeks] will turn against the King accusing him for the policy they themselves forced on him." In desperation the Greek government turned to the major powers and asked for their intervention to secure an armistice. On May 17, the fighting stopped; the war had lasted exactly thirty days. A stunned nation, intoxicated for months with heavy doses of irresponsible nationalism, was forced to come face to face with the harsh reality of defeat. Not unlike a child passing through adolescence, the Greek nation had acted with unrestrained exuberance and rashness—and it had paid a heavy price. By comparison, the misfortunes of earlier years were as innocuous as the scratches on the knees of a precocious child. From now on, it might have been hoped, the nation would mature rapidly, gaining in the process the qualities of moderation, thoughtfulness, and patience that are the keystones of maturity. Mistakes in the future, would surely be much too costly. But as time was to show, the traits exhibited during the nation's growth were to remain part of its deeper nature, reemerging at critical moments with often tragic consequences.

In the wake of defeat

For the next ten years, the nation went through a period of emotional retrenchment. As the thirty-day war of 1897 came to its disastrous end, the Rallis government sought to salvage whatever could be recovered from the ruins. In the end, Turkey did not retain any of her territorial gains except for some minor readjustments along the frontier. The powers stood by a long-established principle that Christian lands liberated from Ottoman rule could never again return to their former masters. Instead of gaining any territory, Turkey actually lost control over Crete. Tired of the recurrent threat to peace posed by the determination of the island's population to be free, the powers decided to grant Crete autonomous status under the nominal suzerainty of the sultan. Ironically, those in Greece who a few months earlier were denouncing any talk of Cretan autonomy as being tantamount to treason were now only too eager to accept the offer. Even more surprising, the powers selected Prince George to become the island's first high commissioner.

The price paid by Greece was largely financial. The powers, with Germany in the lead, imposed on Greece a system of international control. Henceforth, an International Control Commission would set aside annually the funds needed to repay the foreign creditors before any revenues were released to the Greek government for domestic uses. Paradoxically, hardship and disappointment seemed to have a salutary effect on the nation's fortunes. The economy moved out of the doldrums as the investments of the Trikoupis era began at last to pay off. Cured of their infantile braggadocio, the military began for the first time to think seriously of getting properly organized and of establishing an effective training program. It was a time of sober reassessment and introspection. The assassination of Deliyiannis in 1905—by a disgruntled gambler who resented the closing of gambling houses—left the political field to a host of small-time politicians. In the absence of a commanding figure, Georgios Theotokis, Alexandros Zaimis, Dimitrios Rallis, Kyriakoulis Mavromikhalis, and Stefanos Dragoumis alternated in the top posts until the revolution of 1909.

As the country moved into the twentieth century, the nation's interest concentrated increasingly on Macedonia, where the Bulgarians continued to work hard among the Slavic-speaking peasants. Crete was now quiet, under a Greek prince as high commissioner and a cabinet of Cretans; and despite the presence of Moslems on the island, everyone recognized its Greek character. Not so with Macedonia. Much had transpired over those mountains and valleys since the days of Alexander the Great. Under the Romans, Byzantines, Serbs, Bulgars, and Turks, the ethnic composition of the population had become a complex mixture. In fact, Macedonia, lacking any sense of national identity, was nothing more than a name on the map of Europe. For strictly administrative purposes, the Turks had divided it into three *vilayets* (provinces). In the geographic region encompassing the provinces, which stretched from Salonika to Skopje, the Slavic-speaking inhabitants were in the majority. But language was not necessarily a mark of ethnic identity. Many Slavic-speaking families thought of themselves as being Greek while others had no conscious allegiances other than the ties they felt to their kinship group or village.

The Bulgarians who, since the days of San Stefano had coveted Macedonia, consistently sought to give the impression that it was a single region inhabited predominantly by Slavs. In 1902 the Bulgarian government presented a memorandum to the major powers advocating autonomy for the three vilayets of Salonika, Bitola, and Skopje. The plan was for these to form a single province, with Salonika as the capital, under a Christian governor who would be chosen from the prevailing ethnic group. Bulgarian *komitadjis* (guerrillas) moved into the area to reinforce the argument. These efforts found a receptive audience in Europe, especially in Britain. With Greece's prestige at its lowest point, and with the Germans moving ever closer to Turkey, the British saw in Bulgaria a prospective friend and future ally in the Balkans. Although the quest for Macedonian autonomy did not go very far in the face of Turkish opposition, Bulgaria had at least staked her claim for the future. The various governments that came to power in Greece—one following the next as though a mere change of personality would be a solution to the country's problems—did not dare to react too vigorously for fear that they might again expose the nation to disaster. Timidity this time was being confused with prudence. As is so often the case, private initiative came to fill the void. Bands of volunteers moved into Macedonia. Eventually, the government was forced to act, at least behind the scenes. In late 1903 and 1904 Greek officers secretly joined the guerrillas; now the struggle with the Bulgarians over Macedonia was earnestly begun. The Turkish authorities were torn between an understandable delight at seeing two adversaries at each other's throats and the practical necessity to keep order in the area.

While the stealthy and often savage war of the rival guerrilla forces went on in Macedonia, Crete returned to the news. Eleutherios Venizelos, by now the most prominent among the Cretan leaders, came into a serious dispute with Prince George, the high commissioner. If someone were to read today the detailed records of this period, he would search in vain for fundamental differences of opinion between the two men. Yet, as is not uncommon in history, well-intentioned proposals and honest objections were twisted, misinterpreted, and distorted by suspicion into sinister designs for personal gain. In the process the initial arguments were forgotten and Venizelos locked horns in a personal feud with the prince, although both wanted to bring about the island's union with Greece—each in his own way. Ironically, union was out of the question as long as the powers objected; consequently, their quarrel was rather academic and as empty of purpose as it was tragic in its consequences.

Venizelos had for years opposed union with Greece as an impractical objective, and by so doing he had gained the confidence of the British. In 1905 he surprised all concerned by shifting in favor of enosis and raising the flag of revolt in the mountainous village of Therissos. Being well-informed, Venizelos was certainly aware that the powers would not condone enosis. The real objective of his revolt was to oust the prince. The slogan of enosis provided him with a convenient device to generate public support. The revolt was successful: to avoid bloodshed, the prince left the island. As a face-saving device, the powers agreed to transfer to the king of Greece the right to appoint the next high commissioner.

The revolt of Therissos had little immediate effect on the island's status; but it had unintended and unforeseeable wide-ranging consequences. It propelled Venizelos to national prominence, and in less than five years he would emerge as Greece's prime minister. The dispute, and the uncertain policies of the Greek leaders, added to the disillusionment of the Greek public. The military, always a sensitive receiver of public sentiment in Greece, began to complain in muffled tones. The government's so-called correct attitude toward the powers on the question of Cretan union was denounced as a transparent cover for incompetence and timidity. The quest for change—diffuse, uncertain, emotional, and without clear focus at the beginning—began gradually to gather momentum. It would take one more incident to trigger the pent-up resentments. It came from an unlikely source.

The Young Turks take over

In the spring of 1908, with Greek and Bulgarian guerrilla bands roaming the Macedonian countryside, the powers decided to press the sultan on easing the repression of the Christian populations and on restoring peace. A meeting of the czar with the king of England at Tallinn in June generated alarming rumors. The Turkish nationalists, who had formed in Salonika a secret organization, the Society of Union and Progress, saw in the renewed interest of the powers another major move to hasten the liquidation of the Turkish possessions in the Balkans. One of the military leaders of this organization, Capt. Emver Bey, a brilliant army officer of humble origins—his father had been a servant at the sultan's palace— summed up epigrammatically the reasons for action: "We are losing Macedonia. Turkey is being dismembered. There is no more time for idle talk; we must resort to force. It is the only language the Sultan will respect." Later on, the Young Turks, as the members of the society were called, would gain abroad the reputation of liberal reformers. In fact, the genesis of their movement was to be found in their anxious desire to hold on to Turkey's possessions in the Balkans.

In early July the first rebellious units of the Turkish army took to the mountains of Macedonia, where they joined forces with the komitadjis, their former foes. Within days, the Turkish Third Army Corps in Salonika declared its support for the rebels and on July 24 the sultan agreed to restore the constitution of 1876. Turkey was now to be transformed into a state comprised of many nationalities living together in freedom and equality. Even Greek Prime Minister Theotokis hailed the event as the harbinger of better days. Only a few Greek leaders recognized the fact that a revitalized Turkey would be an even more difficult adversary. The call for the freedom and unity of all races in Macedonia, they argued, would blunt, confuse, and delay the national effort to bring the Greeks who were still under Turkish rule into the national fold.

Many others also did not see the revolution of the Young Turks as an untarnished blessing. Russia and Austria, in particular, having their own designs on the region, could easily see that the effort of the Young Turks to turn the Ottoman Empire into a polyethnic community of equal citizens would block their way much more effectively than the enfeebled regime of the sultan. Already the Young Turks were inviting the inhabitants of Bosnia and Herzegovina—temporarily under Austrian administration but legally under Turkish sovereignty—to elect their representatives to the new Turkish legislature, which was provided by the restored constitution. In September the Austrians agreed with the Russians to a virtual partition of the Balkans into two spheres of influence. Bulgaria and the Straits would be in the Russian zone; Macedonia, Serbia, and Bosnia-Herzegovina in the Austrian. Three weeks later, the Austrian emperor issued an imperial decree formally declaring the annexation of Bosnia-Herzegovina. With this, events began to move rapidly. On the following day, October 8, the king of Bulgaria proclaimed the independence of his country and at the same time he fully incorporated Eastern Rumelia, thus ending any Turkish rights—however nominal—over the area. Spurred by the news, the Cretans once again declared, on October 10, the union of their island with Greece.

The Greek government of Georgios Theotokis refused to take a formal stand in favor of enosis. Fearful of a military confrontation with Turkey, Theotokis tried to avoid any provocation that could lead to another disaster such as that of 1897. The Young Turks, unable to take any action against Austria or Russia, sheepishly acquiesced to the annexation of Bosnia-Herzegovina and the proclamation of Bulgarian independence. With Greece, the situation was different. She had no devoted patrons. Encouraged by the hands-off policy of Theotokis, the Young Turks raised the ante and insisted that the Cretan people, still legally under Turkish suzerainty, elect their representatives to the Turkish legislature. They were trying to turn the clock back, but the Cretans had already formed an executive committee, which administered the island in the name of King George. As far as they were concerned, Crete was already an integral part of Greece. The Greek government did not abide by the demand of the Young Turks but played for time.

Already the Young Turks were in trouble with the traditional elements in Turkey and a final confrontation seemed inevitable. It came in April 1909 when Sultan Abdul Hamid staged a counterrevolution. His desperate attempt to revive a dying regime failed dismally. The Young Turks triumphed and he ended up a prisoner in Salonika. Although they placed his brother Mohammed on the throne, the real power was now completely in the hands of the Young Turks. Freed of the old-regime fetters, these advocates of renewed Turkish nationalism rolled up their sleeves and launched an ambitious campaign to modernize Turkey and above all to shore up the foundations of the empire. With renewed confidence, they told Greece that acceptance of Cretan union would lead to war. Shevket Pasha, the leader of the final confrontation with Abdul-Hamid, threatened half-jokingly while talking to journalists that he was looking forward to having his coffee in Athens.

The Greek military seethed under these insults to their national pride. To them, the country's impotence was caused by the low caliber of the politicians, the corruption of the parties, and the inability of the nation's leaders to overcome the emotional trauma of 1897. To a degree these charges were not unfounded. Burned by the experience of the 1897 military disaster, the political leaders were afraid to take any step that might provoke another military confrontation. Inevitably, the throne, too, came in for its share of the blame.

To reduce the mounting criticism, the government decided to take certain steps to streamline the organization of the army and improve the quality of the officer corps. In so doing, it affected the career aspirations of many officers who were bypassed as unsuitable for the new army. When personal grievances were added to the feelings of nationalist frustration, the mixture became explosive. Before long, officers were setting up secret, revolutionary organizations.

In mid-July 1909 the foreign powers that had been keeping the peace on the island of Crete for almost a decade declared their intention to withdraw their units. At first sight this step could have been interpreted as a prelude to the island's union with Greece. But the powers declared at the same time that the supreme authority of the Turkish government remained unimpaired and that any attempt to force changes unacceptable to Turkey would be opposed by the powers. The Greek people and especially the military, who had come to believe that enosis was around the corner, suffered a traumatic shock. Rallis, the red-haired demagogue, again raised the flag of nationalist intransigence and called for the resignation of Theotokis, hopeful that he would replace him in the premiership. The prime minister submitted his resignation and was indeed replaced by Rallis. In spite of his fiery rhetoric when in opposition, Rallis was an extremely cautious man now that he was in power. In fact, his so-called correct attitude exceeded in docility even that of Theotokis. When the Turks demanded a declaration that Greece had no claims whatever on Crete, Rallis bowed to the pressure. Although he did not renounce the objective of enosis, he said everything else he could to mollify the Turkish government. He even went so far as to deliver his reply to the Turkish embassy personally!

The military establishment was in an uproar. A secret organization known as *Stratiotikos Synthesmos* (Military League) had started to hold clandestine meetings. Already one of those meetings had been discovered by the authorities and several participants were arrested. This had merely fanned the flames of rebellion. The officers of the Military League became bolder and more aggressive, but for all their rebellious rhetoric, they were not prepared to take drastic action. They appointed as their leader Col. Nikolaos Zorbas, a mild-mannered senior officer in charge of army logistics. He was hardly the man to lead a revolution. His main role, as he later confessed to a journalist, was to issue the necessary orders, "because officers are accustomed to act only when ordered to do so by a superior officer!"

The absence of a genuine leader was only one of the league's congenital weaknesses. The last military intrusion into the political process was in 1862, when Otho was ousted. Even then, the military had acted under the leadership and the guidance of the politicians.

In 1909 the situation was decidedly different. This time the military were at odds with all political parties, all political leaders. Independence from partisan ties, instead of strengthening their hand, merely deprived them of experienced leadership. More damaging, the rebellious officers had no well-defined objectives, no political program. Still, their movement was drawing strength from a deep-running and powerful public quest for change. For months the halls of the University of Athens had been echoing the heated discussions of students angry with the government's timidity in foreign policy. The trade unions, rudimentary though they were at that time, added their voice to the chorus of discontent, reflecting public concern with economic stagnation, rising prices, and widespread unemployment. But the most serious demand for drastic changes in the country's economic and social structure came from the landless peasants of Thessalia. The transfer of this area to Greece in 1881 had resulted in little change. Most of the peasants continued to work on the large *tsiflikia* (estates) in a state of near serfdom. In 1909 they began to agitate for land reform. Their demonstrations, which often escalated into bloody clashes with the police, gave a social content to the oncoming revolution.

chapter 3
Triumph and Dissension

The revolution of 1909

Like mountains that look more impressive from a distance, certain historic events have a tendency to grow in stature with the passage of time. The revolution of 1909 is one of those events. When it started, it hardly looked like a turning point. In fact, instead of being a deadly serious affair, it had at certain moments the overtones of comic opera. Yet, it did turn an important page in the nation's history.

The revolution broke out almost inadvertently. When Rallis became prime minister, he decided to take a tough stand on the question of military discipline. And, in an effort to break up the Military League, he ordered certain of its key members transferred to military posts in the provinces. The League leaders, reluctant to press for a confrontation, asked Rallis to receive their spokesmen and try to reach some sort of compromise. Rallis, who was no less anxious to avoid a clash with the officer corps, agreed to a meeting on August 27. As it often happens on such occasions, the apostles of moderation were outmaneuvered by the partisans of confrontation. Some of the extremists among the league officers decided to take advantage of Rallis' notorious temper. What they did is worth telling in some detail because it reveals the spirit and the conditions of the time. One of the more radical officers, Lt. Theodoros Pangalos, resorted to a dashing, somewhat comical abduction of two imprisoned officers who had been arrested for their involvement in the Military League. Pangalos hired a horse and carriage in mid-afternoon on August 27 and drove to the jail in full uniform. He passed by the guard at the gate, who dutifully saluted, and then crossed the yard, ignoring a couple of gendarmes who were taking their afternoon siesta. Pangalos woke up the two imprisoned officers, who were also taking their afternoon nap, and before anyone noticed, he walked out of the jail with them. They all drove away through the slumbering town, leaving behind a cloud of dust.

Rallis, who had agreed to meet the league's representatives that same evening, became furious when he learned of this monumental affront to the government's prestige. When the representatives arrived for the meeting they were virtually thrown out. Deliberately misleading reports that the members of the league were badly divided and incapable of anything but inflated rhetoric—reports apparently initiated by the advocates of drastic action against the government—gave Rallis a feeling of confidence and strengthened his resolve to assume a hard line with the military.

Once the last effort to reach a compromise had misfired, there was no turning back. Zorbas, as leader of the league, did his part and issued the necessary orders. The revolution was on. By midnight the first units began to converge on the military barracks of Goudi on the outskirts of Athens. Under a silvery August moon, the units moved through the streets of the capital as though they were going to have a parade. Many Athenians who had stayed up late to enjoy the balmy summer night watched the soldiers and sailors pass by and wished them well. There was no excitement, no apprehension. The following morning elegant ladies with their escorts would drive in the direction of Goudi—to see the revolution!

Around four o'clock in the morning the king was awakened by his son Andreas and told that apparently the army was in revolt. With daybreak, events began to unfold in rapid succession. Rallis resigned and was quickly replaced by Mavromikhalis; the rebellious officers asked for and received amnesty; practically everyone rushed to the side of the revolution. Only Theotokis spoke out in strong terms against the mutiny until he was advised by King George to cool his temper. By the end of the next day, the various units had returned to their regular posts. For another four weeks very little happened. The league had no idea as to what their next move should be; they decided simply to wait for the Vouli to reconvene, whereupon they would ask for the enactment of laws needed for the reorganization of the armed forces and the approval of funds for the purchase of weapons and supplies.

Not surprisingly, several members of the league began to complain that the revolution was running out of steam. Finally, to infuse some life into the enterprise and to show that it enjoyed wide public support, the league, with the help of the trade unions, staged a great demonstration in the center of Athens. Members of the trade unions came with their banners, military officers arrived in their uniforms, delegations of the landless peasants from Thessalia marched with makeshift placards, and curious citizens stood by with their wives and children. Most of the oratory had a familiar ring. The themes were patriotism, the incompetence of the old politicians, the glorious past, and the machinations and intrigues of the ungrateful foreigners who refused to acknowledge their eternal debt to Greece. Only one of the orators who mounted the rostrum raised a point of substance. "No more taxes," was the demand of the chairman of the trade unions. "If more money is needed, let the capitalists pay income tax and carry part of the heavy burden that now falls on the shoulders of the people."

The demonstration climaxed with the appearance of a procession of priests who called the people to take an oath to defend the revolution. Then the multitude in a happy and exuberant mood moved toward the palace, where the demonstrators greeted the appearance of King George with a deafening roar of "Long live the king!"

When the Vouli opened a few days later, the Mavromikhalis government introduced a series of economy measures favored by the military that were designed to provide funds for the supply of the armed forces. Predictably every town, every group, every area affected by the proposed economies raised objections. Everyone wanted someone else to pay the price. Proposals to tax real estate, higher incomes, inheritance, mining and insurance companies, and other enterprises met with obstinate resistance in the Vouli, where the wealthier elements of Greek society continued to exert a great deal of influence. The revolution was drifting into the morass of compromise. The league had neither a leader with the iron fist and personality of a born dictator nor one with the qualities of a born statesman. It continued to be a popular movement in search of a leader.

The rise of Venizelos

In December the league leaders decided to seek help. With their wholesale rejection of all Greek politicians, they had no alternative but to turn to someone untarnished by any involvement in Greek politics. They easily agreed on Eleutherios Venizelos, the Cretan politician who had made a name for himself by standing up to Prince George and leading the fight for enosis during the days of his Therissos rebellion. Venizelos accepted their invitation and came to Athens with a minimum of advance publicity. In a remarkable speech he told the officers who had invited him that they had really made a mess of things and that, if they really wanted his help, they ought to take his advice because it was clear that they were incapable of charting a course for the revolution by themselves. A master politician, he realized immediately that he could not rely exclusively on the league. Since the time for dictatorial solutions had passed, he needed the good will of the king as well as the cooperation of the parties. He refused to accept the premiership, which was urged upon him by the league, and chose instead the role of a mediator. He put the old politicians at ease by telling them that his place was really in Crete and that he was in Athens only for a short visit to help resolve the political impasse.

In his dealings with political leaders he centered his efforts around the election of a National Assembly to revise certain articles of the constitution. It was a clever ploy. In a regular election there was always the possibility that the Cretans might elect their own deputies and send them to the Greek Vouli—and thus conceivably precipitate a confrontation with Turkey and the powers. A National Assembly, by contrast, was a matter for the citizens of the Greek kingdom. At the same time, a National Assembly having twice as many members as a regular Vouli would open the gates to the new political forces that had been spawned by the revolution. After considerable wrangling, all parties agreed to hold an election for a National Assembly, and Venizelos went back to Crete. He knew that he had a future and he was prepared to wait. He did not have to wait too long.

In the election, the old parties won a little over half of the seats while the rest went to a host of new politicians committed to change in one form or another. Venizelos had not campaigned, but his friends had entered his candidacy in Attica. He was elected with the largest number of personal votes. Now he could come to Greece and assume the leadership of the new forces, not as the pawn of the military or the creation of royal favor but as the master of his own destiny. The day after the opening of the National Assembly, the Military League announced its formal dissolution. The revolution was over; or so it seemed. In fact, it was just beginning, with Venizelos as the brilliant new standard-bearer.

When he arrived in Athens he was greeted by a vast multitude of enthusiastic supporters. In his first speech, he showed his mettle in no uncertain terms. When some people in the crowd began to cry in favor of a Constituent Assembly—implying a demand for an end to the monarchy—Venizelos retorted without yielding an inch that he favored a Revisional Assembly—having authority to deal only with nonfundamental articles of the constitution. His stand greatly impressed King George and paved the way for their cooperation. The resentment caused by Venizelos' old feud with Prince George in Crete was quickly forgotten. When Venizelos came to the palace a few days later for his first private meeting with the king, the atmosphere was genuinely cordial. Venizelos outlined an ambitious but at the same time pragmatic program. "Grant me your confidence, Your Majesty," he said, his blue-green eyes sparkling with magnetic excitement, "and in a very few years you will see a different Greece."

King George, visibly impressed, asked Venizelos to assume the premiership. He accepted. A few days later, he appeared before the National Assembly and presented his program. The leaders of the old parties, sensing the threat he posed to their political future, mounted a vicious attack. Venizelos, determined to force the issue, asked for a vote of confidence. Most deputies of the old parties walked out. Venizelos, with calculated emotion, announced his decision to resign. The news fell like a lit match on dry grass. Within hours a huge demonstration had gathered in Constitution Square, bellowing cries of wrath against the "corruption of the old parties" and asking Venizelos to stay on. A delegation sent by the demonstrators to the palace received the king's assurances that "the people should not worry because the King is not going to accept Venizelos' resignation." Two days later, Venizelos received a half-hearted vote of confidence in the assembly. He was not a man to live on borrowed time. That same evening the king agreed to dissolve the assembly and proclaim a new election.

The leaders of the old parties—angered by the king's cooperation with Venizelos—decided to teach both of them a lesson by abstaining from the election in a show of protest. It was the first time in modern Greek history that political parties abstained from an election. But such an act of protest is meaningful only when the voters also stay away from the polls. Otherwise, abstention is simply one very effective way to commit political suicide. This is exactly what happened to the old parties in December 1910. Few voters obeyed the call to boycott the election. Venizelos already dominated the political stage. Without serious competition, his newly-founded political party—the Liberals—won an overwhelming majority in the assembly. No prime minister in modern Greek history was ever more powerful. Venizelos enjoyed the confidence of the crown, the support of the assembly, the trust of the army, and the allegiance of a wide popular following. He was able to govern like a powerful dictator while at the same time enjoying the tremendous advantage of a democratic leader drawing his power from the will of the people, not the bayonets of a politicized army.

Venizelos did not represent the interests of a particular class. If anything he was the apostle of political modernization. For almost three generations, Greece had lived under the control of a peculiar form of feudalism. It was the feudalism of the politicians. Greece had no nobility, no landed aristocracy. The old Byzantine nobility had been swept away by the tidal wave of Ottoman conquest in the fifteenth century. When the free Greek state emerged out of the turmoil of the 1821 revolution, there were no feudal lords to claim divine right to rule over their fellow Greeks. Nonetheless, individuals and families who had gained fame with their deeds during the fighting moved to the center of the political stage. Political prominence became a source of power and wealth. In a land of scant resources, the politician with his access to the emoluments of the state became a most important dispenser of benefits and favors. In the peculiar system that emerged, the politician did not own a large estate as did the erstwhile feudal lords of Europe, but he "owned" a constituency through an intricate system of favors. He could be dislodged only by someone who could convincingly promise more favors from the largesse of the state. Modern political scientists call this phenomenon clientelism. It became a pervasive aspect of political reality in Greece.

Venizelos set out to destroy this system of rousfeti politics, and his electoral triumph seemed to make this ambitious goal more than a noble illusion. It is true that in time he, too, would be defeated by the system, which was not the product of sinister design but an outgrowth of the country's endemic poverty, but in 1911 Venizelos was full of vigor, hope, and self-confidence. Through a revision of the 1864 constitution he tried to speed up the legislative process, strengthen the judicial branch, simplify the amendment procedure, and provide additional safeguards for the protection of civil rights. The term of the Vouli was extended from three to four years. Through a series of measures that were easily passed through the legislature, which his party fully dominated, he tried to fight corruption, improve security in a countryside long plagued by bandits and goat-snatchers, curb the abuses of the press and thereby protect individuals from vicious attacks on their reputation under the guise of freedom of the press, and combat tax evasion and loss of revenue through inefficient and corrupt management. Moreover, he introduced labor legislation that was as advanced as any in Europe at that time. Venizelos also initiated the distribution of tsiflikia land to the landless peasants of Thessalia.

From the outset, Venizelos' major preoccupation was the strengthening of the armed forces. He was rightly convinced that the time for another confrontation with Turkey was fast approaching and that Greece's future would be determined by the quality and effectiveness of her army and navy. The steps he took in the process appeared to many to be inconsistent and even devious. To the grave disappointment of the league officers, he brought back to the leadership of the armed forces Prince Constantine, the diadohos, and chose as his own aide-de-camp and personal adviser on military matters a young captain named Ioannis Metaxas, a brilliant,

pragmatic, highly-trained staff officer whose ties with the diadohos
were well-known and whose name was anathema to many of the
league partisans because of his aloofness, pride, professionalism, and
opposition to the Military League and its revolutionary designs in
1909. When some of the league officers attempted to protest and
block those moves, Venizelos quickly broke any desire on their part
to indulge once again in conspiracies and mutinies by sending a few
of the most obstinate to jail. This vividly demonstrated to the others
that as long as he remained prime minister and had the support of
the overwhelming majority of the people, he would not allow or
condone politics in the armed forces.

On the other hand, he invited a French training mission against
the wishes of King George, who had discussed with the kaiser the
possibility of having a German mission come to Greece to train the
army. To Venizelos the choice between the two powers was not
merely a matter of technical preference—although his explanation at
the time was that the French methods and temperament were more
in keeping with the character of the Greek soldier. He could see that
the Entente Cordiale was bound to come sooner or later into a
major conflict with the Central Powers and there was no doubt in his
mind that Greece—a country surrounded by sea—could never afford
to join the opponents of Britain and France, the real masters of the
Mediterranean. Like Trikoupis he understood clearly the importance of a strong Greek navy in the Aegean and he moved with
unrelenting tenacity to complete the arrangements and find the
money to pay for a valuable cruiser, the *Averoff*, which was destined
to become a legend two years later during the Balkan wars.

In less than a year as prime minister, Venizelos had moved in
many directions, cutting boldly through the cobwebs of backwardness, vested interest, and encrusted habits of procrastination and
inefficiency. He was a man in a great hurry. He had reason to be. In
September 1911 the Ottoman Empire faced another challenge when
Italy invaded Tripolitania, its last remaining possession on northern
Africa. The invasion bogged down after a while as the Moslem
natives made a common cause with the Turkish garrisons and
launched a guerrilla war of attrition against the Italians. To force
Turkey to a settlement, Italy landed on the Dodecanese islands in
May 1912. Venizelos had encouraged this move in the erroneous
hope that the Italian occupation of these Greek islands would be
only temporary, a prelude to their union with Greece. It did not

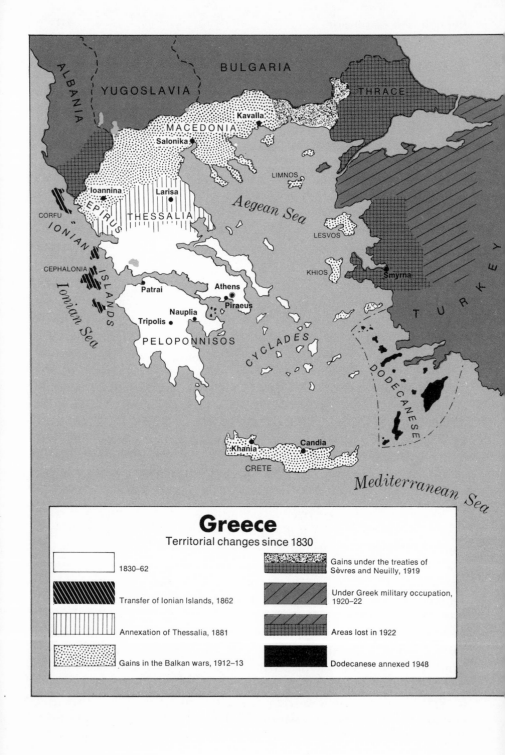

Greece

Territorial changes since 1830

☐ 1830–62	Gains under the treaties of Sèvres and Neuilly, 1919
◼ Transfer of Ionian Islands, 1862	Under Greek military occupation, 1920–22
Annexation of Thessalia, 1881	Areas lost in 1922
Gains in the Balkan wars, 1912–13	Dodecanese annexed 1948

happen as he expected. The Dodecanese remained under Italian rule until 1948.

The Balkan wars

The governments of Greece, Serbia, and Bulgaria saw in the Turkish-Italian war an opportunity to force hard-pressed Turkey to grant more concessions in the Balkans. But this common interest was not easily translated into joint action. Greece, Serbia, and Bulgaria had their own conflicting interests and aspirations over the Turkish-held territories in the Balkans. Bulgaria, with an army of 200,000 men, had ambitious goals over Thrace and Macedonia and saw no reason, at first, to respond to Greek overtures for cooperation. Playing a very astute diplomatic game, the Bulgarian leaders turned to Serbia and in the spring of 1912 signed a treaty of alliance. In this way they drove a wedge between Greece and Serbia. Venizelos faced now the dismal prospect of having these two neighbors to the north swallow up the territories in Macedonia and Thrace without giving Greece a chance to claim her due. For a while Venizelos toyed with the idea of improving relations with Turkey and even offered to forego enosis for Crete if the Turks would allow the Cretan deputies to sit in the Vouli as the representatives of an autonomous region under the suzerainty of the sultan. He even considered having Crete pay a tribute to the Porte. But there was more. What Venizelos wanted to secure by improving relations with Turkey was a tacit agreement that in the event of a Bulgarian attack in the Balkans, the Turkish army would voluntarily withdraw from the areas claimed by Greece and concentrate its forces to defend more vital areas in Eastern Thrace. The Turks were not interested. Venizelos had no alternative but to join Bulgaria, Serbia, and Montenegro without posing any advance conditions for the satisfaction of the Greek claims. A few days after the signing of the alliance in October 1912, the first Balkan war broke out. With the Turkish government mobilizing large forces in Macedonia and Thrace, the four allied governments decided to move. Montenegro was the first to declare war, followed within days by the other countries.

The Greek forces moved into Macedonia under the command of Diadohos Constantine. Hardly anyone expected them to make much headway. In fact, the only reason Bulgaria consented at the last moment to accept Greece into the alliance was that they needed the Greek navy to prevent the transport of Turkish reinforcements to Macedonia by sea. Since 1897 the reputation of the Greek army was quite poor. This turned out to be a blessing in disguise. The Turks were taken by surprise because they expected to face the ragtag forces of 1897. They were forced back in pitched battles. The military successes raised the confidence of the Greek forces, and within three weeks, on November 10, they entered Salonika, and were greeted with a frenzy of enthusiasm by the Greek inhabitants. It had been a deadly race with the Bulgarians, who were also fighting to reach Salonika first. The Greeks won the race and when the Bulgarians reached the outskirts of the city they could only ask permission to quarter a battalion in Salonika, "for humanitarian reasons," to recover from the hardships of their long fight through Thrace and Macedonia. The Greeks gave permission and before long an entire division had made its way into the city. The seeds for the second Balkan war were already sown.

In a gesture aimed at sealing the Greek hold on the city, King George himself moved to Salonika. There, on March 18, 1913, he was shot from behind by what was called a deranged assassin and killed. The real motives for the wanton murder never came to light as the assassin committed suicide a few days later. Rumors of foreign intrigue were never substantiated. If foreign powers were indeed involved—Germany was the assumed instigator—they were engaged in a futile crime because King George had already decided to leave the throne the following October on the fiftieth anniversary of his reign. Whatever the truth, the assassination of King George was to have consequences hardly anyone could have foreseen at the time of his death. Had he lived for a few more years—whether on the throne or in the wings—the disastrous rivalry between Venizelos and newly-crowned King Constantine might have been avoided through his wise counsel and influence. This is one more of those *ifs* of history that are interesting to speculate about but impossible to verify with any certainty.

The first Balkan war ended in May 1913. But the elation of victory was darkened by forebodings of fresh trouble. Both Greece and Serbia were deeply concerned with the intentions of Bulgaria. Before the two governments had time to reach an agreement, the Bulgarian army launched an attack on the Greek positions in Thrace. If the

Bulgarians had hoped to discourage an agreement between Greece and Serbia, they achieved the opposite: the two governments signed a treaty of alliance on June 1.

Four weeks later, the Bulgarian army opened its offensive against the Serb and Greek positions in a determined effort to take them by surprise and drive a wedge between them. Salonika and the rest of Macedonia was the ultimate objective. After a brief pullback, the Greek army with Constantine—now a king—again at the helm passed into a bold counteroffensive and within a few weeks raised their flag over Serrai, Xanthi, Drama, Komotini, Alexandroupolis— all areas that had been seized from Turkey by Bulgaria in the first Balkan war. The Bucharest Conference in August sealed these historic advances. No less than the acquisition of territory or the liberation of Greek populations, the military victories in the two Balkan wars gave the Greek people a new sense of confidence and self-respect. Success had wiped out the humiliating memories of 1897 and removed the emotional fetters that the disaster of that year had fastened on the nation's soul.

War and territorial expansion fostered economic and social advances as well. The merchant marine almost doubled in tonnage in less than five years, growing from 499,000 tons in 1910 to 822,000 by 1915. Athens, which had less than 45,000 inhabitants when King George came to the throne in 1864, had become a large city of almost 200,000 by the end of the Balkan wars, possibly the fastest growing city in Europe at the time. While industrial development remained limited, a strong merchant class had emerged, dealing mostly with the export of the country's agricultural and mineral products and the import of manufactured goods from Europe. The expansion of Greek control over the fertile plains of Macedonia and Thrace added new sources of wealth. Legislation for the protection of labor together with land reforms in the new territories and support measures for the usury-ridden farmers, initiated mostly under Venizelos, blunted the intensity of social conflict, which explains why the dissension of later years was not along economic and social lines. Above all, one success after another in the short span of two years had forged an armor of national unity that appeared to be unbreakable. Venizelos and Constantine were the great heroes of the moment, leading a united, exuberant, confident nation. Within less than two years, this magnificent achievement would be shattered and lost in the convulsions of a dispute centering around Venizelos and Constantine, which pitted one Greek against another for a generation.

Dissension at the top

The outbreak of the First World War appeared to open for Greece fresh opportunities for territorial expansion. True, following the Balkan wars Crete and Epirus in addition to the southern part of Macedonia and Western Thrace were irrevocably united with Greece, but the nation still had unredeemed brethren in Eastern Thrace, the Aegean, northern Epirus, and Asia Minor. Venizelos—convinced almost mystically of Allied victory—was so anxious to enter the arena that he did not even wait to be asked to join the Allies and thus be in a position to bargain for future concessions. He was fearful that the war might end before he had time to become a full participant and share in the fruits of victory. By contrast, King Constantine had serious doubts about Allied victory. He reasoned correctly that if the war were to end quickly, Germany had a better chance to emerge if not totally victorious at least in a strong bargaining position. German successes during the early months of the war seemed to bear him out. But he did not expect the war to end swiftly, and in a prolonged conflict, it would be impossible to foresee the future with certainty. He agreed with Venizelos that Greece's geographic location in the Mediterranean ruled out an alliance with the Central Powers. To the persistent pressures from his brother-in-law, Kaiser Wilhelm, to join Germany, Constantine's reply was a polite but unequivocal no. Neutrality, in his view, was the only realistic policy, at least until the smoke had cleared sufficiently and a sound national policy could be charted safely. In the summer and fall of 1914, with the German armies moving successfully into France and Russia, with the Austrians pressing hard on the Serbs, with Bulgaria waiting for a chance to take her revenge against Serbia and Greece, and with the United States following a policy of neutrality, it could in all fairness be said that confidence in Allied victory had to be more an act of faith than the product of dispassionate and realistic assessment.

In any event, on August 18, 1914, in a secret communication to the British government, Venizelos "with the full approval of King

Constantine" offered to place at the disposal of the Allies the country's military forces and other facilities. This he did without posing any conditions or claims. To his surprise, this most generous offer was politely declined because Britain was afraid that such cooperation would bring Turkey and possibly Bulgaria to the side of the Central Powers. The French also expressed their "deep appreciation" for the offer but they advised caution because in their view "every effort should be made on the part of Greece to encourage Turkey to maintain her declared neutrality." The Russians happily followed suit, anxious to keep Greece away from Constantinople and the Straits; they already had signed secret agreements with Britain and France that promised to give Russia control over Constantinople at the time of victory. In the end, Venizelos was forced by the stand of the Allies, if nothing else, to agree with Constantine on neutrality—and wait anxiously for another day.

It was not easy for Venizelos to wait, especially after Turkey entered the war on the side of Germany. Determined to force a change in policy, he submitted his resignation on two occasions for rather unimportant reasons. In the second instance, for example, Venizelos angrily offered to resign because the king's reply to his demand for the removal of the chief of the general staff, General Dousmanis, had not been delivered by the time Venizelos expected it to arrive. In point of fact, the king's reply accepting the decision of the prime minister had already left the palace and was on its way. The incident was merely a reflection of the growing rift between the two men.

The brewing conflict came to a head in late February 1915, when the Allies decided to invade and seize the Dardanelles (the Gallipoli Operation) and asked Venizelos to contribute forces. To the Allied proposals for joint action, Venizelos responded with alacrity. Unaware of the secret agreements giving Russia control over Constantinople and the Straits, he was already dreaming of the Greek flag being raised over the fabled Polis. The king, on the other hand, following in this the views of Ioannis Metaxas, who was at the time chief of the general staff, expressed serious misgivings about the operation. He said that it would be extremely hazardous, especially in view of the strong fortifications that had been erected in the Dardanelles with German assistance during the intervening months. Moreover, if Greece were to comply with the Allied request and send forty thousand men there, Macedonia would be exposed to a possible attack from Bulgaria. These were no idle fears. The Allies, instead of guaranteeing Greece's territorial integrity, were actually saying that she should give the town of Kavalla in Thrace to the Bulgarians in order to prevent them from joining Germany. Venizelos was not impressed by the king's arguments. He was convinced that timidity and caution at this critical moment would deprive Greece of any influence and bargaining power at the time of victory.

This disagreement between the king and the prime minister over the direction of foreign policy was already becoming the object of public controversy. Agents of the foreign powers seized on the opportunity and used every means to whip up public passions in the hope of forcing on the country those policies that were favored by their respective masters. Greece had experienced for almost a century the stifling protection of Britain, France, and Russia. At the beginning of the twentieth century when Britain became paramount in Greek affairs, erasing the divisive effect of conflicting foreign influences, national unity surpassed all expectations. This unity was now going to be fractured as Germany on the one side and Britain on the other became the two antithetical poles, each, like a magnet, drawing part of the nation. Constantine and Venizelos came to personify the two rival camps, but the rift actually went far beyond the disagreement between two individuals. Whatever the merits of their respective arguments or reasons, the tragic fact remains that these two men who happened to hold the country's destiny in their hands, instead of working together to chart a national policy, retreated more and more into their own fortresses of obstinacy and self-righteousness, suspicious of each other's motives—even of each other's patriotism. A reading of the detailed record of the growing controversy reveals a shocking inability on the part of these two leaders—both of whom unquestionably had the country's best interests at heart—to reason together and plan with detached realism a policy that would best serve the nation at each stage of the war. By the time the Gallipoli Operation, poorly planned and executed by the Allies, came to the anticipated disaster, the time had passed for Constantine to take much comfort in the fulfillment of his prediction.

Unable to join the Allies in Gallipoli, Venizelos resigned on March 5 and was replaced by Dimitrios Gounaris, the leader of the Populist party. The new man at the helm was a capable, intelligent politician of the younger generation who had started his political career as a man of liberal, progressive views. However, in the controversy with Venizelos he sided with the king's cautious policy. Venizelos left the country in a huff vowing never to return to the political stage. The king sought a way out of the controversy by calling the people to the polls. In the election of June 13, Venizelos' Liberal party triumphed. Responding to the public mandate, the king invited Venizelos back to the premiership. For the moment it appeared that the period of confusion and controversy was about to give way to an era of unity and certainty reminiscent of 1912–13. But the old bonds of mutual confidence between Venizelos and Constantine were forever broken.

Before long, the relationship between the two men was put to another critical test. On September 19, 1915, Bulgaria signed a secret treaty of alliance with the Central Powers. All the efforts of the Allies to placate the Bulgarians, even at the expense of Greece, had come to nought. Within two days the Bulgarian army began to mobilize. Venizelos and Constantine agreed that the Greek army should also mobilize. The question was: What should be done if Bulgaria chose to attack Serbia but maintained neutrality toward Greece? Should Greece honor her 1913 treaty and come to the aid of the Serbs, already hard-pressed by the Austrian army? Under the treaty, Serbia was to contribute 150,000 troops in the event of a Bulgarian offensive against the two countries. Now that the Serbian army was engaged in a war with the Central Powers, was Greece still bound by the agreement? Venizelos, with the king's consent, turned to the British and inquired whether the Allies would be prepared to send the necessary troops to Macedonia in order to help Greece in the event of Bulgarian aggression. Britain and France—with the Gallipoli Operation already written off as a hopeless failure—affirmed their willingness to send troops to Salonika. Presumably, Venizelos cleared the matter with the Allies even before he obtained the king's consent because less than two days later Allied troops were already on their way to Salonika.

At this critical moment even Venizelos was taken by surprise. His understanding with the British and French governments was that troops would be sent *only* in the event of Bulgarian aggression. But the Bulgarians had not moved against Greece. In fact, strange reports from London implied that Britain—not knowing the terms of the treaty between Bulgaria and the Central Powers, which remained secret—was still trying to win Bulgaria to the Allied camp.

It was also rumored that the Allied troops in Macedonia would actually be used to turn over part of the area to Bulgaria as the price for her cooperation. Venizelos had no choice but to protest the Allied landing as a violation of Greek sovereignty; nonetheless, having unlimited confidence in his diplomatic skills he apparently was happy that Greece was now forced by circumstances to enter the war. Venizelos doubtless felt that whatever might happen he would be able to expand the country's territory at the conference table as long as Greece was on the side of the victorious Allies. These conjectures and aspirations aside, Greece had no way of preventing the landing in any event. Greek neutrality had been, from the beginning of the war, an illusion that could be maintained only as long as Britain and France considered it to be in their interest.

In a heated debate in the Vouli on October 4, Venizelos spoke openly in favor of "the two Western powers whose interests are more in line with our own." And he added that Greece "cannot ask the foreigners to be her friends; but she must always find her associates and comrades where her interests dictate." Sensible words which at a different time would have deserved only praise. But in the context of the moment, they amounted to an open declaration that Greece was no longer a neutral country but a participant on the side of the Allies. With the Allied troops in Salonika, Greek neutrality was, of course, a battered fiction, but one that Constantine nevertheless opted to preserve. When he met with Venizelos the following day, the issue was clear: Venizelos recommended that Greece enter the war openly and fully on the side of the Allies; King Constantine repeated his objections. Venizelos felt that he had no alternative but to resign. The two men, who only three years before had together doubled Greece's territory, were about to part and by so doing cast the nation into the throes of defeat, revolution, economic chaos, and national disunity. They parted amicably enough, as though they were trying to conceal the gravity of the moment behind a thin smile and a civil handshake.

After an unsuccessful attempt to place Alexandros Zaimis in the premiership, Constantine decided to call another election for December 19. Venizelos, determined to force a showdown, instructed his followers to abstain. This was the second time since 1910 that political parties had opted to stay away from the polls in a show of protest. But in 1910 the old parties had abstained because they knew that they had lost popular support. Their abstention was an acknowledgement of defeat. In 1915, however, Venizelos' abstention was a revolutionary act, a telling warning. In his eyes—and with good reason—the election in June had settled the issue. The voters had given his party 184 seats compared to 90 for Gounaris, with the remaining 36 distributed among the old parties led by Theotokis, Rallis, Mavromikhalis, and Zaimis. The people had spoken out very clearly in favor of his foreign policy. By dissolving the Vouli, the king was ignoring the popular will and imposing his own views. Many agreed with Venizelos' interpretation.

In the election of December 1915 voter abstention reached almost 65 percent. The division of the nation into two rival camps was no longer a matter of conjecture; it could be measured in exact figures. What was even more serious was that King Constantine, by his direct involvement in the controversy, could no longer perform his role as the head of state, that is, as the impartial constitutional arbiter. The king had become a partisan leader. The country was to pay a heavy price for this. Years later, Ioannis Metaxas, one of the king's closest and most trusted military advisers and the man who bore a heavy responsibility for the rift between Venizelos and Constantine, wrote in his diary three weeks before his death in January 1941: "Will God ever forgive us for . . . 1915? We are all to blame. Even Venizelos. Now I feel how much I am to blame."

Constantine is forced out

Underneath the divisive dispute over neutrality, an astute observer of politics could have detected another, subtle current. The old, conservative elite, which had been pushed aside since 1909, had now seized instinctively upon the foreign policy dispute to stage its own comeback. Traditionally this elite had drawn its power from the docile, largely illiterate peasantry. Venizelos had tried to break their hold on the countryside while at the same time opening up new avenues of influence for the growing bourgeoisie. For the first few years, his efforts were successful. But the heavy toll in the Balkan wars was paid primarily by the peasantry, while the benefits that accrued from the country's territorial expansion went primarily to the educated, the merchants, the small entrepreneurial group at the top. The policy of neutrality had a certain appeal to those who expected to carry the heavy burden of war on their shoulders. On every occasion, the leaders of the traditional oligarchy proudly boasted of their success in keeping the country prosperous, safe, secure, and out of war.

Stefanos Skouloudis personified in the highest degree the sterile conservatism of the old political elite. This stubborn, narrow-minded, self-centered man was eighty years old when King Constantine asked him to become prime minister. A native of Constantinople where he had made a fortune in banking, he had come to Greece in middle age, dreaming of a glorious career in politics. But Skouloudis had never succeeded in scaling the heights that he regarded to be within his reach. Now in old age, fate had suddenly decided to smile on him. In reality, the selection of this old man to govern the ship of state in these critical times merely revealed the king's decision to be his own prime minister.

While seeking to protect Greece behind the tattered shield of an unattainable neutrality, King Constantine made one concession after another. He justified his acceptance of Allied demands by inventing another convenient fiction, "favorable neutrality"—that is, favorable to the Allies.* Constantine and his advisers seemed unable to understand that in the event of German victory, Greece's so-called favorable neutrality would be no less damaging than outright participation on the side of the Allies in the war. This was especially true since Germany's allies in the Balkans were the Bulgarians and the Turks, both of whom were eagerly looking forward to the day when they could settle so many old scores with Greece.

In the spring of 1916 Greece was forced to surrender the fortified position of Roupel, in Macedonia, to the Germans as proof of Greek neutrality and as a guarantee against a possible attack on Bulgaria by the Allied troops stationed in Salonika. Within days, the Allied commander, French General Sarrail, declared martial law, seized the island of Thasos, and presented the Greek government with an ultimatum demanding demobilization of the army, the resignation of Skouloudis, the calling of elections, and the purge of several high officials that the Liberals wanted out of the way. Ironically, with Venizelos' blessing, the Allies took out of the closet of history their

---

* For the next eight months, the Allies repeatedly punctured the fiction of Greek neutrality. The violation of Belgian neutrality by the Germans is one of the highly publicized events of the First World War; by contrast it would be a fruitless task to search for references to Allied violations of Greek neutrality.

forgotten vestments as Greece's protector powers and claimed that they had a legitimate right to interfere in the country's domestic affairs. Constantine bowed to the Allied demands; he replaced Skouloudis with Zaimis, and called for an election in the fall. Zaimis was even offered Cyprus if Greece joined the Allies. He refused. King Constantine was not blind to the country's strategic realities, and despite whatever pro-German sympathies he might have harbored in his heart, he fully understood that Greece could not possibly follow a policy openly hostile to the powers controlling the Mediterranean. But he stubbornly clung to his views because he could not shift to the Allies without at the same time having to suffer the return of Venizelos to power. By now the rift between the two men had widened to an unbridgeable chasm.

While the Greek leaders, including Venizelos, were opening their electoral campaigns in August, the German armies seized Rumania, giving the advocates of neutrality new arguments to support their policy. At the same time, the Allies—with the French actually making most of the decisions regarding Greece—became impatient. On September 9 the French staged—with the aid of some *Venizelists*—a fake attack on their embassy in Athens, and demanded that the election be called off. Totally disillusioned, Zaimis resigned. Ten days later, Venizelos left for Salonika, where he formed a rival government. Already the Greek troops stationed there had shifted their loyalty to the Allies. The country now had two rival governments.

For the next two months, Constantine and his government were forced to bow to one Allied demand after another. In exchange for their repeated acquiescence they asked only that the Allies prevent a takeover by the Venizelists and that they allow Greece to remain neutral. They received no guarantees. Instead, the French demanded the closing down of the German, Austrian, Turkish, and Bulgarian embassies in Athens. Moreover, they seized most units of the Greek fleet and finally demanded the surrender of at least one sizeable part of the artillery, including large quantities of war materiel. Most of the civilian and military personnel who were not emotionally committed to Venizelos reacted angrily. Their injured pride swelled into a deep, sullen wave of wrath against the Allies.

The French admiral who visited the king on November 28 reported to his superiors: "The question of the war materiel has so incensed the public and the army that [the king] cannot fight against the current." On December 1, more than two thousand troops from the French naval units anchored in Phaliron bay landed at the outskirts of Athens and moved to seize key positions in the city. Greek forces were guarding the critical points. The king had asked his officers "in the name of our country . . . to avoid any clashes," but this was an impossible request. Tempers were running high. Armed civilians had joined the troops to defend Athens. Rumors that Venizelists were among the advancing French troops raised emotions to fever pitch. Who fired the first shot is not clear, and matters little: before the day was over French soldiers had fallen, while the Allied cruisers at Phaliron were shelling Athens. Shells exploded even in the palace garden while the king was conferring with the Allied ambassadors. The fighting ended when the French agreed to accept twenty-four pieces of artillery as a symbolic gesture of capitulation. The following day, Athens became the stage of ugly incidents of revenge as the king's followers turned against the Venizelists, sacking their homes and stores, beating up those they found in the streets.

The clash with the Allied forces sounded the death knell for Constantine's regime. On December 4 French Premier Aristide Briand, told the other Allied governments that in the view of his government only Constantine's abdication "would give satisfaction for the death of Allied soldiers in Athens . . ." Despite support from Venizelos in Salonika, the French suggestion did not find immediate support in Britain and Russia. The czar was understandably against the overthrow of a king, while the British had no stomach for another attack on Athens. The powers all agreed, however, on one thing—to impose a tight blockade on Greece. The effects were felt by the population almost immediately. Food became scarce, there was no fuel for heating in the midst of winter, and epidemics broke out taking hundreds of lives daily. Ironically, the peasants, who were Constantine's mainstay of support, suffered the least from the blockade because in the villages there was always something to eat. The hardships, imposed by the foreign powers, merely cemented popular feelings for the king. A futile gain. Before long, the fortunes of war would seal Constantine's fate.

After the Russian revolution, the Romanovs could no longer intercede for their Greek relative. In Britain, Lloyd George had taken over as prime minister and his only concern was how to defeat Germany. A more technical problem served as the final catalyst. The

German submarines had played havoc with Allied shipping and, in spite of America's entry into the war, British Admiral Jellicoe told the French in the spring of 1917 that they would have to withdraw from Salonika because it was becoming increasingly difficult to supply their forces there. The French replied that they should instead shorten their lines of transport by "securing the unhindered use of the railway connecting Piraeus with Salonika. This requires a friendly government in Athens. We must therefore take over Athens and the Corinth canal." At a meeting in London on May 28, the Allies approved the plan to occupy Greece and remove Constantine from power. The entire operation was placed under the direction of a high commissioner—French Senator Célestin Jonnart.

Confronted with an ultimatum backed by a strong force, King Constantine agreed to leave Greece. "I do not wish to cause bloodshed," he told the last Crown Council on June 9. Two days later, he left with Diadohos George, his eldest son, from the small coastal village of Oropos. The king was given an emotional farewell by hundreds of simple peasants and fishermen. They thought of him as a national hero and martyr forced off his throne by the bayonets of foreign troops only because he wanted to keep his country out of the maelstrom of war.

Venizelos returns to the helm

Constantine's departure did not mark the end of troubled times. Hundreds of thousands of ordinary Greeks identified with the deposed king and blamed Venizelos for all the humiliations and hardships that the nation had suffered in the past two years. Blind passion on both sides made moderation impossible. Worse, thousands of Constantine's passionate supporters could not see that Venizelos was the choice of the victorious Allies and that it was in Greece's national interest for him to continue stewardship of the country's affairs, at least until the nation's aspirations had been securely fulfilled. With the first opportunity—in the elections of November 1920—they would boot him out and bring back King Constantine.

In June 1917 Constantine was replaced on the throne by his second son, Alexander, a handsome, easy-going, and popular prince in his early twenties. His task was a difficult one indeed. Loyalty to his exiled father clashed with his obligation to work with Venizelos, the man he regarded as the cause of all the trouble his family had suffered. Yet, he succeeded beyond all expectation. As a king, Alexander showed moderation, common sense, and flexibility; as time went on even his relations with Venizelos improved to the point of cordiality.

Venizelos came to Athens from Salonika and assumed the premiership on June 26. Unwilling to set up an outright dictatorship and govern without a Vouli, but also afraid that his party might lose if an election were held, he resorted to an ingenious device. He called back to life the Vouli Constantine had dissolved in 1915. The action was clearly in violation of the constitution and had no precedent in parliamentary history. Already a tendency to ignore the constitution was imperceptibly becoming a part of the nation's political ethos. Supported by a docile majority in the resurrected Vouli, Venizelos governed Greece for three years with an iron hand. Against much popular opposition, he mobilized a strong army— using the firing squad to put down sporadic mutinies—and in September 1918 Greek troops took part in a general offensive in Macedonia with the French, the British, and the Serbs. In less than two weeks, Bulgaria asked for a cease-fire. Germany also was about to fall. Six weeks later the Great War was over. With the victory of the Allies, Venizelos was fully vindicated. Another nation less given to emotion might have cast into oblivion the disastrous—and by now meaningless—dispute between Venizelos and Constantine. The major task facing the nation at this point was how to realize the national aspirations at the peace conference. This could be achieved only by giving Venizelos overwhelming support, but by now the dispute had acquired a perverted logic of its own.

In Paris, Venizelos scored one diplomatic success after another at the peace conference. To strengthen his hand, he agreed to send troops to fight against the Bolsheviks in the Ukraine. He had no special interest in the matter—in fact, he had no clear understanding of what the Bolshevik revolution really meant. But Greece had fought very little during the war and he could not use his country's sacrifices to gain Allied support for Greek claims. Making the most of his personal diplomatic skills—and always keeping before the eyes of the Allied leaders the fact that he had split his nation for their cause—he succeeded beyond his most hopeful expectations. In April 1919, in spite of some Italian objections, he was asked by the Allies to undertake the protection of the Christian populations in the area of Smyrna, in Asia Minor. He immediately accepted. It was a fateful decision—but also an inevitable one. No Greek leader could have refused the opportunity to liberate the Greek population "in the ancient lands of Hellenism." In less than three weeks, on May 13, the first troops landed in Smyrna, where they were greeted by wildly jubilant crowds of Greeks. Their arrival was punctuated by violent incidents of revenge against the Turks. Few could foresee at the time how tragically this historic move to Asia Minor was to end.

Venizelos already visualized a Greater Greece spanning both shores of the Aegean, spreading into Thrace all the way to Constantinople, from the Adriatic to the Black Sea—a "Greece of two continents and five seas," was his triumphal phrase. He was no idle dreamer. In August 1920 he left Paris to return to Greece, his work at the peace conference done. In his pocket he carried the peace treaties, above all the Treaty of Sèvres, which gave Greece not only Western but also Eastern Thrace all the way to the outskirts of Constantinople, where units of the Greek fleet were already flying their flag. Smyrna was formally placed under Greek control with the proviso that within five years the inhabitants of the area would be called to decide in a referendum whether they wanted to join Greece irrevocably. As he was preparing to board the train in Paris, Venizelos was shot several times at close range by two pro-Constantine officers. He was only slightly wounded but the news of the assassination attempt unleashed a hysterical reaction among the Venizelos partisans in Athens. Mobs led by fanatics sacked the houses of royalists, physically attacked suspected adversaries, thus repeating in reverse what had happened to the Venizelists in December 1917 at the time of the French landing. The most reprehensible act was the murder of Ion Dragoumis, an inspired patriot whose integrity was generally acclaimed. He was shot by a detachment of the security battalions in broad daylight in the middle of Athens, as he was ostensibly being escorted to prison for investigation.

The assassination attempt and the violence that followed revealed the intensity of hatred separating the two sides. Venizelos' foreign friends began to have second thoughts, while the Bulgarians and the Turks realized with renewed hope that Greece, torn by internal divisions, would not be able to hold on to her territorial gains without receiving direct Allied support. The Allies, willing though they were to give Venizelos most of what he wanted, had no intention of fighting in his behalf. And to make matters worse, Italy and France, for reasons of their own, were already thinking of their future relations with Turkey.

Upon his return to Greece, Venizelos decided to take the country to the polls. He had extended the life of the resurrected Vouli, which should have ended in June 1919, on the grounds that he had first to complete his task in Paris. With the Treaty of Sèvres a reality, he felt that the time had come to seek a renewed mandate from the people, and he scheduled elections for November 1920. He had reasons to be confident. His policy had been vindicated beyond the most extravagant predictions while that of his opponents had been discredited—or so he thought. To be sure, if logic were the guiding factor, he had every reason to expect an electoral triumph as a fitting reward for his momentous accomplishments. But logic had long since deserted the Greek electorate. The memories of the Allied blockade, the arrests, the executions, the ouster of Constantine, all these unpleasant memories were used by Venizelos' opponents to fan the simmering coals of hatred. But above all, they used the fear of a prolonged war in Asia Minor as their main argument. The territorial gains, they said, could not be held without war. The sultan's government had signed the peace treaties, but a determined group of Turkish officers led by Mustafa Kemal had vowed to recover the lost territories and were preparing an army of their own in Anatolia for the crucial confrontation. Continued leadership by Venizelos, they argued, meant many more years of mobilization and war. They promised peace—but they did not explain how they would achieve it. Unless they were prepared to withdraw from Asia Minor, they would have to face exactly the same problem, and this with the added disadvantage of Allied hostility to their camp. In the frenzy of partisan contention hardly anyone stopped to ask logical questions. The antiwar message fell on fertile ground. Still, Venizelos was confident of victory.

At this critical moment, fate intervened. On September 30, King Alexander was strolling through the grounds of the royal estate in Tatoi, accompanied by his dog Fritz, a German shepherd. Suddenly, the dog got into a fight with a pet monkey and the king rushed to separate the two animals. Another monkey, tied nearby, bit the king in the arm and the leg. At first the incident caused little concern. But within days, the wounds became infected, septicemia set in, and in spite of the desperate efforts of the attending physicians, the king died in the afternoon of October 25.

The untimely death of the young monarch reopened the question of Constantine's return. As long as Alexander was on the throne, the royalists could not openly turn the election into a contest between Venizelos and the exiled king. To advocate openly for Constantine's return would have been legally a crime against the reigning monarch. Moreover, the relations between Venizelos and Alexander had changed markedly since the days of their forced cooperation in 1917. In the last year of his life, Alexander had come to feel very close to Venizelos. When many objected to Alexander's proposed marriage to Aspasia Manou, the daughter of a prominent Athenian family with Phanariot ancestry but nonetheless a commoner, Venizelos sided with the young king. The hopeful prospects arising out of their rapprochement vanished with Alexander's death.

Dimitrios Gounaris, by now the leading light in the royalist camp, raised the issue of Constantine's return sharply. To Venizelos' suggestion that Prince Paul, Constantine's youngest son, be elevated to the throne, Gounaris replied that the decision should be left to the people. With this, the election was openly transformed into a contest between Constantine and Venizelos. Whatever the outcome, the constitutional system of vasilevomeni dimokratia had received a fatal blow because the king was turned into a partisan figure, supported by one section of the people and voted down by another. For a brief moment, Venizelos thought of asking Constantine to resign and turn the throne over to his constitutional successor, Prince George, the diadohos. This was indeed the most sensible solution. The death of Alexander justified a postponement of the election and the beginning of discussions for the succession of Diadohos George to the throne. Venizelos was persuaded by his closest associates to drop the idea. They were confident that an electoral victory would end the matter once and for all. They were in for a surprise.

The Asia Minor disaster

In the election of November 14, 340,000 voted for the royalists, 300,000 for Venizelos' Liberal party. The difference in absolute figures was not great, but because of the large, multiseat districts and the plurality system used in Greece at the time, the Liberals won only 110 seats out of 360. Together with all the other Liberal candidates in the Athens electoral district, Venizelos was defeated. Within days he left Greece and went into self-exile in Paris. Two weeks later, a sizeable majority voted in a plebiscite for Constantine's return. His arrival on December 19 was greeted by a jubilant multitude.

Constantine's return to his throne was to prove an empty victory. The Allied leaders who had supported the Greek aspirations had confidence in Venizelos. But even when he was at the helm, they had made it clear that they had no intention of giving military support to a campaign against Kemal's nationalists. In fact, Venizelos had been thinking prior to the election of pulling back the Greek forces from the advanced positions they held in Asia Minor. He was planning to make at the same time a diplomatic effort to reach a compromise with Kemal. He would offer to withdraw from Asia Minor in exchange for a Turkish recognition of Greek sovereignty over the territory of Eastern Thrace, which had been transferred to Greece by the Treaty of Sèvres. Venizelos believed that in making such an offer he would hold a trump card. The Treaty of Sèvres provided that in the event Turkey failed to comply with the peace treaties, she would be forced out of Constantinople.

The outcome of the election gave the reluctant Allies an excuse to revise their policies toward Greece. In less than two years, the French would openly shift to the side of Kemal in order to protect their own interests in the Middle East. The Italians, always opposed to a strong Greece, and having their own aspirations in Asia Minor, would have no trouble reaching an accommodation with the Turks. Even the Soviet government would discover in Kemal a revolutionary who merited their support to the tune of 10 million gold rubles. Paying Greece back in good measure for sending troops against the Red Army in the Ukraine, they signed in 1921—after centuries of Russo-Turkish rivalry—the first accord for friendship and cooperation. In Britain, Lloyd George had no reason to bail out the opponents of his friend Venizelos. A warm, personal friendship existed between these two men. Lloyd George, a radical Welshman in his youth and a liberal to the depths of his soul, had much in common with Venizelos, himself a radical revolutionary in his Cretan days and the embodiment of liberalism in Greece. Besides, Britain had no intention of becoming involved in another war

(above) The trial of the six leaders who were later executed, 1922.   Author's archives
(below) Refugees from Smyrna, 1922.   United Press International Photo

venture. Greece, her people divided and tired of fighting, her capabilities overextended, her security threatened by the lack of reliable friends, now had to face a vigorous new Turkey under the command of a capable, determined, iron-fisted leader, Mustafa Kemal.

The political leaders who won in the November election—with Gounaris as the dominant figure in their midst—soon came face to face with a harsh reality: Either Greece would remain in Asia Minor and risk a war with Kemal's forces or she would have to withdraw and leave almost a million Greeks to the tender mercies of Kemal's nationalists. The second alternative was virtually unthinkable. Sheer pride could not allow the king and his associates to give up the territories their hated antagonist had brought to the national fold. Furthermore, the Greek inhabitants in Asia Minor could not return to the old days as though nothing had happened. Their relations with the Turks had changed radically from the moment Greek troops landed in Smyrna. Once they had openly sided with these forces, they could not remain in Asia Minor if the troops withdrew. A compromise solution was possible only with strong Allied support.

Unable to reach an agreement with Kemal, the royalists discarded their electoral promises "to bring the boys home," and in a desperate move they decided to launch a preemptive attack against the Turkish positions. They did so in full knowledge of Allied hostility to such a move. They compounded the hazardous nature of this fateful decision with a series of diplomatic blunders. When their own prime minister, Dimitrios Rallis, proposed to include Venizelos in the delegation he was to take to London to discuss Greece's future moves, he met a stone wall of opposition. Dimitrios Rallis, already seriously ill with cancer and freed by his proximity to death of the blinders of partisan hate, was thinking only in terms of best serving the national interest. Disillusioned, he resigned. The delegation that went to London in February was offered a last chance for a compromise. Under the proposed scheme, Greece would have retained Eastern Thrace all the way to the outskirts of Constantinople (Catalca). The city of Smyrna would have been placed under a Christian governor appointed by the League of Nations. Greece in return would have withdrawn from all other parts of Asia Minor. It was a most sensible solution.

The reply came from Athens in the form of a unanimously

approved Vouli resolution. In ringing words of defiance, all 360 deputies, Venizelists and royalists in a rare display of unity, declared that "Greece finds it absolutely impossible to accept any revision of the Treaty of Sèvres." After all those years of bitter dissension this was certainly the worst possible move on which to be unanimous. Through intermediaries Venizelos urged Gounaris to accept the proposed scheme. But his advice could not easily be accepted by those who so deeply distrusted his motives. Interestingly, Metaxas— a man with unimpeachable royalist credentials—spoke in March with Gounaris and his closest associates in favor of withdrawing from Asia Minor in order to save Eastern Thrace. Venizelos and Metaxas stood at the opposite ends of the political spectrum. But both were men of brilliant intellect and political acumen; they could see that without strong Allied support, the Asia Minor campaign was doomed. Both were out of power and they could afford a cool, detached view of the situation. Metaxas was offered the position of commander in chief in the Asia Minor army, but he declined; he would have participated in the government only to pursue a compromise solution, not to pursue war.

Historian Foivos Grigoriadis has recently brought to light evidence that seems to indicate that certain elements in the British government hinted to Gounaris that they would favor a campaign against Kemal although they could not offer outright material support. They indicated that success in such an effort would strengthen Greece's bargaining position. The British suggestion appears to be in conflict with their support of a compromise; in fact, the reasoning behind the suggestion shows considerable political adroitness. London continued to deal with the sultan in Constantinople as the legitimate government of Turkey. They also hoped that his spiritual influence as the Khaliph would help them control the Arabs more easily. But ever since July 1919, when Kemal raised his standard of revolt in Anatolia, the sultan's regime had been tottering on the brink of collapse, propped up only by the presence of Allied troops in Constantinople. The clever British wanted to use the Greek troops in Asia Minor to humble Kemal and shore up the sultan's government. Gounaris apparently thought that the British were in reality favoring the Greek campaign and he fell for their ploy. Without adequate preparation, the Greek army launched a major offensive hoping to advance in a pincer movement, encircle

Kemal's forces, and destroy them. Kemal did not fall into the trap. He rapidly withdrew his forces toward the center of the Anatolia plateau.

In April 1921 Gounaris personally assumed the premiership and moved to strengthen the Asia Minor forces for a more decisive encounter. Within two months, the Asia Minor army had reached 200,000 men although only half this number were front-line combat troops. The Allies again offered to mediate for a compromise. Gounaris turned a deaf ear. The former advocate of neutrality had now become a determined warrior, following precisely the policies he had so vehemently attacked eight months earlier when he was campaigning against Venizelos. Those who will search for socioeconomic explanations for Gounaris' turnabout are likely to be disappointed. The premier's actions can only be attributed to an understandable ambition; he wanted to be remembered as the man who had preserved "the Greece of two continents and five seas"— not the man who dismantled it. A noble aspiration, perhaps, but one rendered totally unrealistic in the face of Allied hostility and British duplicity.

On June 12 King Constantine came to Smyrna as though to signify by his presence that there was no turning back. A month later, more than 100,000 troops opened a major offensive against the Turks. For eleven days, they repeated the pincer movement of the previous March, only now it was staged on a much larger scale. Once again Kemal's troops slipped through the ring. Two weeks later, the Greek high command decided to advance through the arid Anatolia plains in the direction of Ankara, Kemal's capital. King Constantine, now playing only a symbolic role, had serious misgivings about such an operation. He remained silent, however, when Gounaris insisted on the big push at the final war council.

While these momentous decisions were being made at the front, life in Athens continued with little apparent change. Reports on the retreat of Kemal's forces were given banner headlines and treated as the harbingers of final victory, firing the imagination and the nationalist feelings of the populace. Shortages and rising prices were accepted as necessary sacrifices for the realization of the nation's most cherished aspirations. Even those who had misgivings kept such thoughts to themselves for fear that words against the war would be condemned by their neighbors and friends as unpatriotic. In the Vouli, the revision of the 1911 constitution—ironically along the very lines suggested by Venizelos prior to the November 1920 election—occupied much of the attention of the lawmakers, with the discussions often seeming to take place in a vacuum as though the country were at peace. Characteristically, at the very time the Greek army was preparing for its major offensive into Anatolia, the Vouli was deeply immersed in a debate as to whether the *dimotiki* (vernacular) should be introduced in education side by side with the *katharevousa* (the pure or high Greek) used in the schools. The issue was not merely a question of linguistics; the dimotiki was championed by the more progressive elements while the katharevousa was defended by the traditional elites.

For ten long days in the middle of August, the Greek soldiers marched through the dry Anatolia plateau, baked by day under a relentless sun, shivering after nightfall in their sweat-soaked uniforms. They met only sporadic fighting, as Kemal in a strategically sound move withdrew his forces all the way back behind the Sakarya river and took up positions along the rocky hills that form a protective barrier around Ankara. His forces, well-supplied in friendly territory and fighting for their native soil, were ready to face an enemy exhausted after so many days of marching. Kemal had chosen his ground well.

The Greek high command, without allowing the troops time to rest and recover from the hardships of the previous ten days, ordered a frontal offensive on August 23. For the next ten days, they fought with almost superhuman determination against the Turkish strongholds. Losses were heavy on both sides. At one point, the commander in chief and the diadohos escaped capture only by sheer chance. The battle was over by September 5. The Turks had stood their ground. Having no choice, the Greek high command ordered the return of the troops to the positions they held before the march through the Anatolia plain. The campaign had cost the Greek army 3,897 dead, almost 20,000 wounded. The new front line stretched from north to south across Asia Minor, with a bulge jutting out eastward in the area around Afyon. A year later this bulge would become a fatal trap for the Greek forces.

The Allied governments quickly grasped the meaning of Kemal's successful resistance. It was time for the powers to discard all pretenses. The French were the first to come out openly on his side. In late October they signed an agreement for the withdrawal of French forces from the southwestern part of Asia Minor with the exception of those troops at Alexandretta. In return, the French gave Kemal all the weapons, ammunition, and supplies they had stored there. The Italians followed suit by evacuating the areas they occupied south of Smyrna. The British plan to destroy Kemal by using the Greek army had failed, so now London proposed to Gounaris that Asia Minor be evacuated. All those Christians who wanted to leave the area would be assisted in doing so. Gounaris, who was at the time in London searching for a desperately needed loan to shore up the country's finances, raised no serious objections. In Athens, however, rumors that the government was willing to compromise provoked howls of public disapproval, especially in the press. Metaxas, who wrote articles in favor of giving up Asia Minor to save Eastern Thrace, was denounced in flaming editorials as a traitor.

In late February 1922 Gounaris returned from London empty-handed. No loan, no compromise solution, no Allied support. Kemal, of course, was in no mood to even consider a compromise solution. He could already smell victory. At this critical juncture, Gounaris lost a vote of confidence 162 to 155, accused by the deputies of surrendering to Allied pressure and agreeing to give up Asia Minor. Most of the opposition to a compromise came from the Liberals—who disregarded the advice of their own self-exiled leader. The Liberals, being in the minority, did not have enough votes in the assembly to bring Gounaris down. Some opposition also came from the royalists. In a contest of superpatriotism in speech after speech, Venizelists and royalists denounced any thought of a compromise and made the unfounded prediction of new military victories in Asia Minor. Gounaris' opponents had little in common and could not form a cabinet to replace him. By necessity, he stayed on.

In April 1922 the Allies again suggested a compromise. This time, Greece was asked not only to withdraw from Asia Minor but also to pull back in Eastern Thrace, away from Constantinople. Kemal agreed, requesting only that the evacuation start immediately and be completed within four-and-a-half months. Kemal's willingness to accept a compromise stiffened Greek confidence and opposition to the idea of evacuating Asia Minor reached a hysterical crescendo. One cabinet crisis followed another. The Venizelists were adamant against a compromise because most of the people in the liberated territories credited Venizelos for their good fortune. The Venizelists could not ignore the pressure applied by these people. Be that as it may, the last chance for a compromise was lost. After another cabinet crisis, all royalist parties agreed to form a coalition government under Petros Protopadakis. On May 22 the new cabinet received an overwhelming vote of confidence. Six months later, Protopadakis and four of his cabinet members would die facing a firing squad.

The Protopadakis government compounded the errors of its predecessors. It replaced all the key officers in the high command, including the commander in chief, Gen. Anastasios Papoulas. Gen. Georgios Khatzianestis took over, but he was a man who had been away from active duty since 1916 and who had no familiarity with the terrain in Asia Minor. Frantically responding to a barrage of diverse suggestions, the government transferred from the Asia Minor front to Eastern Thrace nineteen badly needed battalions with their artillery and cavalry support. The government decided to advance and seize Constantinople—a grandiose scheme that fired public imagination in Greece only to be hastily abandoned on July 30 when the Allies told the Greek government that they would use their troops guarding the approaches to Constantinople to force a halt to the advance. Another strategic blunder was the government's decision to transform the occupied territories in Asia Minor into an autonomous region—a plan that had no other effect than to fire the nationalist feelings of Kemal's soldiers.

The decision to seize Constantinople apparently convinced Kemal that the time was ripe for his offensive. The Greek army, seriously weakened by the transfer of battalions to Eastern Thrace, still had to defend a long front stretching over five hundred miles from north to south. Kemal could select the most favorable points for his attack, concentrate superior forces at those places, and then break through the lines by using artillery to soften the enemy positions and cavalry to spearhead the offensive. The bulge at Afyon was the obvious choice for the major assault.

The offensive opened on August 21 with a fake attack on the southern flank of the bulge. Then, with a heavy artillery barrage, bold cavalry sorties, and direct infantry assaults from the north side of the bulge, the Turkish troops forced their way through the Greek lines. At this crucial moment, General Khatzianestis, with his headquarters three hundred miles away in Smyrna, ordered the retreating troops to hold their ground at all cost. Kemal had escaped disaster three times in 1921 by retreating rapidly to avoid possible encirclement. Facing a similar danger Khatzianestis chose the opposite tactic. Kemal exploited the error, launched small pincer movements, and split the Greek forces at several points. On September 2 his troops captured General Trikoupis, the commander of the First Army Corps. Communications with the front were in such disarray that three days later the Greek government appointed General Trikoupis commander in chief to replace Khatzianestis. Whereupon, Kemal triumphantly announced that Trikoupis had already been his prisoner for days.

With the First Army Corps and the Second Army Corps broken up by heavy concentrations of artillery, the retreat turned into a rout. Kemal, most likely, had not anticipated such a decisive victory. He had probably expected to push the Greek lines further to the west and thereby simply improve his bargaining position. Instead, he had found a confused, demoralized opponent. Within fourteen days, the first Turkish units entered Smyrna. The remnants of the Greek army hastily boarded waiting vessels and left for the nearby islands of Khios and Lesvos. Hundreds of thousands of Asia Minor Greeks crowding the Smyrna waterfront were frantically searching for the means to escape from the oncoming Turks. The advancing armies immediately set the Greek section of the city to the torch. Metropolitan Khrysostomos of Smyrna was arrested and then turned over to a mob that literally tore him to pieces. The officers and men of the Allied naval units anchored in the harbor watched with personal horror—but official neutrality—the last agony of Hellenism in Asia Minor. All along the coast, thousands of destitute, frightened human beings eventually made their way to the neighboring Greek islands. In the course of a few fateful days, the Hellenism of Asia Minor, which could trace its beginnings to the days of Homer, had come to an end.

The ouster of the monarchy

The disaster inevitably set in motion a train of momentous events. Hastily reorganized army units under the command of Gen. Stylianos Gonatas and Col. Nikolaos Plastiras sailed across the Aegean and landed in the vicinity of Athens on September 25. The revolution was on. Within a day, King Constantine left the country for the last time, a broken, dispirited man. Hundreds of royalists, including the members of the last cabinet, were thrown in jail. The uprooted refugees, the returning soldiers, the Venizelists who hungered for revenge, all demanded that the axe of retribution fall without pity. In this heavy climate, Gounaris and his closest associates, including General Khatzianestis, were brought to trial before a revolutionary tribunal. Accused of high treason, six of them were sentenced to death on November 28. Within hours, they were executed by a firing squad. British efforts to save their lives came too late.

With the death of the six leaders, the rage of the public suddenly subsided. Even the most radical lost their taste for blood. Years later, Plastiras—the man who had the final word on the execution—admitted that the six who were executed were not really guilty of treason. He was right. They did not deliberately bring about the disaster. If anything, they hoped to win the war no less passionately than the men who sent them to the wall. But they were caught in the web of a policy from which it was impossible to extricate themselves. Until the very end, they were hopeful that they would succeed in saving the Greeks in Asia Minor.

Kemal, now the undisputed master of Turkey, imposed the terms of a victor. At Moudania, the Allies sided with the Turks and forced the Greek representatives at the armistice conference to accept the withdrawal from Eastern Thrace. This was the first time that Christian territories were returned to Turkish rule after having been liberated. Emboldened, the Turks demanded Western Thrace as well. At Lausanne, where a peace conference started in November 1922, Venizelos—now the revolution's choice as chief delegate— fought a losing battle against Turkish arrogance and Allied indifference. His old friend, Lloyd George, had lost his commanding position as prime minister. The Turkish delegates pressed on. They insisted on heavy reparations, the dismantling of the Greek fleet, and the ousting of the patriarchate from Constantinople.

With Eastern Thrace irrevocably lost, the Greeks focused on Western Thrace. Gen. Theodoros Pangalos, one of the key personalities of the revolutionary regime in Athens, took over as commander in chief. Within a few months he organized, with whatever weapons and materiel he could salvage, a strong fighting force, which he deployed along the new frontier, the river Evros. In Lausanne, Venizelos agreed to an exchange of populations, a move that was aimed at eliminating once and for all the scourge of territorial disputes in the troubled area. At this point, out of a million Greeks in Asia Minor, only 200,000 remained on Turkish soil. By contrast, 480,000 Moslems still lived in Macedonia and Thrace. Throughout the war they had been treated well, as Greek citizens. Under the special treaty for the exchange of populations, signed in January 1923, 388,000 Turks were transferred to Turkey, and 150,000 Greeks went to Greece. One hundred thousand Turks remained in Western Thrace and approximately an equal number of Greeks stayed on in Constantinople. Fifty years later, the Turks in Western Thrace would number 120,000 while the Greeks in Constantinople would have dwindled to less than 30,000, driven away by the subtle but incessant harassment of official Turkey.

In May, Venizelos was instructed to reject the exorbitant demands for reparations and the surrender of the fleet and to leave the Lausanne conference in protest. Pangalos in Western Thrace was ready to cross the Evros river and push swiftly all the way to Constantinople. The plan was not as foolhardy as it may seem. Under the terms of the armistice, the Turks had less than three thousand men in Eastern Thrace, mostly gendarmes assigned to maintaining internal order. The Pangalos army was an effective striking force that was well-equipped and enjoying high morale. Before Venizelos had time to walk out of the conference, he was asked by the British delegate to allow Ismet Pasha Inonu, the Turkish representative, to take the floor for a brief announcement. Ismet told the conference in a terse statement that Turkey was withdrawing all additional demands and would be satisfied with the territorial changes already accepted by Greece. Informed by the British of the Greek plan to push toward Constantinople, the Turkish delegation had moved quickly to consolidate in a treaty what they had already won in the peace talks. Both in the military and the diplomatic fields, the leaders of the new Turkey were proving resourceful and imaginative.

The revolutionary leaders in Athens received the news of the agreement with barely concealed disappointment. In a telegram congratulating Venizelos for his arduous efforts, they let their true feelings show: "Our military soul is saddened by the unjust fate that suddenly pushes us away from the realization of our national aspirations, the achievement of which was made certain by our enormous military effort. We feel, nonetheless, that hopes to have another opportunity have not disappeared. It is possible, as a result of Turkish intransigence toward the Allies, to find in the future more favorable circumstances." Pangalos went even further and telegraphed Venizelos that he no longer recognized him as representing the Greek interests at Lausanne. The government quickly brushed this aside but the incident revealed the internal divisions that were already developing within the Venizelist camp. In fact, it revealed a profound change. Venizelos had been the standard-bearer of the Great Idea in the twentieth century. He had pursued the vision with missionary zeal. The Treaty of Sèvres embodied the final success of his drive, but then the November election in 1920 struck his aspirations a fatal blow. Two years later, the military disaster in Asia Minor merely sealed the tomb of the Great Idea.

Historically, Venizelos' political role ended with his defeat at the polls. New forces were now moving to the forefront, using his name and his irrelevant feud with Constantine as their standard, but with new motives, new aspirations, and new goals, all of which had little in common with the man they worshipped as their leader. The same applied to the partisans of Constantine. With his death in Palermo a few weeks after his forced departure from Greece, he could obviously no longer serve as a living symbol; he was a memory. Inevitably, the royalists transferred their loyalty to the throne as an institution. Sooner or later, the Venizelists would also transfer their hatred for Constantine to the royal institution itself. The confrontation with King George II, who had succeeded his father to the throne, was only a matter of time.

The Treaty of Lausanne was barely signed when Greece faced another unexpected challenge. The new Italian government of Benito Mussolini seized the island of Corfu on the pretext that Greeks had murdered General Tellini and four members of his mission to the International Commission. The men had been working on drawing the new Greek frontiers with Albania. Many years later, Count Sforza revealed that Mussolini had ordered the murder. But in 1923 the Fascist government—only a few months old—used the incident as an excuse to tell the world that Italy was now governed by a new breed of men. The Italian troops evacuated Corfu twenty-seven days later but not before the Allies had forced Greece to pay Italy 39 million francs as an indemnity for the death of Tellini.

This new humiliation played right into the hands of royalists, who chafed under the control of Plastiras and his revolutionary regime.

They began to conspire even with Venizelists, who had their personal reasons for resentment. In October they decided to launch a counterrevolution. Metaxas, who knew of the plot, tried to convince them that their revolt should start in Athens and Salonika. He felt that if the Plastiras-Pangalos group were allowed to keep control of these two cities, the revolt would be doomed to failure. They ignored this sound advice and his prediction came true. Implicated in the revolt, Metaxas had to leave the country.

The inept and confused revolt had no other effect but to strengthen those who wanted to oust the monarchy. That Venizelos himself opposed such a constitutional change seemed to matter little to many of those who still identified themselves by his name. The blunder of the October revolt was compounded by the decision of the royalist politicians to abstain from the election of a Constituent Assembly. Predictably, the Venizelists won an overwhelming victory —385 seats out of 394. More important, the advocates of a republic, though outnumbered by the orthodox Venizelists, enjoyed the advantage that determined zealots usually have over uncertain, lukewarm dissenters. King George made a last, wise move to save his throne. In keeping with the constitution, he invited Venizelos, the acknowledged leader of the victorious Liberal party, to form a government. Venizelos refused—probably because he realized that the power was in the hands of the republican firebrands in the army. The fate of the throne was now sealed. Four days later, King George was asked to "take a trip abroad," and stay out of the country until the Constituent Assembly had completed the drafting of a new constitution. He left with his wife for her native Rumania. At the pier in Piraeus, the republicans contrived a final humiliation. They sent a detachment of soldiers to see him off, but when he passed in front of the soldiers, they remained pointedly at ease. At the very last moment, General Stylianos Gonatas, who was prime minister at the time, rushed to the pier to bid a friendly farewell to the departing royal couple. He was a royalist when the course of events at the time of the Asia Minor disaster thrust him to the leadership of the revolution. For many years King George would remember the humiliation as well as Gonatas' decent gesture.

The official ouster of the monarchy was now only a matter of time. At this critical moment when the country needed national unity to cope with crushing problems, the fate of the throne was hurled into the cauldron of political passions. One of the most difficult of the current problems, the rehabilitation of the refugees, would have been enough to break the back of even a wealthy and powerful country. In the course of only a few months, the country's population had increased from 5,043,800 to 6,204,600, while its territory had been reduced by the loss of Eastern Thrace and the coastal areas of Asia Minor. The country's economy, exhausted after ten years of almost unceasing warfare, was called upon to feed, clothe, house, and employ hundreds of thousands of refugees who had reached safety with only what they could carry on their backs. A largely agricultural country, Greece could not find work for all these people immediately. Only a part of this desperate group could be settled on the lands left vacant by the departing Moslems in Macedonia. Help for the others would have to come from the nation's meager resources. The trade deficit, which in 1922 amounted to 90 million gold francs, went up to 278 in 1923 and 430 in 1924. A general strike, instigated with surprising skill in 1923 by the nascent Communist party, failed to bring down the government and lead to a Communist take-over, but nevertheless it gave one more indication of the growing discontent.

A few days after the king's departure, Venizelos received persistent calls from the leaders of the Liberal party, from liberal republicans, from leaders of the revolution, and from others to return to Greece and assume the premiership. This time, he accepted. He had wanted to play the role of a national statesman, to heal the deep wounds of national disunity. He might have been able to do so together with King George but he had chosen to reject the king's invitation. Now Venizelos was seen by his friends as the archangel of revenge and retribution. His policy of moderation was bound to clash with the intransigence of the extremists. They were searching for scapegoats. But the radical republicans did not turn against the capitalist socioeconomic system.

Socialism had not attracted much attention in Greece—except among intellectuals—because the peasants in the countryside, as well as the shopkeepers, small businessmen, and civil servants in the towns, to say nothing of the big family concerns in industry and commerce, were more interested in keeping and augmenting their property holdings than in any socialization schemes. Besides, social legislation protecting the lower income groups was already advanced in Greece. Communism, too, with its collectivist bias, held little attraction among the peasantry or the petty bourgeoisie in the towns. Individualism and the high value traditionally placed on private ownership worked against communism. Then the association of the Communist party (KKE) with its Slavic counterparts—especially in Bulgaria—added another barrier to popular acceptance. Finally, the party's early advocacy of Macedonian independence gave it an unpatriotic, treasonous coloring because this policy meant the detachment of territories won in the Balkan wars after heavy sacrifices. For many years, the KKE remained faction-ridden, an ineffectual organization with few adherents and a constant turnover of leaders. For Greek radicals during this period, the ouster of the monarchy was a much more meaningful target.

Venizelos stayed as prime minister for only twenty days. Faced with the pressures of the diehard republicans, he resigned. Although he still believed at that time that vasilevomeni dimokratia was the system best suited for Greece, he had no desire to oppose the republic. But he could easily foresee that any attempt to oust the monarchy by an overt or concealed coup would merely perpetuate the old feuds and rob the republic of national legitimacy and acceptance. History was to prove how right he was. But, in spite of his prestige, he was powerless to stem the tide. On March 7 he told a meeting of liberal deputies:

I came to Greece to offer my services in an effort to reconcile the two opposing camps and bring tranquility to the country. My efforts have failed because of the prevailing extremism. My political opponents resent my presence and hurl the most monstrous charges at me, while my friends and especially the advocates of the republic tell me that I should leave Greece. Discouraged by this chaotic situation I have come to the conclusion that I have no other choice but to depart as soon as possible.

A few days later Venizelos left the country. Now, nothing could stop the ouster of the monarchy. After the royalist revolt of the previous fall, officers whose loyalty to the revolution was in doubt were dismissed. This was the fourth time in less than a decade that the officer corps was purged for political reasons—the first instance of this was in 1916, when Venizelos broke with Constantine; the second came in 1917, when Venizelos returned to power; the third was in 1920, when Constantine was restored to the throne. An officer's career no longer reflected his competence; instead, it was a reflection of his partisan ties and his good luck in being either obscure or on the winning side. In 1923 the majority of the officers, and especially those holding key command posts, were on the side of the republic. With such backing, the radicals decided to move. Alexandros Papanastasiou, a scholarly Venizelist with mildly socialistic leanings, emerged as the new prime minister and the principal advocate of swift action. He would have preferred, of course, that at least some royalists accepted the republic and to this end he made a last effort to strike a bargain with Metaxas—still a fugitive abroad since the revolt—and with others in the opposite camp. The effort foundered on the rocks of mutual suspicions and fixed notions.

On March 25, 1924, the Papanastasiou government placed before the National Assembly a resolution "on the ouster of the Dynasty and the proclamation of a Republic." Since the royalists had boycotted the election, the assembly was almost entirely made up of Venizelists. Yet many deputies, knowing of Venizelos' reservations about arbitrary action, refused to support the resolution. Still, it passed, and a referendum on April 13 ratified the change. Of 1,084,065 votes cast, 758,472 (69.95 percent) voted for the republic. Nearly 200,000 of the yes votes came from the newly enfranchised refugees.

The advent of the republic meant above all that those who had made a common cause with the monarchy during the years of the schism were now virtual pariahs on the political stage. Still, the republicans, with their aim now achieved, continued their efforts to win over prominent royalists and broaden the republic's popular base. In a gesture of conciliation, the government granted amnesty to those involved in the revolt of the previous fall. Metaxas returned to Greece and to the surprise of many of his friends he made a statement recognizing the legitimacy of the republic. With this, Panagis Tsaldaris, a close friend of Gounaris, emerged as the leader of the uncompromising royalists. He restored Gounaris' Populist party, and refused to accept the validity of the change. The divisions within the nation remained as deep as ever.

chapter 4
From Republic
to Dictatorship

A season for coups

The president of the assembly had greeted the proclamation of the republic "as the dawning of a bright future for our country and our nation." The prediction could not have proved more inaccurate. The country was to experience many more years of political turbulence.

As the republic was setting out on its course through history, life in Greece, especially in the Athens-Piraeus region, was rapidly changing. Almost 400,000 refugees gravitated to the area around the capital, particularly in Piraeus. Makeshift housing was hastily put together, while special legislative measures were taken for the settlement of refugees on vacant lands around Athens. The water shortage, which had always been a problem in Athens, reached crisis proportions, with noisy housewives battling around the public water fountains. The American ambassador once complained to the prime minister that he could not "have tea and take a bath on the same day." Late in 1924, the Mikhalakopoulos government, which was in office at the time, contracted with an American company for the construction of the Marathon reservoir. Five years later, Athenian homes received tap water for the first time. City transportation became—and was to remain for many years—a serious problem since many of the refugee settlements around the city were too far from the few tramway terminals. But the most pressing necessity was to find employment for the thousands of refugees who milled around idly in the streets of Athens.

The agitation of the Communist party for "an end to the capitalist system to solve the country's economic problems" had surprisingly little effect on the destitute refugees or the poorly paid workers. Marxist ideology seemed to most of them to be outlandish and irrelevant. The ousting of the monarchy had given a large measure of emotional gratification to those who were seeking scapegoats for the Asia Minor disaster. The radical politicians and their supporters in the army, who had forced through the National Assembly the resolution for the republic, had no interest in Marxism. In fact, they knew little and cared less about the Communist ideology. Greece was well-insulated from the effects of Communist agitation at that time by a number of important factors: the association of the early Greek Communists with their Bulgarian counterparts; the prevailing notion that communism was an instrument of Slavic imperialism; and the support of the Greek Communists for the separation of Macedonia to form, with the Slavic-held parts of this geographic region, an independent state. The national elite—politicians, military, clergy, businessmen, educators, journalists from both camps—almost without exception took such a strong stand against communism that the party could not gain mass support until many years later.

Solutions to the country's pressing economic problems were sought not through socialism but through private enterprise. In the midst of all the partisan quarrels, coups, military rebellions, at times tragicomic incidents, that made headlines during the first four years of the republic, the governments that came and went followed a surprisingly consistent economic policy. It was designed primarily to help local businessmen set up industrial enterprises to provide employment and to meet at least some of the consumer needs. To help those fledgling industries, the various governments erected protective barriers against foreign competition. Wages—in a labor market glutted with unemployed refugees—were low, and the government made no effort to change this because the primary necessity at the time was to have people employed even though their pay might be a pittance. Poor quality and high production costs priced the few industrial products out of foreign markets while the import of badly-needed consumer goods caused ever-increasing deficits in the balance of trade. The upshot of these economic policies was a strange mixture of capitalism with welfare statism. Low productivity, a cumbersome bureaucracy, and the frequent turnover of governments resulted in a low standard of living, with only few individuals—mostly in industry and wholesale commerce— amassing large fortunes by paying their debts in inflated drachmas.

That the refugees were overwhelmingly Venizelist added a political motive to the overriding necessity of providing relief to those uprooted human beings. Much of the burden was inevitably borne by the native, established bourgeoisie, who paid most of the taxes and whose way of life was being eroded by the new realities. At the same time a new bourgeoisie was emerging, and it was made up mostly of the expanding host of salaried employees in the state bureaucracy, in industry, and in commerce.

As though to strike back against the demons of humiliation, disunity, pettiness, and confusion, the poets and writers of those years turned with almost desperate intensity to the classical glories. Angelos Sikelianos, an idol of Greek youth and a legend in his own lifetime, sought in the late twenties to revive the Delphic Ideal as a source of inspiration, hope, and pride. Kostis Palamas, another poet whose name was revered by every Greek, spoke of the cruel present but then he gave the inspiring prophecy that when Greece reaches the lowest depths she will regain her "broad, early wings" and fly high again. George Seferis the poet-diplomat, decried the nightmarish present, the men "who kill each other and become smaller and smaller, drifting like specks of dust in the wind," but he, too, sought in the ancient past the "speaking fountain" that would show the way to a new beginning. This notion of rebirth is a constant theme in Greek literature and culture and may explain why the national symbol is the mythical phoenix reemerging from its own ashes, and why Easter is the greatest religious holiday of the year.

In a lighter vein, the theatrical revue, with its irreverent and often

Only six worn columns remain of the great Temple of Apollo, seat of the Delphic oracle.

Photographs on pp. 139–43 taken by David O. Johnson in April 1973. Converted from color to black and white.

(*left*) Ruins of the Tholos of the sanctuary of Athena Pronaia at Delphi.

(*above*) The clear Greek sunlight highlights the beauty of ancient ruins atop the Acropolis in Athens.

Two of the six caryatids (female figures) that support the roof of the Maiden Porch of the Erechtheum on the Acropolis.

(*top*) A distant view of the Maiden Porch and a portion of the temple to the mythical King Erechtheus on the Acropolis.

(*left*) A close-up of the gigantic pillars and slabs of Pentelic marble on the Acropolis attests to the incredible accuracy and genius of ancient Greek masterminds.

(*below*) The archaic temple of Apollo, built around 550 B.C., stands above the excavated ruins of the agora of ancient Corinth.

Corinthian columns of a Roman temple, known as temple E, in ancient Corinth.

Modern-day tourists marvel at the perfect acoustics in the well-preserved theater at Epidaurus where 14,000 spectators could hear every word of the Greek dramas performed in the fourth century B.C.

caustic political satire, became in the twenties and thirties the most popular form of public entertainment. The more sophisticated were attracted by the National Theater and by the dramatic companies presenting serious contemporary works as well as classical plays. Actors like Aimilios Veakis, and actresses like Marika Kotopouli were greatly admired. No less known were the great comedians Vassilis Argyropoulos, Vassilis Logothetidis, and others who relieved, with their talent, the pressing anxieties and disappointments of the interwar years. Most of this cultural activity was centered in Athens. The provincial towns were forgotten most of the time, remembered only by second-rate theatrical groups which, nevertheless, attracted large crowds seeking a respite from a monotonous and barren life.

The dramatic shock of the Asia Minor disaster found powerful expression in the novels of Elias Venezis and Stratis Myrivilis, both of whom wrote with poignancy about the lost world in Asia Minor. Other writers, like Pandelis Prevelakis, extolled the simple village life which was solid, surefooted, and anchored securely in tradition. This celebration of the simple life was a reaction to the frustrations, the pettiness, the confusion, and above all the baseness of city life. By contrast, men like Grigorios Xenopoulos and Georgios Theotokas sought to understand and explain the realities of city life in the wake of war and disaster. Nikos Kazantzakis, another well-known writer, went beyond the confines of the national context and sought to explore universal themes concerned with man's destiny, the mysteries of life and death, and the meaning of life itself. But even Kazantzakis could not escape the impact of the national environment. As it often happens in the wake of great national tragedies, the interwar years produced a rich harvest of literary works in the midst of political mediocrity, economic uncertainty, and national disunity.

Popular discontent was reflected in the instability that marred the republic's early days. In less than fifteen months, the country went through three major cabinet crises, two unsuccessful minicoups, several interventions of ambitious officers into the political process, a series of strikes and demonstrations by disgruntled workers, the ouster of Patriarch Constantine from Constantinople, and the arrest of hundreds of Greeks in Constantinople by the Turkish authorities. The Venizelist majority in the National Assembly broke up into several rival factions, each of which clustered around one of the personalities that Venizelos had elevated to prominence during his more prosperous days. At the same time, the National Assembly continued to struggle through the final stages of shaping the constitution.

Exploiting popular dissatisfaction with the political leadership, Gen. Theodoros Pangalos, who had left the army for a full-time career in politics, decided to use his army connections and take over the government. His action was triggered by another cabinet crisis and the hasty enactment of an electoral law that introduced into modern Greek history the system of proportional representation. On June 25, 1925, he gave the signal to his fellow-conspirators in the army, who immediately placed Athens and Salonika under their control. President Pavlos Kountouriotis tried to pacify Pangalos by asking him to participate in a new government, which was to be again placed under veteran republican Papanastasiou. Throughout the day, the various political leaders dashed from one meeting to another, bargaining, cajoling, conspiring against each other. The public had little to do with all these frantic political maneuvers. Life continued its regular rhythm throughout the day. Finally, when it became clear that the army was steadfastly behind Pangalos, the president gave him the mandate to form a new government. Five days later, Pangalos appeared before the National Assembly as though nothing irregular had happened and received a vote of confidence—185 to 14, with 9 blank ballots; 189 deputies stayed away from the voting in protest.

Pangalos immediately moved to consolidate his position. "For us," he said, striking a statesmanlike pose, "there are no longer Venizelists and royalists. Venizelos is politically dead, and Constantine is physically dead." Up to a point he was right; the old dispute was surely no longer valid. New problems that had arisen in the wake of defeat and revolution cried out for decisive action by a strong government resting on genuine popular support. But Pangalos had neither the temperament nor the intellectual gifts needed to play such a historic role. Yet, the pettiness of the other politicians and the public craving for a strong, talented leader generated an undercurrent of support for Pangalos. Even the British seemed pleased by the emergence of his regime.

Finding an empty treasury, Pangalos resorted to the obligatory sale of government bonds and a drastic devaluation of the drachma. With the money thus raised he took steps to supply the army with a hundred thousand new rifles and the navy with six submarines. To stamp out corruption, he displayed his intolerance of such illegal activities by hanging publicly two officers who had been accused of embezzling public funds. In the next few months, he put down two attempted minicoups and came to blows with Bulgaria over a border incident. Facing the growing opposition of most Venizelist leaders— his former comrades, who were alienated by his arbitrariness—he turned to the royalists for support and accepted some of them into his cabinet. In September, he pressed President Kountouriotis to sign a decree dissolving the assembly. Most people heard with a sigh of relief the end of the one-sided legislature. But Pangalos did not set a date for another election; instead, he began acting more openly as a dictator. Moreover, he ignored the constitutional draft that had been prepared by the assembly.

The Venizelist leaders turned to Nikolaos Plastiras, who had retired from public life and was spending his time in his native village. He came secretly to Athens to prepare for another coup to unseat Pangalos. Before he had time to put his plans into effect, he was arrested late one evening in October while trying to escape over the rooftops of the houses adjoining his hideout. The satirical magazines, which enjoyed high popularity in Greece in those troubled days by lampooning with relish all political leaders, immediately dubbed Plastiras "the black cat." This was a reference to his wartime nickname, "the black horseman." Plastiras was put on a boat and sent into exile abroad.

At this point, Pangalos realized that he had either to reach an agreement with the Venizelists or move boldly to stop all political activity and openly set up a dictatorial regime. For three days in December he talked with political leaders about a timetable for the full implementation of the new constitution. There were so many different points of view that in the end the talks collapsed in total confusion. Within a few weeks, Pangalos took over "all remaining constitutional and legislative powers," arrested and sent to exile most of the Venizelist leaders, and successfully snuffed out another planned coup. When President Kountouriotis decided to resign in protest against Pangalos' actions, the dictator decided to become president; in fact, he decided to change the entire system of government to that of a presidential republic, based on the American model. His reply to one of the constitutional experts he called for assistance is at once a classic display of cynical disregard for constitutional sanctity and a shrewd assessment of the public mood. "My dear Thrasyvoulos, I'll tell you with what right I can [change the constitution] . . . On the first day, the people will be surprised. The following day, they will say: 'Let's see; maybe, it is all right . . .' Five or six days later, they'll have forgotten all about it." Pangalos had correctly anticipated the public reaction. Even the political leaders raised no serious objections at first and they even decided to run their own candidate—Professor Constantine Demer-tzis—opposite Pangalos. Only when Pangalos changed the electoral law to assure his own victory did they take Demertzis out of the race and call on the people to boycott the election. Without opposition, Pangalos won by a landslide. Somewhat surprising was the very large number of voters who ignored the call for boycott and voted for Pangalos.

He now appeared at the pinnacle of his power. Apparently he thought that this time he could try to realize his ambition to recapture Eastern Thrace—an ambition frustrated two years before by the signing of the Treaty of Lausanne. The British dispute with Turkey over the oil fields of Mosul offered, in his eyes, a new opportunity for invading Eastern Thrace. In March 1926 he approached Mussolini and proposed some form of joint action against Turkey. When Mussolini showed no enthusiasm for the idea, Pangalos turned to the Yugoslavs and offered them several impor-tant concessions, including a free zone in the harbor of Salonika. Before he had time to put these plans into effect, he was overthrown. Ironically, the blow came from the very same Republican Battalions that had helped him stay in power for thirteen months. These units of professional soldiers—selected for their staunch antiroyalist convictions—turned against Pangalos because he had taken steps to reduce their privileges and their pay in his efforts to placate the royalists and broaden his popular base. So, while he was vacationing on the island of Spetsai, Gen. Georgios Kondylis, with the help of the Republican Battalions, seized the major government buildings and installations in Athens on August 22, 1926, and declared that the rule of Pangalos was over. The deposed dictator made an attempt to escape by sea, but his boat was intercepted and he was captured.

Kondylis assumed the post of prime minister and called Koun-touriotis back to the presidency. Two weeks later he used regular troops to break up the Republican Battalions. Obviously, he had no intention of allowing those troublesome units to do to him what they had done to Pangalos. But Kondylis did not have enough personal support in the army to set up a dictatorship. Pressed by the political leaders, he agreed to hold elections and stay out of the race to ensure impartiality. In November 1926 he conducted the first parliamentary election using the proportional system. Out of a total of 958,392 valid ballots, the Union of Liberals, a new party coalition formed by Georgios Kafandaris and Andreas Mikhalakopoulos, received 303,000 and 102 seats; the Republican Union under Papanastasiou 62,000 and 17 seats; the Populist party under Tsaldaris 194,240 and 60 seats; the party of Free Thinkers, established by Metaxas, 151,042 and 51 seats; and the Popular Front (Communists) 41,982 and 10 seats. Another 46 seats went to various small parties and independents. In spite of some new party titles, the political forces in the Vouli could still be identified along the lines of the old Venizelist/anti-Venizelist dichotomy. Viewed in this light, the two major camps had come out almost equal in strength (119 to 111). Neither side had a clear majority in the 286-seat Vouli. After twenty days of talks, both sides agreed to form a broad coalition cabinet under the premiership of Alexandros Zaimis, the aging "Prime Minister of the difficult moments." This coalition of Venizelists and anti-Venizelists lasted until June 1928, even though Tsaldaris pulled out in August 1927 and Papanastasiou left in February 1928. Metaxas stayed in the coalition until the end in an effort to bridge the gap between the two camps. By so doing he succeeded only in eroding his political base, as most royalists turned to Tsaldaris, whose intransigence was more in keeping with their feelings.

In June 1927 the text of the republic's constitution was at last published in the Official Gazette, but the country's new charter began its life under a cloud. Its legitimacy was seriously undermined by the royalist ministers in the coalition government, who refused to affix their signatures and thus give their formal sanction to the republic. Nonetheless, Greece now formally had a republican constitution. This meant, above all, that the office of the head of state was occupied by an elected president instead of a hereditary monarch. Still, the authority of the president and his relationship to the cabinet or the legislature was not much different from that which the king once had. The president's term of office was set at five years, but he could be reelected for two additional terms. The constitution now expressly required that a cabinet should enjoy majority support in the Vouli. The term of the Vouli remained four years, but now a second chamber was added, a *Gerousia* (Senate). Senators were to be elected for nine years, but one-third of the Gerousia was to be renewed every three years. In general, the constitution followed the Western principles of democratic government.

The coalition cabinet came to an end in June 1928, when Venizelos decided to reenter the political arena. He had returned from abroad in April 1927 and had lived as a private citizen at his home in Crete. Responding to the persistent prodding of many influential Venizelists, he called on the government to resign. His influence was such that within days he was asked by President Kountouriotis to form a new government and hold a parliamentary election. The end of the coalition was hardly lamented by anyone. Whatever the talents or the intentions of the participating leaders, the country's problems defied easy solutions. The rehabilitation and settlement of the refugees was a costly enterprise that was being paid mostly by Greek taxpayers. Inevitably, the blame for these economic burdens fell on the government. Moreover, the people, after so many years of war, revolution, coups, and military disasters, were searching for new life styles, for more enjoyment, for a higher standard of living. The old rivalries, though by no means extinct, came to seem less and less relevant to the new realities. With the Great Idea a discarded dream, the nation subconsciously searched for a new lodestar, a new national myth. But the politicians dominating the stage lacked the breath of vision that was needed to chart a new course for the uncertain and groping nation. Only one man had the qualities of leadership and the charismatic personality that this moment in history required: Eleutherios Venizelos. Sixteen years before he had galvanized the nation and had led the campaign to make the Great Idea a reality. Now, with the old vision gone, he was called upon to rekindle the nation's confidence in itself and to give new direction and new meaning to the nation's life. A tall order even for a personality of his stature.

Venizelos comes back to power

Before holding an election, Venizelos pressed Kountouriotis to sign a decree reestablishing the plurality system. With this, all Venizelist leaders—with the exception of Kafandaris—rushed to seek political shelter under Venizelos' mantle. The Liberal party, with 61 percent of the total vote, won 223 out of a total of 250 seats.

Some 32 percent of the voters held on to their anti-Venizelist loyalties. The Communist party, which in the previous legislature held 10 seats, disappeared from the stage as only 14,000 faithful cast their ballots for the Popular Front candidates.

In 1928 Venizelos was no longer the liberal revolutionary, the fiercely nationalist idealist of his younger days. The change had come with dramatic finality as the myth of the Great Idea was buried under the wreckage of the Asia Minor disaster. Under the banner of reconciliation and moderation, he had returned in 1924, hoping to lead the country through the difficult days ahead. But at that time the wounds were still gaping, the memories too vivid, the hatreds too overpowering, and he had been forced to leave. For another four years the country had gone through the spasms of readjustment—the ouster of the monarchy, the military coups, the cabinet crises, the Pangalos dictatorship—and then through the efforts to shelve outdated rivalries and work together in a broad coalition government. Whatever the accomplishments of those years—and, considering the staggering problems, much was done—public dissatisfaction with the nation's leadership was growing. Venizelos was received by the nation as a savior in 1928. Few realized, of course, that his ideas had changed radically and that he was no longer the man they remembered from earlier, bygone days. The label of the liberal was still there, but the man who carried it had by now become a true conservative: Venizelos was determined to keep peace with the country's neighbors, to end deficit spending, to preserve internal order, and to stimulate economic development through careful management of the nation's finances.

Tempering his old attachment to Britain, Venizelos forged in 1928 new ties of cooperation with Mussolini's Italy, which was a rising force in the Mediterranean. In 1930 he boldly discarded centuries of Greek-Turkish rivalry and animosity, and laid the foundations of friendship between the two countries. Greece, he declared, had no territorial aspirations that might cause problems with her neighbors. On the domestic front, he reversed the policies of deficit financing for refugee rehabilitation, cut down on military appropriations, raised taxes, and pressed hard on tax-dodgers. He even reduced the salaries of civil servants to save money for productive projects. Convinced that labor unrest undermined his efforts to stabilize the economy, he took a firm stand against strikes and especially against disturbances instigated by the Communists.

True, communism remained a marginal nuisance in Greece, shunned by most people, above all because of the party's commitment to the separation of Greek Macedonia. Nevertheless, in December 1928 Venizelos initiated special legislation that made agitation against the socioeconomic system a punishable, *sui generis* crime. Venizelos also made a concerted effort to push forward the country's economic development. With foreign assistance in the form of reparations and the proceeds of foreign loans already contracted under the coalition government, he financed land reclamation, irrigation, and flood-control projects, the improvement of roads and harbor facilities, and the construction of schools.

For the first two years, Venizelos moved boldly, heartened by wide public support. In the spring of 1929, in the first election for the Gerousia, the royalist candidates received only 26.6 percent of the votes cast. Venizelos was indeed all-powerful. But clouds were already gathering above the horizon.

The first signs of opposition came from Venizelist leaders, who began to cast irreverent aspersions against some of the policies of their idol. More than a few of his economic policies in particular had been rather painful to the very groups that had been the backbone of his popularity. The reality of his conservatism was now coming into conflict with the liberalism of his closest associates. The opening salvos were fired shortly after the election of Zaimis as president. Kountouriotis had resigned, professing old age, though it is most likely that he left because he was angered by Venizelos' refusal to increase expenditures for the navy. Venizelos, to prevent the selection of another strong personality who might try to curb his power, opted for Zaimis, who by now was an old, weak, indifferent man with no emotional ties to the system he was supposed to symbolize and defend.

Kondylis was the first to charge that "the government's errors open the door to political anarchy." A few weeks later, Kafandaris and Papanastasiou published articles in which they accused Venizelos of gathering too much power in his hands. Charges of scandals—many without foundation—shocked public opinion, especially since the accusing finger belonged to Venizelist leaders. The press, in a veritable orgy of yellow journalism bandied around all kinds of charges about the mishandling of public funds. Tsaldaris, secretly enjoying the spectacle, kept a polite silence. A by-election on the island of Lesvos in July 1931 showed that the Liberal party was losing ground. A few months earlier, the party's candidate for mayor in Salonika had received only 37 percent of the vote compared to the 68 percent that was given the party candidates in the August 1928 parliamentary election.

Venizelos placed a large part of the blame on the press and tried to curb, through legislation, the abuse of freedom. The bill was eventually enacted but not before it pitted Venizelos against most of his former comrades. Still, he might have survived these internal assaults; his final undoing came from events that were entirely beyond his control.

The international waves of turbulence, set in motion by the economic collapse in the United States, reached Greece around the end of 1931. Already some of the sources of foreign exchange that Greece so desperately needed to offset the endemic deficit in her balance of trade were drying up. No more flow of dollars and pounds from the remittances of emigrants to the United States, from shipping, from foreign loans or reparations. There were now few buyers abroad for tobacco or raisins. Still, the economy continued to move on, sluggishly perhaps, but without a catastrophic breakdown. The turning point came in September 1931, when Britain broke away from the gold standard. In January, Venizelos travelled to Rome, Paris, and London in search of a loan to shore up the country's dwindling exchange reserves. Italy had little to spare and France was beset with problems of her own, not the least of which was Hitler's star rising across the Rhine. In London, Venizelos expected a friendlier reception since only a few months earlier he had condemned an uprising of the Cypriots against their colonial rulers. Vain hope. He returned to Athens empty-handed. In April the council of the League of Nations took up the question of financial aid to some European countries, including Greece. But the major powers were too worried about other pressing problems—the Japanese invasion in Manchuria, Hitler's increasing popularity in Germany, falling prices, unemployment, Communist agitation—and in the end Greece received no succor. Before the end of April, with gold reserves down to the equivalent of a little over $2 million, Greece abandoned the gold standard and declared a unilateral moratorium on the payment of her foreign debts.

Venizelos was at his best when he enjoyed the warm embrace of success and the adulation of faithful worshipers. Failure had always had a shattering effect on his temperament. In the summer of 1932, he was confronted with failure on the economic front, desertions from his supporters, and attacks from the leaders that he himself had once propelled to the center of the political stage. He feared that in an election he would lose, and he did not want to end his political career in the midst of failure. In 1920 he had been defeated at the height of his political career by what he called an ungrateful electorate. Now, defeat would be a pitiful epitaph; he was too old to expect another grand opportunity for a final vindication. Yet, the calendar moved relentlessly toward the day the current term of the Vouli would come to an end and he would have to face the electorate. In a desperate effort to revive past loyalties, he rekindled the old hatreds and the fears against a return of the monarchy. He authorized General Othoneos to form a paramilitary organization— a new Military League—ostensibly to defend the republic but in reality to prevent the rise of Tsaldaris and his royalists to power. Speaking on September 4, 1932, in his native city of Khania, Venizelos said: "The civil conflict that has lasted for seventeen years can only be terminated in two ways; either the two camps agree to come to terms and restore peace, or one camp will overpower the other until it is finally defeated and accepts unconditional surrender." Neither this transparent reference to old passions nor the threat of military intervention seemed enough, however, to quell the discontent and opposition.

Fearful that the plurality system would give the royalists a majority in the Vouli, Venizelos went back to the system of proportional representation. In the elections of September 25 the two major parties, the Liberal and the Populist, came out with almost equal strength: 391,521 Liberal votes to 395,974 Populist votes. Another 389,000 votes were scattered among seven other parties, including 58,000 for the Communist candidates. This fragmentation of forces was reflected in the Vouli. No political party had sufficient strength to form a viable government. After long and involved discussions, President Zaimis asked Tsaldaris to form a cabinet on the condition that he would formally acknowledge the legitimacy of the republic. He did so in a letter to the president, who immediately and with considerable fanfare made the declaration public.

Tsaldaris formed a cabinet with the participation of Kondylis, who was now openly breaking away from the Venizelist camp, and Metaxas. In addition, he had the support of Kafandaris and

Papanastasiou, who led their own separate parties. General Othoneos, speaking on behalf of the Military League, declared that
Tsaldaris' recognition of the republic had removed the reasons for
the existence of the paramilitary organization, at least for the time
being.

The Tsaldaris cabinet, resting on a narrow and unreliable majority, survived for a little over two months. When the Vouli reopened
after the Christmas holidays, Venizelos, as the leader of the
opposition, initiated a vote of nonconfidence against the government and forced its resignation. He then formed a cabinet with the
help of other key Venizelists, but, knowing that he could not rely on
his unpredictable associates, he pressed Zaimis to dissolve the Vouli
and call another election. Then, encouraged by the ambivalent
results of the September election, he brought back the plurality
system and formed a grand electoral coalition with the other
Venizelist leaders. The lines were now clearly drawn. The election
was set for March 5.

The royalist camp regains control

On election night, reports showed that the Venizelist
coalition was losing the fight. Shortly after midnight, Plastiras
decided to seize power, annul the election results, and set up a
dictatorship. Although the initial response of many commanders in
the army was favorable, the coup collapsed by the end of the
following day amidst much confusion. The irrepressible revolutionary gave up in disgust and walked—literally—home. With Venizelos
still in the post of prime minister, a coup by Plastiras was the
epitome of absurdity—unless it would have had the approval and
support of his idol. Since Venizelos had no intention of becoming a
dictator and therefore refused to give his support, the coup lost any
meaning and simply faded away.

With the collapse of the coup, Zaimis called Tsaldaris, the leader
of the victorious coalition, to form a government. The country was
now entering a new period. The royalists had returned to power for
the first time since the advent of the republic. They had already
declared their loyalty and their intention to avoid provocative
changes. Deposed King George, living a quiet, lonely life in London,
was almost forgotten. He had never commanded the adulation and

the passion his father had once inspired. A government by Tsaldaris promised to solidify the republic's legitimacy and assure national acceptance of the government, thus relegating to the attic of history the dichotomy in the political life of Greece. But to many fanatical Venizelists, the rise of Tsaldaris to power was nothing less than the takeover of the republic by its enemies. As far as they were concerned, the royalists could not rest easy as long as the Venizelists dominated the armed forces. Of course, any personnel changes in the officer corps would inevitably affect the seniority and promotion prospects of those who had benefited in the past by the forced retirement of undesirable royalists. Those affected were bound to resist. The more intransigent royalists continued to see Venizelos as an evil spirit waiting for the appropriate moment in which to strike again. With the members of various political factions in such a state of mind, anything was possible. Something finally happened shortly before midnight on June 6, 1933.

Venizelos and his wife Elena were returning to Athens from a dinner engagement in the fashionable suburb of Kifisia. Their car, followed by another vehicle carrying their bodyguards, was halfway to Athens when suddenly a third car appeared through the darkness and moved between Venizelos and his bodyguards. The occupants of this third car began shooting in both directions, immobilizing the automobile carrying the bodyguards. The driver of the Venizelos car, though wounded, opened up speed to escape the assassins. After a gangster-like chase, the pursuers abandoned their prey and disappeared into the night. Venizelos escaped unharmed, but his wife was wounded, although not seriously.

Reports of the assassination attempt fell like a live grenade on the political stage. Tsaldaris immediately issued a statement damning "the dastardly act" and, wisely, gave a free hand to the investigators. Within hours enough evidence was found to warrant the arrest of the chief of state security. The car used by the assassins was traced to his brother, who was also identified as one of the participants. The investigation revealed that two other police officers were in the car together with a notorious brigand named Kostas Karathanasis.

For the rest of the year, the two camps spent much of their energy on mutual recriminations; the Venizelists charging the government with complicity in the assassination attempt, the royalists zeroing in on the Plastiras coup. Behind these internal divisions one could feel the subtle influence of what was happening in Europe at the time.

The French, alarmed by Hitler's growing audacity, worked to construct regional alliances with an obvious anti-German thrust. Venizelos, with his policy of maintaining neutrality and good relations with all sides, seemed out of step with his erstwhile friends. By contrast, Kondylis—an old friend of the French—and the Populist leadership were now in favor of closer cooperation with the other Balkan states against possible expansionist ventures by their neighbors. The Balkan Pact was signed in February 1934 by Greece, Yugoslavia, Rumania, and Turkey. Protracted diplomatic efforts to bring Bulgaria into the group failed. The pact had reversed in effect Venizelos' policy of noninvolvement. His objections may not have prevented its signing, but they did force the Tsaldaris government to stress that the treaty in no way be able to bring Greece into conflict with Italy. In an ironic reversal of roles, Venizelos was now the advocate of neutrality while the royalists came out in favor of the French plans for cooperation. In a way, Venizelos was following his old axiom that Greece's foreign policy should be in line with that of the powers controlling the Mediterranean. In his view, Mussolini's Italy was now the power to watch. That Britain also was rather lukewarm toward the Balkan Pact strengthened his opposition.

All these conflicting foreign interests no doubt had their effect on Greek politics, but to say that the flare-up of passions was the work of foreign agents would be an exaggeration. There was enough domestic hatred, suspicion, and willfulness on both sides of the political fence to keep the fires of dissension going. The accused assassins were repeatedly brought to court but their trial was postponed time and again on one pretext or another. In contrast, many officers involved in the Plastiras coup were tried and convicted while others were expelled from the armed forces. In a series of newspaper articles, Venizelos and Metaxas engaged in a verbal duel over the issues that divided the nation during the First World War, reviving the old disputes and deepening the rift between the two camps. Through it all, the country's economy continued to suffer from a combination of stagnation, unemployment, and rising prices. By the end of 1934 the Populist government was rapidly sliding downhill. So was the republic and the parliamentary system. The reelection of Zaimis, who was by that time too old to matter, symbolized the republic's incurable malaise. The spectacle of deputies exchanging heavy insults and even coming to blows on the floor of the legislature, the petty wrangling of the political leaders,

(above) Tsaldaris and Za-
imis, 1934, after the recognition of the Republic by
Royalists. Courtesy, VIMA,
Athens

(left) Eleutherios Venize-
los and Madame Venizelos.
United Press International
Photo

and the incessant recriminations, filled many citizens with a feeling
of contempt for the system and for the nation's leaders. Still, the
republic might have survived if it were not for a fateful decision by
Venizelos, ironically one of the republic's most prominent champions.

The revolt of March 1, 1935

In a long and incredibly detailed letter to a rather obscure
naval officer, Venizelos left future historians an unusually candid
report of his motives and involvement in the preparation of the
military revolt that broke out during the evening hours of March 1,
1935. In his letter, Venizelos revealed that "more than a year ago
. . . I encouraged the formation of democratic institutions . . . and
promoted the organization of true republican officers in the armed
forces who alone could prevent effectively the restoration of the
monarchy or an attempt by Kondylis and Metaxas to impose a
dictatorship." He went on to say that in the previous August he had
disallowed a military coup "not only because it was at variance with
the plan I had drawn, but also because its haphazard preparation
doomed it to failure." He had decided to give the green light "about
three months ago" because he was alarmed by demonstrations in
favor of the monarchy and the possibility that in the forthcoming
election for the Gerousia, the royalists might gain a majority and
then move to replace Zaimis with Prince Nikolaos as a prelude to
the restoration of the monarchy. "I have no doubt now that if we
wish to avoid enslavement, we must rise before the election for the
Gerousia. I told the revolutionary committee that I not only have no
objection, but that I advise that we move as soon as possible."
     In a letter to General Othoneos, written ten days later, Venizelos
repeated the same views with one important addition:

The unholy alteration of the seniority list in the army threatens to
destroy irrevocably its soul. . . . The majority of the Supreme
Military Council is now controlled by the government. Therefore,
there is no longer any safeguard against the removal of more
republican officers. . . . Under these circumstances, the republican
camp will commit a crime by waiting passively for the monarchists to
choose the moment of attack. By then, it will be too late. For these

reasons, I believe that the republican camp must launch a defensive attack that will save Greater Greece from its oncoming destruction.

Venizelos also had personal reasons for wanting to see the overthrow of the royalist government. To his closest associates he repeatedly expressed his personal anguish: "I cannot stand to be hunted like an animal in the jungle," an obvious reference to the June 6 assassination attempt and his constant fear that the real assassins were just waiting for another chance to cut him down. We know today that this despicable act so unnerved Venizelos that many of the fateful actions that he took following the attempted assassination can be traced to the unsettling emotional aftermath of the experience.

The revolt, which started on March 1 with a take-over of several naval units and the Salamis naval base, will remain in history as a classic illustration of bungling and confusion. The officers who seized the ships, instead of sailing for Salonika as the plan provided, sailed for Crete, where Venizelos was staying at the time. Then, they moved from one island to another carrying the message of rebellion. By the time they finished their rounds, it was too late to go to Salonika. The army units stationed there kept control of the city and arrested many would-be revolutionaries. More important, the government kept complete control in Athens. Kondylis, as minister of military affairs in the Tsaldaris cabinet, became the chief decision-maker. He was promoted to lieutenant general, whereupon he immediately took charge with his customary brusque determination. After brief clashes along the Struma river in eastern Macedonia, the rebellion fizzled out. It had lasted ten days. Poor preparation, disorganization, unwillingness on the part of the ordinary soldiers to fight, conflicting objectives among the rebels—some being more interested in a Fascist type of government than in the preservation of the republic—and even the belief by top republicans, including Papanastasiou, the so-called father of the republic, that no real threat against the constitution existed, compounded the indecision and ineptness of the protagonists and thus hastened the revolt's ignominious demise. The axiom that whoever holds Athens has the odds in his favor was again borne out.

Shortly before dawn on March 12, Venizelos, convinced that he had lost his final gamble, boarded the cruiser *Averoff*, which still was under rebel control, and sailed with his wife and a few close associates for the Dodecanese, then under Italian sovereignty. The group eventually reached Naples. As he was coming ashore he admitted ruefully to his wife, "The great masters make great mistakes . . ." He had indeed made an egregious error. Although he was already seventy years old, he was yet dreaming of changing the constitution to install a presidential system with himself as a virtual dictator. Quite openly he was telling his friends that with him in power only individuals devoted to his new regime would be allowed to serve in the armed forces and the police. The defense of the republic was a smokescreen.

Prior to the March revolt, few were seriously favoring the restoration of the monarchy. Metaxas was shrewd enough to realize that if King George were restored to the throne, a reconciliation with the Venizelists would have to be achieved in order to strengthen his own position. Tsaldaris had found in his two years as prime minister that he could govern just as well under a president. In fact, compared to the senile Zaimis, King George was bound to be a more difficult head of state. Kondylis, with his close ties to the French, would have been the last man to raise the flag of the monarchy in spite of his growing disillusionment with the republic. The March revolt wiped out the reservations held by all these leading political figures. Metaxas was the first to come out openly in favor of restoration. With Venizelos out of the way and the entire Venizelist camp in disarray, he was no longer fearful of a reconciliation between the king and the defeated republicans. Venizelos had once prophesied that the dispute would end in the unconditional surrender of one of the two camps. His opponents were now ready to put his prediction to effect.

Metaxas could also detect a major shift in public sentiment. The middle class, which was interested primarily in economic and political stability, was now fearful of a Communist-inspired upheaval that threatened to result from the weakening of the political structure and the continuing economic stagnation. Therefore, the middle class was rapidly losing confidence in the republic. Metaxas tried to capitalize on this, and on March 29 he openly came out in favor of the vasilevomeni dimokratia. Tsaldaris could also see the changing mood of the middle class, but at first he thought that the Populist party could benefit from this change without having to raise the flag of the monarchy. The past, however, did not allow such options. Venizelos had tried to act as a man of stability, as the leader of a conservative middle class, but his radical past stayed with him until the very end, when he was driven by these contradictions to a mad, desperate venture. Tsaldaris also was burdened with his past. To his supporters as well as to his adversaries he was a royalist; now that the issue of the restoration had been raised he could no longer hold onto the fiction of his respect for the republic. To do so would have been to risk political suicide. Although he said in mid-May that "the republican system is not at issue," he reversed his position ten days later and declared that a referendum on the constitutional system would take place in the near future.

The restoration of vasilevomeni dimokratia

In the wake of the March revolt, the victors brought to trial 1,130 civilians and military officers, as well as most Venizelist political leaders. Venizelos himself was sentenced to death, but he was safely beyond reach in Paris. Most of the other political leaders were either acquitted or given relatively light sentences. Three individuals were executed—a cavalry officer named Volanis, and two retired generals, Anastasios Papoulas and Miltiades Koimisis. Interestingly enough, the generals were not executed because of their part in the revolt, which was virtually nonexistent, but because of old scores, namely, their damaging testimony at the trial of the six leaders accused of high treason in 1922. Both were former royalists; Papoulas, in fact, had been the commander in chief of the Asia Minor army until he was replaced almost at the last moment by the hapless Khatzianestis. The execution of these two old generals was no less a political murder than the execution of the six royalist leaders in 1922.

The major victim of the unsuccessful revolt, of course, was the republic. The government, dominated now by the dynamic personality of Kondylis, issued in April four constitutional acts, all of which were unquestionably in violation of the constitution. With these acts the government abolished the Gerousia, suspended both the life tenure of judges and the rules protecting civil servants from arbitrary dismissal, and ordered the purge of the state machinery of all "disloyal" employees. At the same time, the constitutional acts issued a call to the voters for the election of a new Vouli. President Zaimis was too feeble in his old age to fight against these violations of the constitution.

The Venizelist leaders pressed for a return to the proportional electoral system, hoping in this way to improve their chances at the polls, but the royalists refused to accommodate them. In protest, they decided to boycott the June 9 election, thus making the same error the royalists had committed in 1924. Other analogies to that other election are also pertinent. In 1924 Venizelos was not pressing for a republic—but he was unable to resist the pressures of the extremists. In 1935 Tsaldaris was rather reluctant to press for the restoration of the monarchy, but inevitably, he, too, would surrender in the end to the pressures of the extremists. In spite of the call by Venizelists for a boycott, 1,026,196 cast their ballots in 1924 compared to 1,141,330 in 1933. Surprisingly, the Communist candidates received nearly 100,000 votes, an unprecedented feat under the plurality electoral system. To a large extent this broadening of the KKE's popular base was due to its decision the previous April to change its policy on the Macedonian question. Freed of this burden, the party could at this time exploit the economic problems and prepare more effectively for the "approaching decisive struggles."

Now that the Vouli was dominated by the royalists, the end of the republic was only a matter of time. Those who favored the restoration of the dynasty were apparently encouraged by influential circles in Britain, even in France. The British in particular were active behind the scenes in promoting the idea of restoration and pondered the question as to who would be an effective prime minister to help the king with a strong government. The situation in Greece was viewed in the broader context of Western strategy—and under this light the republic appeared as a tin shield. At first, Kondylis was the clearly preferred choice of the British and the French. He was a man who had supported the Allied cause in the Great War and who had shown toughness combined with intelligence. The French were especially pleased with this Francophile, whom they saw as a suitable counterpart to the Anglophile King George. For the next six months, Kondylis—the erstwhile republican—would be the prime mover for the restoration of the monarchy.

On July 10, the newly elected, one-sided Vouli passed a resolution stating that "no later than November 15, 1935, a referendeum shall be held to allow the people to decide whether they wish to retain the existing republican parliamentary system or to establish the vasilevomeni dimokratia." Tsaldaris had misgivings. Like Venizelos in 1924, he realized that constitutional change should be the result of a truly free choice, otherwise the throne would come to rest on a shaky foundation. But Kondylis and the determined royalists had no intention of letting this crucial matter be decided by such a risky device as an honest vote. In fact, they wanted to do in reverse exactly what the diehard republicans had done in 1924, that is, have the assembly change the constitution arbitrarily and then call the people to a referendum to ratify the change. With almost two thousand republican officers purged from the ranks after the March revolt, the army was now dominated by the royalists. On October 10 the chiefs of the three services—General Papagos, Rear Admiral Economou, and Air Force General Reppas—acting with Kondylis' blessing, forced Tsaldaris to resign. Kondylis emerged as the new prime minister. The Italian invasion of Ethiopia a few days earlier apparently underscored in the eyes of the royalists the need for decisive action.

The new government appeared before the assembly as though nothing irregular had happened. After giving an angry report to the deputies on the events that had led to his forced resignation, Tsaldaris left the chamber. He was followed by 165 deputies. Only 82 deputies stayed on. Without hesitation, Kondylis presented a draft resolution abolishing the republic, restoring the constitution of 1911, and appointing himself as regent until the king's arrival. As an afterthought, the Vouli set the referendum for November 3, but there was no longer a matter of true choice. The Kondylis government had already imposed martial law. Papanastasiou, who had called on the armed forces to intervene and assure an honest referendum, was arrested and sent into exile. King George in London was displeased with these arbitrary steps but he, too, had little choice.

In the referendum 1,491,992 voted for the restoration, 32,454 against. In their anxiety to assure success, the champions of the monarchy went overboard; not only was the 97.8 percent majority unbelievably one-sided, but the number of voters had suddenly increased by 350,000 over those who voted in 1933. Three days later, the king issued a statement calling for national conciliation and an end to the long years of dissension. Venizelos had already advised his followers to accept the change. In October British emissaries had spoken to him in favor of a reconciliation with the king. In Greece the Liberal party, now headed by Themistocles Sofoulis, began talks with the Populists for a coalition government that would help the king in his efforts to break away from the grip of Kondylis and the more intransigent anti-Venizelists.

King George II, accompanied by his younger brother Paul, the Diadohos, left London for Greece a few days later. During a brief stopover in Paris, the king assured the French that Greek foreign policy would follow the lead of the Western democracies. In Rome he told Mussolini that the friendly ties forged by Venizelos in 1928 would not be affected by his return to the throne.

On November 25 the light cruiser *Helle* with King George aboard sailed majestically into the Saronic gulf. A new chapter was opening in the country's checkered history. Kondylis swiftly found out that the king had no intention of becoming a pawn in the hands of the extremists. When Kondylis handed the king at the pier the text of the first royal proclamation, the monarch took out his golden pen and immediately set about making several significant changes, stressing the theme of conciliation and national unity. A few minutes later, as the king was about to climb into his automobile for the triumphant ride to Athens, Kondylis made a move to take a seat next to him. The king politely but firmly indicated that he wished to ride into the city with only the diadohos at his side.

The royal proclamation left no doubt that King George was determined to be the sovereign "of all [his] people, without exception." To the painful surprise of the extremists, he declared in no uncertain terms: "I wish to cast the past to oblivion, determined to secure equal justice for all." In keeping with these words, he invited all major leaders from both camps to consult with him. Tsaldaris and Metaxas responded affirmatively to his invitation for a meeting. They suggested a general amnesty and the calling of a parliamentary election under the proportional representation system. From the Venizelists, only Mikhalakopoulos accepted the invitation for a meeting. Sofoulis sent a letter saying that the Liberal party did not recognize the restoration of the monarchy as legitimate but that it was prepared to operate within the new constitutional order. He, too, suggested general amnesty and the holding of elections under the proportional representation system. Kafandaris, Papandreou, and Papanastasiou declined to consult with the king because, as they said, they did not recognize the legitimacy of the regime.

The king, determined to pursue a policy of national conciliation, did not take offense but instead agreed that an amnesty and a new election were two indispensable steps toward achieving his goals. He replaced Kondylis in the premiership with Professor Constantine Demertzis, a neutral and generally respected personality. At this critical moment of transition, General Papagos visited the king and indicated that if the Venizelist officers who were purged from the army after the March revolt were granted amnesty, they would have the right to return to active duty. This, he cautioned, was too drastic a step and would cause great unrest in the army. The king realized that at this early stage he could not push too far the people who had been instrumental in securing his return to the throne. He reached a compromise. To the officers, he would grant only a pardon. In Paris, Venizelos criticized this compromise because it treated the political protagonists of the revolt who received amnesty more favorably than low-ranking officers. But Venizelos placed most of the blame on the Venizelist leaders who he claimed were not helping the king in his efforts at conciliation. Sofoulis, taking his cue from Venizelos' friendly attitude, asked immediately for a meeting with the king.

Since all the political leaders seemed to favor proportional representation as a means of toning down the rivalry between the two camps, the king agreed to go along. He had serious reservations as to the wisdom of this electoral system, which he felt was bound to lead to a fragmentation of the political forces. In his view, the country needed a strong government supported by a cohesive majority in the legislature. Apparently, he was planning to have another election soon, with the plurality system. He was not to have the opportunity.

In the election of January 26, 1936, the two camps emerged with almost an equal number of seats—the four royalist parties with 143, the five Venizelist with 141—with 15 seats going to the Communist-led Popular Front. One seat went to Sofianopoulos' Peasant party. Unless the two rival camps agreed to put aside their differences, neither one could form a government without the support of the fifteen Communist deputies. The electoral success of the extreme Left reflected more profound changes. Under the leadership of Nikos Zakhariades—a Stalin appointee—the KKE was broadening its popular appeal by exploiting the economic conditions and the popular disillusionment with the political system. Strikes with only barely concealed political motives were already playing havoc with production.

The Liberal party with 126 seats and the Populist party with 72 could have formed together a viable coalition government. But such cooperation required an agreement over the return to active duty of many Venizelist officers who had been purged after the March revolt. Tsaldaris would have gone along on this thorny issue if it were not for the diehards in the army. Inspired by Kondylis, they were prepared to use force to prevent the reinstatement of the purged officers. A conspiracy was already afoot. Kondylis asked to see the king on February 1, at which time he planned to demand that such officers be kept out of active service. He was in touch with fellow-conspirators in the army who were ready to back his demand by force. The day before the crucial meeting, Kondylis died of an apparent stroke. He was fifty-seven.

With the passing of Kondylis, the domestic and foreign advocates of a strong government focused their attention on Metaxas. This military strategist was no less versed in the secrets of political power. With a brilliant, calculating, devious intellect, he was a great deal more formidable than Kondylis. But Metaxas had only seven deputies from his party in the Vouli, and no one expected the other leaders to accept him as a compromise prime minister. Yet, in less than four months, Metaxas was to gain the premiership. Moreover, his government would receive an unprecedented vote of confidence, 241 in favor and 16 against, with 4 abstentions.

Dictatorship or revolution

Metaxas did not reach the summit by a miracle. His rise was made possible by the rapid disintegration of the parliamentary system. At a time when the menace of war was no longer a matter of speculation, Greece remained without a strong, political government. All the king's efforts to forge a coalition of Liberals and Populists foundered because of the intransigence of extremists on both sides. The fate of the Venizelist officers remained the one issue on which agreement seemed impossible. In late February, Sofoulis signed a secret pact with the Communist deputy, Sklavainas, pledging the support of the Popular Front deputies for the election of Sofoulis as president of the Vouli. Having the declared confidence of the Vouli, Sofoulis could then form a government. The Communists, of course, did not promise their support without some strings attached. Their terms included the repeal of the law that made agitation against the socioeconomic system a punishable, *sui generis* crime, the freeing of all Communists held in prison or committed to restricted residence in remote islands, the suppression of all Fascist organizations, the abolition of the state security agencies, the making of proportional representation the permanent electoral system, a five-year moratorium on peasant debts, a drop in the price of bread, and a few other changes along these lines. Although the agreement remained a well-kept secret, there were rumors circulating about some form of cooperation between the political parties and the Communists.

On March 3 Gen. Alexandros Papagos, minister of military affairs in the Demertzis cabinet, informed the prime minister that "the army will not remain indifferent in the event of collaboration between the bourgeois parties and the Communists." Confronted with another attempt by the military to meddle in politics, the king turned to Metaxas and asked him to take over the ministry of military affairs. In this move, the king was apparently encouraged by the British, who were anxious to see a strong and friendly government in Greece. To the utter surprise of many, Venizelos wrote a letter from Paris on March 9 to a friend in which he said: "It is not necessary for me to tell you how overjoyed I am at the king's decision to put down at last the interminable interventions of the military . . . and appoint Metaxas to the ministry of military affairs. With his action, the king has regained his prestige in full, a factor indispensable for restoring the emotional unity of the Greek people and moving the country to a normal political life. . . . From the depths of my heart I say: Long live the king!" Considering the many years of rivalry between Venizelos and Metaxas, the puzzling statement can be understood only in the light of British views at the time.

Three days before Venizelos wrote his letter, Sofoulis, with the aid of the Communist votes, was elected president of the Vouli. In keeping with parliamentary practice, the king called Sofoulis and asked him to form a government. At this crucial moment, Sofoulis took a step that infuriated the Communists. Instead of forming a cabinet—which would have been constantly under their thumb—he turned to Tsaldaris and proposed a coalition government. The discussions between the two sides, however, were again torpedoed by extremists. Sofoulis advised the king to keep Demertzis' nonpolitical cabinet in office until the major parties agreed on a coalition. The king was very anxious to see the impasse terminated. Almost two months had passed since the election, and the Vouli still was unable to provide the country with a political government. The king's anxiety was justified. That same week, Hitler's armies moved into the Rhineland, and the outbreak of a war in Europe seemed, at least for the moment, to be imminent. In a reshuffling of the Demertzis cabinet, Metaxas emerged as deputy prime minister. Anyone familiar with the personalities involved could easily tell that Metaxas was to be the dominant figure. Besides, Demertzis was ill and spent most of his time in bed.

The Communists took revenge for what they considered to be Sofoulis' perfidy in a rather original fashion. On April 3 *Rizospastis* —the Communist newspaper—printed the entire text of the Sofoulis-Sklavainas agreement. The disclosure left most people aghast. The Communists did not stop there. A few days later, when the Vouli was debating a motion to censure Sofoulis for his agreement with the Communists, they casually tossed in the information that the other major party, the Populists, had also sought their collaboration. The confidence of the middle-class in the parliamentary system sank even lower when 188 deputies voted against censuring Sofoulis, thus indirectly excusing his collaboration with the Communists.

Sofoulis' position as the man appointed by Venizelos to head the Liberal party in his absence received a serious blow when Venizelos, the man who had dominated the political stage for a quarter of a century, died on March 17 of a stroke in Paris, where he had been living in self-exile. He was seventy-one years old. The man who had given his name to the two rival camps—commonly known as Venizelists and anti-Venizelists—was no longer there to draw the emotional adulation of one-half of the nation and the unthinking hatred of the other half. Sofoulis, in the hopes of strengthening his position, brought the late statesman's son, Sophocles, into the leadership of the Liberal party. Sophocles Venizelos, had none of the physical presence or personal magnetism of his father. A graduate of the military academy back in 1915, he had long ago retired from active service. Now in his early forties, he was to play a crucial role in Greece's destiny, primarily because of the legacy of his name.

Soon another death would bring Metaxas closer to the pinnacle of power. On the morning of April 13, prime minister Demertzis was found dead in his bed. He had died of an apparent heart attack during the night. At this point, the king asked Metaxas to move up to the premiership until the parties could agree to form a coalition government. Metaxas was not an ordinary caretaker prime minister. He was a political figure, the leader of a small party in the Vouli to be sure, but he was also a strong, dynamic personality. Sofoulis and Tsaldaris made one more effort to reach a compromise and form a coalition government. But now, with Venizelos gone, Sofoulis was no longer the anointed leader of the Liberal party. Kafandaris, who had been Venizelos' stand-in during the twenties, long aspired to inherit the party and now at last he saw his chance. He raised vehement objections to a compromise solution on the question of the Venizelist officers, and in so doing he gained stature among Venizelist circles at the expense of Sofoulis.

With the growing unrest in the country and the international horizon dark and foreboding, King George received with grave disappointment the news that the formation of a coalition government was again made impossible. On April 25 Metaxas appeared before the Vouli and asked for a vote of confidence. If the parties were unable to give the country a political government, Metaxas said, the Vouli should at least give his cabinet a vote of confidence so that he could govern more effectively. Sofoulis, encouraged in this by Sophocles Venizelos, declared that the Liberal party was prepared to give a vote of confidence to Metaxas. He then went on to condemn in the most damning words the disintegration of the parliamentary system, which had made such action necessary. Tsaldaris, who had never liked or trusted Metaxas in spite of their common royalist orientation, agreed to give a vote of tolerance. Kafandaris, stating that "ideological differences or personal rivalries no longer divide the people," added his support for Metaxas. Papanastasiou decided to abstain in a show of protest against the major parties "which have failed in their primary responsibility of giving the country a government." Only George Papandreou, one of the most prominent Liberals, attacked the Metaxas government as being a prelude to a dictatorship. When the votes were counted, the Metaxas government had received 241 out of 257 votes cast, with 4 deputies abstaining. Sofoulis then introduced a bill making proportional representation the country's permanent electoral system. King George was against this system, which threatened to condemn the country to permanent instability, but four days later the bill was passed with the aid of the Communist votes. With this, all hope to have a new election under the plurality system, which alone could produce a cohesive majority in the legislature, all but vanished. Half an hour later, the Vouli decided to adjourn until September 30.

Within a few months, the parliamentary system had been reduced to a mockery. For many years, the political process had been controlled largely by a very thin layer of political activists at the top. In reality political parties were shallow, oligarchic, personalized structures with hardly any organization reaching the grass roots of the electorate. Yet, they had been able to command the support of the voters, who were not confused by the changing party labels or the kaleidoscopic shifts in partisan affiliations. The voter was guided by two overriding political allegiances. First, there was a personal attachment to his favorite deputy, the man representing his area in the Vouli. Often this relationship was determined by personal favors. Second, there was a very broad, almost above party allegiance to the *parataxis* (camp). Still, in the absence of durable, well-structured party organizations, the voter had little influence on decisions that were made at the top. Much of the arbitrariness and tampering with rules and institutions could be traced to the oligarchic nature of the political system. The press, which could have played the role of custodian over political morality and constitutional propriety, seldom did so because its partisan ties ruled out truly independent criticism. Pressure groups only reinforced the weaknesses of the system, since the habitual disregard of constitutional restraints only made it easier for politicians to enact legislation granting special privileges. In 1936 the weaknesses of the political system became intolerable. While Europe was facing the possibility of war, Greece had become a country without a strong government, its political parties had turned into cabals of feuding politicians, and its democratic institutions had lost the respect of the people. The idea of a dictatorship as the only effective defense against "anarchy and communism" began to gain ground.

With the disintegration of the parliamentary system, the Communists felt that the time was ripe to move to a "higher form of struggle." Those who advocated a Communist revolution found their influence growing among the lower income groups and among some disillusioned intellectuals. The Communist battle cry was "the struggle against monarcho-fascism"—a rather clever combination of words. They avoided any references to the dictatorship of the proletariat and called instead for a "democratic-bourgeois" revolution, which presumably would safeguard individual freedoms while promoting more socially-oriented economic policies. This was in keeping with Stalin's directives on a Popular Front strategy at the time. To strengthen the party's hand, the Communist leadership discarded its advocacy of Macedonian independence. The stepped-up agitation had its effect. In the first four months of the year, the Communists and their fellow travelers instigated more than three hundred politically-motivated strikes, often with demonstrations and clashes with the police.

Strikes, demonstrations, street fights, and riots followed one another with increasing intensity until they came to an explosive climax on May 9, 1936, in Salonika. Earlier in the month, tobacco-workers had gone on strike demanding higher wages. The Communist party had always had strong support among these workers. On the morning of May 8, five to six thousand workers joined in a demonstration and marched toward the general administration building to present a petition to the governor-general. The gendarm-erie tried to block the way and a violent riot erupted. Several people were wounded before the demonstration was broken up by force. The brutality of the gendarmes angered the entire city. By midnight, many more unions joined in a twenty-four hour strike. The Third Army Corps, stationed in Salonika, declared a state of emergency. The next day, May 9, fresh bloody clashes with the gendarmes gave the signal for another demonstration. This time, tens of thousands of people from all walks of life poured into the center of the city. When some demonstrators tried to seize an armored car, the gendarmes lost their nerve and opened fire into the crowd while mounted police charged the multitude with drawn swords. The demonstrators fell back, leaving on the bloodied pavement twelve demonstrators dead and dozens wounded.

As soon as Metaxas realized the seriousness of the situation, he ordered the gendarmes back to their barracks and assigned police duties to the regular army. But the military units stationed in Salonika were made up mostly of local residents who had no intention of fighting against their own kin. One of the companies sent to disperse a demonstration joined the demonstrators instead. The commander of the Third Army Corps was forced to give permission for another protest demonstration that same afternoon. With a volcanic outpouring of emotion, a tremendous crowd took possession of the streets, where they paraded, shouted, cursed, and cheered. The authorities made no attempt to interfere. Power had passed to the demonstrators. Needless to say, only a very small fraction of the thousands who flooded the streets were Communists or even sympathizers. But under the circumstances, this fact was unimportant; the volume and the aggressiveness of the demonstrators showed that the people, angered by the brutal use of force, and lacking confidence in the nation's political leadership, had become "masses" in the Leninist sense of the word. They were ready to be manipulated by self-appointed but determined leaders. Today we know that the Salonika organization of the Communist party had become the unseen but effective guiding force behind the disturbances.

The next day, more than 150,000 people attended the funeral of the May 9 victims. Although the scene was highly charged emotionally, there were no violent incidents, probably because no state officials made any attempt to interfere. Public authority was not restored in Salonika until May 11, when army units arrived from Larisa and four naval ships sailed into the harbor.

The Salonika eruption played straight into the hands of the advocates of dictatorship. On May 10 Metaxas had discussed with the king the necessity of taking some restrictive measures in view of the worsening international situation and the increasing intensity of Communist agitation. Despite the "absolute certainty" of the KKE's leaders that "a rapid and decisive clash was forthcoming between the people's anti-Fascist forces welded around the KKE and the Fascist reactionary forces gathering around the king," the dichotomy was not as portrayed in this statement. The KKE still remained a small party. But in the summer of 1936 popularity was not a decisive factor. The Communists had correctly understood that once the democratic leaders had virtually deserted the stage, the initiative had automatically passed to the two extremes of the Right and the Left. Between these extreme positions was the majority of the people, who remained uncertain, frustrated, and vacillating. In this state of passive equilibrium, the scales could be tipped by either side.

The events in Salonika had revealed how easily public authority could be swept away by an angry and frustrated populace. The revolutionary agitation that had started a few months earlier with strikes of limited and localized significance had now escalated to violent clashes, to what the Communists called "higher forms of struggle." Metaxas decided to outpace the advocates of revolution. He found a valuable ally in the person of Sophocles Venizelos, who was deeply concerned with the rise of Communist agitation. He was in close contact with Metaxas through Theodore Skylakakis, the minister of interior. Venizelos had served with Skylakakis as a fellow cadet in the Military Academy and, although Skylakakis had become a staunch royalist, the two had remained personal friends through the years.

Sophocles Venizelos played a decisive political role in late July, as the news of civil war in Spain raised the specter of a similar threat in Greece. Many Greeks in those days had interpreted the events in Spain as a Communist effort to take over a strategic country at the other end of the Mediterranean. On July 22, with the newspapers emblazoned with headlines reporting the alarming news from Spain, Sofoulis went to the palace with "great news." At last, a coalition government appeared within reach. Tsaldaris had died suddenly on May 17 of an apparent heart attack, and his death fed the wild speculation that the successive deaths of major political figures had not been an accident of fate but rather the sinister plot of a mysterious hand. With Tsaldaris removed from the political stage, other Populist personalities moved to the foreground. One of them, Ioannis Theotokis, had been among the most intransigent royalists. During the previous months, his unyielding objections over the fate of the Venizelist officers had undermined time and again the efforts for a coalition government. Now he reversed his stand and agreed to form a coalition government in the fall, after the opening of the Vouli. The king, however, had little confidence in Sofoulis and even less in Theotokis, who had suddenly made this complete aboutface from dogged intransigence to total cooperation with the Liberals. The king felt that he could not wait until the fall. The die was cast when Sophocles Venizelos assured him that Sofoulis did not speak for the party and that in his view the country needed a strong, temporary dictatorship under Metaxas. In fact, Venizelos had already agreed with Metaxas on the key aspects of this move. The dictatorship would last for about two years, solve the question of the Venizelist officers without destroying the unity of the army, suppress Communist agitation, strengthen the country's military forces, and activate the economy to cope with unemployment, stagnation, and rising prices. In taking this stand, Venizelos had been apparently encouraged by some of his highly influential British friends, and was even prepared to participate as deputy prime minister in the dictatorial government.

The intervention of Venizelos dispelled whatever reservations the king might have had. That same evening he told Metaxas that he would agree to a temporary suspension of the constitution. Now the contest was between a Metaxas dictatorship and a Communist-led revolution. The man in the street could sense something was afoot but only a handful of insiders had any real knowledge of what was coming. For the next ten days, Communist-inspired strikes and demonstrations broke out in the vicinity of Athens. A fire in the Salamis naval base threatened for a moment to blow up the ammunition stores of the fleet. Another fire broke out in the Patrai military depots. The fires may have been accidental, but in the emotional climate of the moment suspicion of sabotage gained easy and wide currency. Then, the General Confederation of Labor (GSEE), which was strongly influenced by the KKE, proclaimed a "general political strike" set to begin in the early hours of August 5. Determined to outpace the revolution, Metaxas made his move at a cabinet meeting on the evening of August 4.

The dictatorship

The ministers—most of them nonpolitical personalities who were initially appointed to cabinet posts when Demertzis was prime minister—came to the meeting on August 4 unsuspecting that history was to take a dramatic turn. No special police precautions were in sight as they entered the Ministry of Foreign Affairs, where Metaxas had his office. They did not know that the two evzone guards at the entrance had orders to allow them to enter but to prevent anyone from leaving the building until Metaxas had given permission. As they arrived, they were led individually to his office, where they were told that he had decided, with the king's consent, "to dissolve the Vouli and suspend certain articles of the Constitution." They were asked to sign two decrees that he had prepared—or resign from the government if they disagreed. Only three refused to sign. Then, with the signed decrees in his briefcase, Metaxas went to the palace.

The dictatorship was imposed with a stroke of the pen. Confident of military support, Metaxas did not mobilize any units prior to his coup. He was already the prime minister and he had the king's sanction. He anticipated no opposition from the army commanders, who were much more likely to receive the news with a sigh of relief. The next morning, curious citizens clustered around the posted announcements. No newspapers were allowed to come out on August 5. Neither was there a general strike. Several Communist leaders had been arrested during the night. The scales were tipped in favor of the dictatorship, and no one rose to challenge the move. Metaxas justified his action to the people by saying that "Communism had come to believe that the moment was at hand to overthrow the social system . . . by using a systematically and intensively organized general strike . . . [to] provoke civil war." The war in Spain seemed to give a sense of urgency to these words. Venizelos did not join the cabinet as originally intended and two days later he left for Europe. For the next two years he continued to support the dictatorship as a necessary expedient.

The political leaders, stunned by the sudden blow, remained speechless, at first. Then by September they began to address memoranda to the king protesting the dictatorship. The king made no move to respond to their protests. The Communist party, with most of its cadre arrested or in hiding, remained paralyzed. All its revolutionary rhetoric had suddenly evaporated.

For the next four years, Metaxas combined the instrumentalities of a police state with a series of socioeconomic measures designed to tone down social discontent and activate the sagging economy. The press was censored, opponents were arrested and sent to the islands, strikes were prohibited. At the same time, the government took steps to improve the workers' pay and working conditions. After years of delays the Social Security law, which had been initiated in 1930 by Venizelos, finally came into effect. The government wrote off the debts of farmers, passing the burden on to the country's taxpayers; increased the procurement price of wheat; and started a series of public works in the countryside. Unemployment gradually fell off while the per capita income inched upward until by 1938 it stood at approximately one-tenth the level in the United States at the time, almost a 45 percent rise over the prevailing levels in the mid-twenties. The fear of war, leading to a renewed drive for armaments

A stately cedar on the acropolis of Mycenae overshadows spring flowers and groves of young olive trees.

Photographs on pp. 176–85 taken by David O. Johnson in April 1973. Converted from color to black and white.

A layer of early morning mist gives the impression of a lake in this view from the balcony of a modern hotel in Delphi.

Neat gardens and terraced fields meet a line of rocky boulders from heights above on the island of Mykonos.

Modern fireproof construction typifies new housing near Delphi.

Massive clusters of flowers brighten a rustic home on the island of Ios.

On the extraordinary island of Thira, homes cling tenaciously to the sheer cliffs that form the inside edge of the volcanic crater.

The vertiginous descent to the harbor of the island capital of Thira is made down a zigzag cliff path of cobblestone steps.

The tiny settlement of Yerake is crowded between the sea and the nearby mountains of the Peloponnisos.

Patiently awaiting its next load, a burro rests beside the road overlooking Mykonos harbor.

Minimal tides and a strong jetty allow whitewashed homes to hug the waterline of the harbor of Mykonos.

A glass-bottom bucket helps a fisherman sight octopuses in the harbor of Ios.

(*top*) No blueprints are needed for the experienced Greek boat builder to fashion any size caique on the island of Spetsai.

The interisland ferry dwarfs fishing boats in the harbor at Naxos.

Boys at play with a modern toy next to ancient bollards on a dock at Ios.

The ferry from Egion in the Peloponnisos prepares to dock at Itea where, according to tradition, Apollo landed when he came from Crete on the sacred dolphin.

A miller keeps his weather eye on the wind, the source of power for grinding grain in this 300-year-old windmill overlooking the harbor of Mykonos.

in Europe, had acted as a stimulant to the world economy, which thus began to move out of the throes of depression. The Greek economy reflected this general improvement.

Whatever the king's initial intentions, the specter of war made a return to parliamentary democracy a difficult and risky enterprise. True, the British were fully aware that the Metaxas regime, being a dictatorship, was not popular, and in many diplomatic exchanges between London and the British embassy in Athens there was a shadow of uncertainty as to whether the regime could actually manage to rally the people in the event of war. At the same time, these exchanges reveal that at no time did the British doubt Metaxas' determination to stand by their side in a general conflagration. Ironically, through the years of the dictatorship, Metaxas introduced practices copied from the totalitarian regimes of Germany and Italy—certainly a bizarre way for preparing the ground to fight on the side of the Western democracies.

Through the next four years, several politicians made efforts to organize some form of resistance to the dictatorship. One of the earliest conspiracies was initiated by Papanastasiou in the fall of 1936. He was in contact with some Cretans and was about to discuss joint action with Theotokis when he died of an apparent heart attack on November 17. Metaxas ordered that he be given the funeral dignities accorded to a prime minister dying in office. The death of the "father of the republic" did not end the conspiracy; within days, Mikhalakopoulos emerged as the new leader.

Metaxas was not overly alarmed by the rumored threat of a coup. He was much more concerned with the king's real views about the regime. Contrary to the prevailing opinion at the time—a view that has persisted ever since—King George was not wholeheartedly committed to the regime, which had been forced on him by the course of events. He had agreed to a dictatorial regime as a temporary measure in the face of rising Communist agitation and political stalemate, during which time the peace of Europe was in jeopardy. Similar thoughts had apparently led the British and Sophocles Venizelos to accept or even encourage Metaxas' move. It is not clear whether Metaxas saw the dictatorship as a temporary expedient. The king's feelings were obliquely revealed on the occasion of the regime's first anniversary. Vacationing on the island of Corfu, the king sent Metaxas a telegram of congratulations in which he included two phrases heavy with meaning: "Recalling today

the great and imminent danger which made necessary the extraordinary and, I hope, *temporary measures* . . . I wish that the
achievements of your government will *shortly make possible the
cooperation of all* in a spirit of unity for the sake of the common
good" (italics mine). Metaxas did not publish the cable. Few knew
that the king was already pondering how to end the dictatorship, and
Metaxas, to be sure, was not unaware of the king's true feelings, but
there was little he could do. He realized that his regime would not
last very long if the king openly withdrew his support. The army was
loyal to the king, and Metaxas had no illusions on this score.

The king and Metaxas did not disagree on matters of foreign
policy. In spite of the prevailing public assumption in those days,
Metaxas was not pro-German. In fact, he had long been committed
to a policy of cooperation with the Western Allies. The fascist-like
trappings of his regime created a misleading facade. The issue that
cast a shadow over the protagonists' relations centered on the
question of the nature and, above all, the duration of the dictatorship. King George was ideologically in sympathy with the British
form of parliamentary democracy. Even in those days when Hitler
and Mussolini were treated as statesmen and admired by many, King
George had no respect and certainly no admiration for them or their
systems.

In the last months of 1937, with the threat of a Communist-led
revolution removed, with the economy improving, with national
confidence restored, and with the army freed of the irritant of
constant politicking, King George began to think seriously that the
time to end the temporary suspension of parliamentary life was at
hand. A cautious man by nature, however, he wanted first to check
personally with high British and French officials about the prospects
of war in Europe. His talks in London and Paris were decisive. When
he returned to Athens in mid-December, he had no illusions: Europe
was inexorably drifting toward the maelstrom of another war. Under
the circumstances, he had no option but to let Metaxas stay on.

Changes in the country in the face of impending war were barely
understood by most people in those days, but they were clearly
reflected in several steps taken by the government. In early January
the Athenians saw for the first time units of the National Youth
Organization (EON) parade through the streets of the capital with
their blue and white uniforms, their Fascist salutes, their songs.
Previously the king had objected to any organization that would rival

the Boy Scouts, which reflected the British, democratic tradition. Now, Metaxas was given permission to go ahead with his youth organization. As if to make a counterpoint, the political leaders launched another "paper war" of clandestine proclamations against the regime. This time, Metaxas had most of his opponents arrested and sent into exile in the islands or in remote villages. Mikhalakopoulos was among them. By the middle of February, as Metaxas was about to travel to Turkey for another agreement to strengthen the ties between the two countries, he was able to make this entry in his private diary. "Everybody is now quiet. The rumors and every opposition has stopped. The people as a whole are satisfied because order has been assured and the government is strong. The January turbulence came from the people's doubts as to whether the government had the inner strength to prevail, or that it was being prevented from doing so by the throne. All these hesitations, doubts, skepticism have disappeared. So important was it to make this show of strength." Mikhalakopoulos fell victim to this show of strength; his death on March 27, after a short illness, removed from Metaxas' path another potential rival.

Metaxas was now in full control. Surprising though it may seem, his popularity, especially in the countryside, was increasing. In foreign policy, he was strengthening ties with Turkey while playing a leading role in the councils of the Balkan Pact. With the specter of war already clearly within sight, most people in Greece were against a return to the anarchy and confusion of the pre-Metaxas days. Hitler's takeover of Austria in March 1938 seemed to give substance to the worst fears. Furthermore, the regime's propaganda could use the daily reports from the disastrous civil war in Spain as a vivid illustration of what Greece had escaped thanks to Metaxas' bold action. In the armed forces, few turned a nostalgic gaze to the old days. Even the change of uniforms, which now followed the British style, seemed to underline a new spirit of professionalism. Defense outlays were receiving high priority and although few Venizelist officers were returned to active duty, many came to be absorbed in other areas of administration. Above all the economy was doing well, and virtually all segments of the population shared in the benefits. Most citizens appeared willing to live with the dictatorial regime.

Such was the public mood when at dawn, July 29, 1938, a group of Venizelist politicians with droves of armed villagers entered the city of Khania, Crete. Taking advantage of the initial surprise, they disarmed the regiment stationed there, broke into the arsenal and took a large number of rifles; then, joined by a large crowd of excited townspeople, they seized the General Administration building and the wireless station, and issued a proclamation declaring the end of the dictatorship and calling on the people and the armed forces in the rest of the country to rise in support of the revolution. To the dismay of the rebels no one else responded, not even the other Cretan towns. Even if some had answered their call, it would have mattered little because so long as Metaxas retained control in Athens, the revolt was doomed. By noon, the rebels lost heart. Two or three planes flew over Khania and the other Cretan towns and dropped leaflets with a statement by Metaxas, calling on the people to remain calm. Members of the Communist organization in Khania tried to revive the revolutionary spirit and give some sense of direction to it, but they were already too late. The leaders of the stillborn revolution left the city in the evening and sought refuge in the mountains. They tried to organize another uprising in October but again they found little response. Finally, they asked privately for amnesty. Metaxas ignored the request but authorized Constantine Maniadakis, his minister of public security, to help them "escape" to the Dodecanese and then to Cyprus.

The Cretan uprising appeared as the last echo of an era that had long since passed. In the late summer days of 1938, Europe was facing war as Hitler's demands over the Sudetenland threatened to plunge the entire continent into the abyss. Before the end of September the British and the French would meet Hitler and Mussolini at Munich and bow to the German dictator. The Allied powers had to gain time in order to prepare for the inevitable confrontation. For a while the threat of war was muted as Chamberlain assured a frightened world that at Munich they had secured "peace in our time."

King George and Metaxas were not deceived by these hopeful words. With the international situation becoming increasingly uncertain, Metaxas knew well that there was no alternative to his rule. Before the end of the year he moved to eliminate any remaining fissures in his regime. As soon as he returned from the funeral of Mustafa Kemal, who had died on November 10 at the age of fifty-nine, Metaxas reshuffled his cabinet, replacing with individuals of his personal choice all the ministers he had inherited from Demertzis. Some of those who were removed were closely associated with King George, but no objection was raised from the palace. In spite of his reservations toward the regime, the king could not easily find another political personality with the strength of character, ability, and competence to match Metaxas. The short, corpulent, bespectacled prime minister, who resembled a retired schoolteacher, was not only an astute politician but a first-rate military strategist as well. In view of the international situation, the king had no choice but to go along with Metaxas. As a gesture of goodwill and support, the king even asked Prince Paul, the diadohos, to become the honorary leader of the National Youth Organization, although they both detested the organization's Fascist trappings. Maybe the king, seeing that most young people had already joined this organization, wanted to establish closer ties between the throne and the country's younger generation.

In the early months of 1939 one major preoccupation united the king with his prime minister: that is, the need to strengthen the country's defensive capabilities. The Balkan Pact was already a rather tattered shield, as Yugoslavia and Rumania were concerned with the growing menace of the Axis while Turkey was interested only in ways to avoid entanglement in the oncoming war. Greece was making every effort to avoid any action that might be regarded provocative by Italy. Intelligence reports indicated that Mussolini was about to strike in the direction of Albania or Greece. The reports were accurate. On April 7 an Italian expeditionary force invaded Albania. A small, poor country of less than 2 million people, Albania was to serve as Mussolini's bridgehead in the Balkans. But for the time being, the Italian leader had to be content with this first gain. He assured the Greek government that his action in Albania posed no threat to Greece. Metaxas accepted the statement, but he was not fooled by it.

The Italian move ended all thought of overthrowing Metaxas. As late as March, several political personalities in Greece and abroad— mostly in Paris—had continued to talk about plans to remove Metaxas. Most of them believed at the time that he was pro-German and would some day deliver Greece to the Axis. Now, in April, they indicated to the Greek authorities through various channels that, as good patriots, they were not going to add to the country's problems. The realization that the threat of war had now reached the borders of Greece apparently had a sobering effect. Europe indeed was living through the last days of peace. On September 1 the German armies crossed into Poland. The war was on.

In Greece the government made every effort to tone down the impact of the dramatic events. The press was ordered to avoid hysterical headlines or the overt support of either side. Greece was to remain neutral. On this, the king and the prime minister were in agreement. Behind the scenes, Metaxas moved methodically but quietly to strengthen the country's defenses. His was an impossibly delicate game. Outwardly calm, almost indifferent to the war, he was preparing for the crucial moment he knew would eventually come. As though the Stalin-Hitler pact had made communism even more dangerous, Metaxas and his minister of public security, the resourceful and earthy Maniadakis, renewed their war on the KKE with astonishing results. The remnants of the party organization were so deeply infiltrated with police agents that in June 1940 Maniadakis was able to create his own temporary administration of the party. The confusion in the party ranks was so pervasive that most Communists, including Nikos Zakhariades, the party's jailed leader, regarded Maniadakis' administration as the genuine leadership of the party. The old central committee of the KKE, moreover, was being dismissed as "a bunch of stool pidgeons." The public, of course, knew nothing of this.

For the first six months of 1940 Mussolini maintained a friendly stance toward Greece. But with the fall of France and Italy's entry into the war, this situation changed abruptly. Mussolini regarded the Balkans as his sphere of influence. Besides, he needed some achievements of his own to match the spectacular victories of his Axis partner. He had already selected Greece as his target.

In July sporadic air attacks on Greek ships in the Aegean were used by Mussolini as a warning against the use of Greek waters by the British fleet. Metaxas continued to appear calm. Earlier in the year, he had rejected a foolhardy proposal by General Papagos, the army's chief of staff, to launch a preemptive attack against the Italian forces in Albania. Metaxas had even rejected suggestions for military mobilization; instead, he resorted to an ingenious device of strengthening the army by calling men to the colors through "individual summons." His policy was clear. He would not take any provocative steps but be ready to strike back if the Italians moved against Greece.

In early August, Metaxas received intelligence reports indicating that Italy was about to strike. Immediately, he instructed the Greek ambassador to Berlin to ask for Hitler's intercession. Hitler spoke to his fellow dictator and the operation was aborted, but not before an Italian submarine sank the Greek light cruiser *Helle* on the morning of August 15 as it was anchored off the island of Tinos. It appears that the commander of the submarine did not receive in time the orders cancelling the attack. The Greek government easily verified the nationality of the submarine from the fragments of the torpedoes used but nothing was said in public. The people, of course, also had no doubt as to the identity of the culprit.

Mussolini had been made to postpone his attack on Greece not only because of Hitler's intervention—the German dictator was already planning his attack on Russia and had every reason to avoid additional complications in the Balkans—but also because the Italian military commanders told him that their forces in Albania would be sufficient only if Greece accepted her fate without resistance. In the event of war, they said, the forces would be inadequate. Mussolini ordered reinforcements. To gain time, he instructed the Italian ambassador in Athens, Count Grazzi, to settle the sinking of the *Helle* amicably, explaining to Metaxas that the submarine had apparently mistaken the Greek vessel for a British warship. But the calm was deceptive. With the collapse of France, the focus of the war was shifting to Eastern Europe and the Balkans.

In late August, Hitler and Mussolini met in Vienna and settled, as they saw fit, several territorial disputes affecting Hungary, Rumania, and Bulgaria. Rumania was forced to give up Transylvania to Hungary and Dobrutsa to Bulgaria. Hitler had already begun planning Operation Barbarossa, the attack against Russia. In mid-September, while setting the foundations of the Tripartite Pact with Japan, Germany agreed that "Greece and Yugoslavia belong exclusively to the Italian sphere of interest . . . and the search for solutions belongs to Italy alone." For a while, Mussolini felt that his German partner was paying proper heed to Italy's interests in the Balkans. But then, in early October, General Ion Antonescu seized the reins of power in Rumania, expelled King Carol, and invited the German troops to enter the country. To restore the equilibrium, Mussolini decided to move on Greece—this time without Hitler knowing in advance.

At 2:50 on the morning of October 28, the Italian ambassador,

Count Grazzi, handed Metaxas an ultimatum. Accusing Greece of aiding Britain, the Italian government asked Metaxas "as a guarantee of [Greek] neutrality . . . to allow the Italian armed forces to occupy certain strategic points. . . . Should the Italian troops meet with resistance," the note went on, "they have orders to suppress such resistance by force [and] the Greek government will bear the ensuing responsibility." Faced with these alternatives, Metaxas chose to stand up and fight.

chapter 5
The War Years

Unexpected victory

Mussolini was so sure that Greece would fall within days that he even managed to assure Hitler of this. When the German dictator arrived on October 28, 1940, for a meeting with Mussolini, his plan was to dissuade his Italian partner from carrying out the operation against Greece and to propose instead a possible joint action to seize the island of Crete, which was strategically important. The Italian ambassador in Athens had been, to some extent, the architect of Mussolini's optimistic expectation. He had either "deliberately deceived" his government—as the British ambassador in Athens suggested—or he had been successfully taken in by Metaxas' low profile and overcautious policies. Whatever the truth, Mussolini was in for a painful surprise.

After a modest advance of approximately fifteen miles into Greek soil, the Italian troops were forced to retreat. World public opinion, which was by now accustomed to hearing the dazzling successes of the German blitzkrieg techniques, could not believe the reports from the Greek front. Yet, what was happening on the mountains of Epirus was hardly a miracle. The Italians had 59 infantry battalions, 400 artillery pieces, 150 light tanks, and 300 airplanes. The Greeks had secretly deployed in Epirus and western Macedonia 39 infantry battalions and 120 guns. They had no tanks, and their entire air force consisted of 115 planes, more than 65 of which were outdated. Italian supremacy in armor and air power was soon rendered a meaningless advantage by the mountainous terrain and the bad weather. The mountains of Epirus—craggy, forbidding, with only goat paths snaking through the ravines and along the sides of the precipitous slopes—were hardly suitable for a blitzkrieg. Then, the heavy rains at this time of the year turned even the few suitable passes into muddy graveyards for the heavy instruments of war. Low clouds reduced the Italian airforce to a somewhat irrelevant luxury. Even the superiority of the Italians in artillery was offset in the end by the astounding mobility of the Greek mountain artillery, which was able to climb to impossible places and hit the enemy with deadly accuracy. In the end, the fighting came down to man-to-man combat on the ground. In spite of serious shortages in food supplies, winter clothing, and even ammunition, the Greek officers and soldiers fought with such dogged determination that by November 8 no Italian troops remained on Greek soil.

Those who had predicted that the unpopularity of the Metaxas regime would undermine all efforts for a successful defense were proven wrong. Metaxas had become a national hero overnight. Even Zakhariades of the KKE thought it expedient to issue a proclamation two days after the Italian attack, saying, "in this war, directed by the Metaxas government, we shall all give every ounce of our strength without reservations." A month later, with the Greek forces already advancing into Albania, Zakhariades changed his mind and spoke in favor of an "armistice effected through the good offices of the Soviet Union." Of course at the time, Russia was a friend of Germany. Zakhariades was not alone in his efforts. Others, such as the metropolitan of Ioannina and even Nikolaos Plastiras, who at the time was living in Nice, France, made efforts to terminate the war. But the Germans were posing one impossible condition, that is, the withdrawal of all British units from Greek soil. These efforts at securing an end to the fighting remained mostly unknown to the public at the time.

While it is certainly true that an end to the fighting would have been welcome, the fact is that it was no longer possible to achieve this goal. Italian aggression had irrevocably placed Greece on the side of the British. In early December the German high command discussed Operation Marita (against Greece) as part of the major offensive of Operation Barbarossa (against the Soviet Union). Hitler wanted to eliminate the British presence from his southern flank. He was, of course, thinking in terms of the future. At the moment the British contingent in Greece was quite modest. By the end of December it consisted of thirty-nine fighter planes and eighteen bombers with their crews. Together with communications, antiaircraft, and engineering units, the entire British force did not exceed forty-two hundred men. The British fleet—a formidable force in those days—had not been very actively involved in the Greek-Italian war. It had made no serious effort to block the reinforcement of the Italian troops in Albania across the Straits of Otranto.

In January 1941 the British proposed to deploy Allied forces in Salonika but Metaxas replied that the projected force of only two or three divisions with no more than sixty or sixty-five tanks was totally inadequate. "We are determined," he said, "to face a possible German attack by whatever means and sacrifices may be necessary, but in no way do we wish to provoke such an attack. . . . In any event we shall do our duty to the end . . . as devoted and loyal friends." This official declaration announcing his determination to resist if attacked by Germany was Metaxas' last. Eleven days later he died at the age of seventy. For three days, long lines of ordinary people braved the winter cold in order to pass by the bier where the Greek leader's flag-draped coffin lay in state. Throughout his long, turbulent career, he had never been truly popular—except during the last, dramatic weeks since October 28, 1940.

The passing of Metaxas left King George as the principal decision-maker. By February the threat of a German attack was quite visible. Hitler had already begun to prepare the ground. To prevent Turkey from spoiling his plans, he pressed for a Bulgarian-Turkish treaty of nonaggression. The treaty was signed on February 17. Only two days later, Hitler set the dates for the first part of Operation Marita. Bulgaria had already indicated her willingness to join the Tripartite and allow the use of her soil for the attack on Greece. The price offered by Germany was the transfer of Western Thrace to Bulgaria. At the same time, Hitler pressed Yugoslavia for permission to use her transportation facilities for moving military supplies to the front. The Yugoslavs tried to gain time, but when the first German troops began to pour into Bulgaria they realized that the ring was closing around their country. Worse, there was no evidence of strong British forces coming to their aid through northern Greece. King George and Prime Minister Alexandros Koryzis, the banker who had succeeded Metaxas, told the British that regardless of what Britain was prepared to do, Greece "as a faithful ally, is determined to go on fighting . . . even if she can only count on her own forces." The forces the British were able to spare at the time from the North African front were too small to withhold the oncoming German onslaught.

The Yugoslav government eventually succumbed to the German pressures and joined the Tripartite only to be overthrown the following day by a military coup. To the dismay of the British, the new Yugoslav government disregarded their advice to attack the Italian forces in Albania. Instead, they tried to placate Hitler. Then, in response to popular pressures, they hastily signed a treaty of friendship with the Soviet Union. Vain gestures. Early in the morning of April 6, German planes blasted Belgrade mercilessly. At the same time, Hitler's armored divisions crossed the Yugoslav and the Greek borders.

Vastly superior, the German divisions pushed through to Belgrade in the north and toward the Vardar valley in the south. For four days the Greek soldiers defending the fortifications of the "Metaxas line" along the Bulgarian frontier fought with a determination that impressed even the enemy. But when the Yugoslav front around Bitola collapsed, and the German tanks rolled down the Vardar valley toward Salonika, the battle of Macedonia was over. Now the Greek forces in Albania were facing encirclement from the southeast. Already on April 11, Koryzis had given orders to the fleet to prepare to move to Crete, where the government was also planning to go, since little hope of effective resistance remained. The fifty-three thousand Allied and British troops that had come to Greece in February and March were engaged in a desperate effort to retreat to the south and make an orderly evacuation possible. The waves of people pouring in from the north trying to escape the fighting, the whining of the German stukas diving from the skies with their deadly cargo, the anguish of soldiers shedding their uniforms to escape capture, the complete breakdown of normal daily life for civilians, all contributed to a nightmarish canvas of despair.

On the afternoon of April 18 the cabinet met in the presence of the king to decide on a request by the military command in Epirus for a cease-fire. No decision was reached. That same afternoon, Prime Minister Koryzis left the meeting in a state of extreme agitation, went to his home, and shot himself. The king turned to another banker, Emmanuel Tsouderos, a Cretan, and asked him to take over as prime minister. Three days later, with all hope gone, General Tsolakoglou signed—without government approval—the instrument of surrender. Up to that moment, Italian troops had not been able to enter Greek soil. Two days later at dawn, the king and most members of the cabinet, together with the British ambassador, flew to Crete. Gen. Alexandros Papagos resigned from his post as commander in chief and stayed in Athens. The city was now in the grip of chaos. Public authority was practically nonexistent; food supplies were scarce; transportation and other elementary services had come to a standstill. The port of Piraeus was being devastated by the German air force. Through the last few days, the remnants of the Allied expeditionary force made their way to the south, using every little port as an evacuation point.

On the morning of April 27 a long column of motorcycles appeared on the main thoroughfare of Athens from Kifisia. At the entrance to the city a small deputation of Greek officials waited to surrender the city. The German officer in command of the column moved on through the empty streets in the direction of the Acropolis, where his soldiers raised the German flag. Two days later, General Tsolakoglou formed a puppet cabinet in Athens, thus initiating the dark years of Nazi occupation.

Crete was now the only unconquered part of Greece. The German high command immediately faced a serious dilemma. Any attempt to take Crete at this time would involve a delay in the upcoming Operation Barbarossa, and this did not seem wise. But then again it appeared equally dangerous to allow Crete to remain under British control, for then the island could become a strong naval and air base. Hitler decided to postpone Operation Barbarossa and attack Crete. He launched an airborne operation on May 20 and after nine days of fierce fighting with heavy losses on both sides, the island fell. King George and the Tsouderos cabinet escaped through the southern coast and found temporary shelter in Egypt. Operation Marita had lasted fifty-four days and had caused a delay in the launching of Operation Barbarossa that was to prove fatal. In 1943, when the fortunes of war had turned against Germany, Hitler was asked by a Bulgarian visitor if he would have started Operation Barbarossa had he known how difficult it was going to be. "I would have started earlier," he replied.

Under Nazi occupation

No cheers, no flowers, no welcoming speeches greeted the Germans as they entered Athens. During the first few weeks of occupation their only friends were some unrepentant Germanophiles, a few inevitable opportunists, and some misguided Communists who earnestly believed that Germany was a sincere friend of the Soviet Union. Politically, the Germans found an almost complete vacuum. The structure of the Metaxas regime had totally disintegrated. The leaders of the old parties, forced out of touch with the public for more than four years, had been reduced to politically impotent individuals who spent most of their time in aimless discussions with their friends. The Communist party organization was in disarray.

Most citizens in the summer of 1941 were primarily concerned with merely surviving under the deadly efficiency of Axis occupation. With food and other supplies rapidly running out and with no prospect for regular imports in the future, all the customary patterns of life began to change radically. The traditionally downtrodden peasant found himself in a rather enviable position with his ready access to food and fuel, while the people in the towns stood in line for a piece of bread or a bowl of soup. The most naively optimistic predicted a rapid return of the Allies, especially after Hitler's invasion of Russia on June 22.

The fateful launching of Operation Barbarossa freed the Greek Communists of their brief camaraderie with the Germans. In the three weeks before the German attack on Russia, more than a thousand Communist cadres in prison or in exile had either escaped in the confusion or were freed by the Germans. On July 1 some of the most capable of them met to form a new central committee and chart a new course of action. They called on the party faithful to abandon the "police agents and the other reactionary elements" of the old party organization and to work for a "reconstruction of the Greek Communist party." The basic duty of the Greek Communists, they said, was "to organize for the defense of the Soviet Union and for the overthrow of the Fascist yoke." The central committee also urged that while Communists must focus on the everyday problems of the people and at the same time organize "armed resistance against the conquerors," they must be sure to "explain to the people that only a people's government of workers and peasants can for ever free the country from foreign dependence and exploitation." With the social, economic, and political foundations of the nation crumbling under the crushing weight of defeat and occupation, the Communist party was emerging as a commanding force.

The king and the Tsouderos government were already too far away to provide direction and leadership to the nation. While still in Crete, they had asked British permission to transfer the seat of government to Cyprus, where the island's Greek population would keep the ties alive. The British refused, fearful that this might raise hopes that they were preparing to give up colonial rule on the island and let it become part of Greece. The government went to Egypt instead, and a month later it moved to South Africa. Then, after a long journey by sea, they reached Britain late in September. In London, King George was received with great honor as a faithful and noble ally. From this point on, political developments occurring in the name of the Greek people would move in a fragmented, disconnected fashion, with unrelated protagonists having varied, conflicting objectives. In London, the Tsouderos government saw as its major task the securing of Greek territorial claims in northern Epirus and the Dodecanese, and the adjustment of the frontier with Bulgaria. In occupied Greece, Communist leadership was preparing for an armed struggle against the Axis forces, and the politicians were training their arrows against King George, whom they blamed for the Metaxas dictatorship.

With the Tsouderos government far away in London, with the king's position as the national symbol seriously weakened, with the old political leaders lacking the experience or zeal for armed resistance, the initiative passed largely to the Communists. In September 1941 a meeting of the KKE's central committee decided on the formation of a National Liberation Front (EAM), a broad resistance organization to undertake the struggle. Realizing that if they used a strictly Communist line their chances of expanding the EAM's mass basis would be uncertain, they made patriotism and love of liberty the rallying cry. Still, the EAM's message included subtle references to social changes that were designed to remove economic disparities and create a "more just and equitable society" after the war. The EAM found many followers. Nazi occupation and the breakdown of the economy had seriously weakened the prewar middle class. To survive, people had to sell for a pittance their prized possessions, even their homes. Destitution, like a gigantic bulldozer, had leveled the social distinctions of the past.

Early in the spring of 1942 the first guerrilla bands of the Greek People's Army (ELAS), which had been organized by the EAM, made their appearance in the mountains of Central Greece. Before long, another resistance organization, the Greek Democratic Army (EDES) took the field in Epirus. The EDES, which was ostensibly connected with Plastiras, was actually organized by Napoleon Zervas, a republican officer. Of the two organizations, the ELAS was the strongest, with bands in most parts of the mainland.

Relying mostly on their own resources, the guerrillas engaged in small-scale, hit-and-run attacks on isolated enemy soldiers, gaining weapons, supplies, and experience in the process. Before the end of 1942 the British authorities in the Middle East began to take the resistance bands more seriously. Several emissaries were sent to make contact with them and, if possible, provide expertise and direction. One of these efforts had a tragic end. Major Tsigantes, a well-known officer of republican fame, entered Greece secretly. A daring but somewhat careless man, he failed to cover his presence properly. In the end his hideout in Athens was betrayed by some anonymous informer and in a desperate gunfight with Italian carabinieri he was killed.

At about the same time, on September 29, a commando unit under Brigadier General Myers parachuted into Central Greece. Their mission was to sabotage the railway line between Athens and Salonika and disrupt the supply of Rommel's Afrika Korps, which was then pressing hard in the direction of Egypt. Myers hoped to enlist the aid of the local guerrilla units to overcome the troops guarding the selected targets. At first, Aris Veloukhiotis, the leader of the ELAS units in the area, failed to respond but when he realized that units of the EDES might participate and thus share in the glory he changed his mind. Myers's saboteurs, with the aid of both ELAS and EDES guerrillas, blew up the vital bridge at Gorgopotamos on November 25.

The original plan was for the Myers group to proceed to the Ionian coast and then return to the Middle East by submarine. Instead, they were ordered to stay in Greece and establish a British Military Mission (BMM). This auxiliary military force was to concentrate on organizing, training, and supplying the guerrilla bands. The resistance movement was now part of the Allied war effort. Most of the costly mistakes of the next two years stemmed from this view that the guerrillas were purely a military element that could be used at will by the British in the Middle East. The Greek Communist leaders, showing greater perspicacity, saw the ELAS as a political force as well. In the December 1942 Pan-Helladic Conference of the KKE, George Siantos, secretary of the central committee, reminded his audience that the party's ultimate objective was "the struggle for socialism" and that "our present policy will open up the way for the realization of our ultimate strategic objectives." For the next crucial months, British policy would follow two contradictory paths. The military authorities would look to the resistance forces exclusively from the point of view of possible military deployment, without any concern for future political consequences. On the other hand, the foreign office, becoming increasingly aware of the oncoming political entanglements, would try to prevent the excessive strengthening of EAM/ELAS and to keep open the channels of communication with other organizations and political groups in Greece. Secret papers published recently by the British government show very clearly this duality in policy. The Tsouderos government tried to stay out of this conflict and in fact out of all political activities as much as possible, focusing primarily on the support of the Greek territorial claims. But this did not avert trouble, and finally in 1943 the brewing conflicts came out into the open.

Politics in the midst of war

By the beginning of 1943 the constant trickle of individuals coming from occupied Greece into the Middle East provided the human material necessary for organizing regular military forces in Egypt and Palestine. Many of those who escaped the Nazi occupation were prorepublic in their sympathies and some were Communists or fellow travelers. The ELAS controlled most of the escape routes and usually saw to it that only friends made it through safely. By the end of 1942 political sympathies and affiliations were beginning to divide the Greek armed forces. In February 1943 many loyalist officers submitted their resignations on the grounds that "the Greek Forces/Middle East have departed from their primary objective and are now engaged in politics . . ." The officers were arrested and then imprisoned behind barbed wire in Merj Uyun, while committees and soldiers circulated petitions calling for a new "democratic" government and the purging of the armed forces "of all Fascist elements."

To quell these demands, Tsouderos flew to Cairo in the middle of March. On the advice of the British he brought into his government several individuals with strong republican credentials. Byron Karapanayiotis became minister of the army, and a few months later Sophocles Venizelos joined the government as minister of the navy. The crisis subsided. At the same time, Tsouderos, who was now taking an active part on the political stage, established contact with the old politicians in Athens and asked for their aid in broadening the base of the government. He invited a three-member delegation to discuss the details. Sofoulis, dean of the old politicians, sent a reply stating that cooperation was impossible until the king agreed to submit to a "free vote after the country's liberation." Another communication in May set the condition that the king should not return to Greece "until the people had voted on the issue . . ."

The British government at that time favored the return of King George at the head of the Middle East armed forces. The election of a constituent assembly or a plebiscite could take place afterward. This view was not shared by the Americans, who disapproved "of any action which might give the impression that [the Allies] want to impose the King on the Greek people." These views of the State Department reflected the reports of the American agents in the Middle East, who saw the king as the principal cause of friction between the political leadership and the Tsouderos government. The Americans held to this view even later, when events began to reveal that the real danger to free institutions did not come from the king but from the growing strength of the Communist controlled EAM/ELAS. The British were already well-informed as to the extent of Communist influence on the Greek forces in the Middle

East. In a secret British report dated March 17, the identity of key
individuals and the role of paramilitary organizations in each of the
three services were spelled out in considerable detail. In any event,
to placate the republicans and ward off more trouble, the British
pressed the king to make a statement at least alluding to a future
vote on the question of the monarchy. On July 4 King George spoke
over the radio and affirmed that elections for a constituent assembly
"will be conducted within six months after the liberation . . ."
Although the question was now openly raised, the crucial point of
when the king would return remained unsettled. The next day new
disorders broke out in the Greek military units in Egypt. Sailors and
soldiers defied orders from their superiors and openly declared that
they would obey only the EAM. The mutiny was put down with
British aid and two soldiers were executed, but by now the
infiltration of the Greek Forces/Middle East was far advanced.

Pressures on the king

In Cairo the chief political conflict for the Greek government centered on the fate of the throne. In the Greek mountains
another, more sinister rivalry was gathering momentum. The ELAS
had opened a determined drive to eliminate all other resistance
organizations. In the early months of 1943 a guerrilla force under
Col. Stefanos Sarafis—another well-known republican personality—
was successfully dispersed. After a few weeks of captivity, Sarafis
agreed to join ELAS and become its military commander. Then in
May, ELAS bands dispersed the guerrilla force of the National and
Social Liberation (EKKA), led by Col. Dimitrios Psaros—another
republican officer. However, British pressure was brought to bear and
the ELAS soon afterward let Psaros take the field again. During the
same period of time, the ELAS also attacked the forces of Stelios
Houtas, but the effort was unsuccessful. After the failure of this
operation, thoughts of moving against Zervas' larger and stronger
force were shelved for the time being.

Brigadier General Myers was not overly concerned with the
political implications of the ELAS actions; he was annoyed, however, with the damage the quarrels among resistance groups was
doing to Allied military plans. Following instructions from Cairo,
the BMM (British Military Mission) called on all guerrilla groups to

respect each other's territory and obey the orders of the general headquarters for Allied Forces/Middle East. The Communist leaders ignored these demands. They hoped that with the Allied advances in North Africa, Greece would soon be liberated and that if EAM/ELAS were to seize power at the moment of German withdrawal, it should enjoy near monopoly. But the summer dragged on with no signs of either a German withdrawal or an Allied invasion. Still needful of British supplies, the Communist leaders decided to adopt a more moderate line. Besides, the dissolution of the Comintern in May seemed to indicate that Stalin also wanted to strengthen his ties with his Western allies by eliminating this obsolete but abrasive relic from the earlier revolutionary days. After what has been described by the deputy chief of the BMM at the time as considerable "tacit blackmail and counter-blackmail," the Communist leaders agreed to the "National Bands Agreement," which in June set up a joint general headquarters for the ELAS, EDES, and EKKA.

For a moment it appeared that this agreement, together with the decisive suppression of the July mutiny of soldiers and sailors in Egypt, would restore unity. Events would soon crush such hopes. The politicians in Greece renewed their demands for a clearcut statement from the king that he would not return until a plebiscite decided on the fate of his throne. This demand was soon reinforced by the arrival in Cairo of six representatives from the guerrilla organizations. Instead of discussing military questions as originally planned, the visitors—with the three Communist members taking the lead—plunged into a fierce drive to force a declaration that the king would stay out until a plebiscite decided the issue. A week later, several cabinet members also agreed that for the sake of national unity the king should make such a statement. In the face of these concerted pressures, King George turned for advice to Churchill and Roosevelt, who were then conferring in Quebec. Both answered that the king should return to Greece as soon as the country was free of enemy troops, and then submit the constitutional question to the people. Roosevelt in his reply appeared to shift away from the previously expressed views of the state department, which opposed the king's return before a plebiscite. Apparently this was one of those occasions when Roosevelt acted on his own, probably having been influenced by Churchill. The British prime minister went even further and ordered the British authorities in Cairo to "refrain from

(left) Athens after the December, 1944, uprising. Author's archives

(below) Communist weapons captured by the Greek army during the guerrilla campaign, 1949; King Paul is in the foreground. Author's archives

encouraging those elements [EAM and republican leaders] to put forward political claims at this time . . ." Brigadier General Myers, who was thought to be too sympathetic to the EAM/ELAS, was replaced by Col. C. M. Woodhouse, who had served as his deputy since November 1942.

Civil war in the mountains

When Italy surrendered to the Allies on September 8, 1943, most of Greece was under Italian administration. The Germans held under their direct control only the island of Crete and a few other strategic points. The Bulgarians occupied Western Thrace. Most Italian officers and soldiers in Greece surrendered to the nearest guerrilla bands, which acted as representatives of the Allies. The ELAS, which operated in most of the areas where Italian units were located, took over large quantities of materiel. Prior to the Italian surrender, the ELAS had relied primarily on British assistance for their activities. But now they acquired more weapons and supplies than the British would ever have furnished, even under the most favorable circumstances. Thus the BMM and the Cairo authorities lost their major trump card in dealing with the ELAS. The consequences were soon to follow.

In the fall of 1943 the prospects of an early liberation seemed to brighten up. North Africa had been cleared of Axis troops; Sicily had been successfully taken over by the Allies; King Boris of Bulgaria had died mysteriously; and on the Russian front the Red Army was advancing steadily toward the borders of Rumania. Closer to home, Greek and Allied troops had landed on two islands of the Dodecanese and on the island of Samos, where, as Ambassador Leeper wrote in a secret report to his government, "to the surprise of certain British military authorities which had been misled by the vocal opposition to the government," the temporary administration of the island immediately recognized the authority of the Tsouderos government and issued decrees under the label "kingdom of Greece." On September 29 Cairo ordered the guerrilla bands in Greece to prepare for major sabotage operations against six major airfields. To top it all, the Germans began to move their units in several directions as though they were preparing to withdraw.

Those in the Communist leadership who favored drastic action were given free hand by the moderates. Less than three months after signing the National Bands Agreement, the ELAS launched a major drive to eliminate the EDES and other guerrilla bands and strengthen its power position in anticipation of the critical moment of the country's liberation. In the process, some of the smaller groups were driven to a position where they had either to disband, join ELAS, or quit the mountains and join the Security Battalions. The latter were being formed by the puppet government of Ioannis Rallis in the larger towns as a defense against a Communist takeover. Many officers and ordinary citizens had enlisted in those German-sponsored units during the last year of occupation, at a time when the defeat of Germany was already in sight. This apparent paradox had its explanation. By the end of 1943 the key issue in occupied Greece was not the fate of the monarchy or the merits of Nazism but the growing power of the Communist party and its EAM/ELAS. George Papandreou, in a hard-hitting letter to the Communist leadership, openly accused the EAM/ELAS of "being guilty of unleashing civil war . . . its ultimate objective being to destroy every opponent and thus assure its own total and exclusive dominance."

For several weeks, the Greek countryside was engulfed in the flames of civil war. In November the war council in Britain reviewed the situation and agreed to suspend all assistance to the EAM/ELAS. The Americans, and even the Russians, spoke for the need to form a common front against the enemy. But the end to the internecine fight came not so much in response to such advice as to the changing prospects of an early liberation. The KKE had revealed its true intentions too soon. The Germans were not preparing to evacuate Greece; on the contrary, taking advantage of the civil war, they had started a campaign of their own to eliminate both the ELAS and the EDES. In the clashes that followed, it seemed doubtful that any of the guerrilla organizations would survive. In late February the Plaka Agreement ended the fighting between the ELAS and the EDES.

During this terrible struggle the life of the ordinary people had become even more miserable. Many villages were put to the torch by the Germans, countless people were killed in the crossfire of civil war and German oppression, and the fields lay untilled. In January 1944 Themistocles Sofoulis, gave a vivid and accurate description in a letter to Tsouderos.

Approximately one thousand villages and small towns have been burned down so far. Not only have we lost last year's harvest, but new cultivation has become impossible. More than a million and a half are homeless, wandering about, hungry and in rags, condemned to die. Despair and anguish hold in their grip the soul of our people. A loaf of bread sells today for 140,000 drachmas and prices climb daily by the tens of thousands. No longer is it a rhetorical phrase to say that the existence of our nation is at stake. If this situation is allowed to continue, only the blackmarketeers and the guerrillas, who do not share with the people these conditions of famine, will survive. . . . Only if the [Allies] give a severe warning and a threat that they will cease any contact with the EAM may they bring about a compromise [on the part of the Communists], but even then no one can guarantee that it will last, since the EAM's basic aim is to monopolize the resistance and become the only force to impose its own objectives.

In the cities and towns the impact of the EAM was less evident, but the galloping inflation fed by the indiscriminate printing of money had completely shattered any respect for the monetary system and for orderly trade patterns. Disaffection with the socioeconomic system would have turned many to the EAM if it were not for the realization that an EAM/ELAS takeover meant a Communist regime with its suppression of individual freedom. These were the conditions in Greece as the last year of foreign occupation began.

Mutiny in the Middle East

While the fate of the throne remained the visible part of the controversy, concern was inexorably shifting to the more serious danger of a Communist takeover at the moment of liberation. At this critical stage Gen. Alexandros Papagos broke his long silence and entered the arena. Using his prestige as the erstwhile commander in chief of the Albanian campaign, he made a serious effort to form a force that would be capable of maintaining order during the critical period between the withdrawal of the enemy and the arrival of Allied troops. Papagos was soon arrested by the occupation authorities and his plan collapsed.

For the first three years of enemy occupation, the KKE had used the EAM very successfully as a device to gain broad public support.

In the spring of 1944, however, the designs of the Communists had been revealed and the party was facing Allied ostracism and public opposition. Should the Tsouderos government return with the Greek forces and Allied support, the EAM/ELAS would either have to cooperate or fight against the legitimate authorities. To strengthen its position, the KKE leadership moved on two fronts. In Greece they managed to form a shadow government with the cooperation of some respected personalities from other parties; in the Middle East they instigated a serious revolt within the Greek military forces. On March 26 a broadcast from the Greek mountains announced that a Political Committee of National Liberation (PEEA) had been established with several republican personalities in its ranks. It appears that many of these individuals—with Professor Alexandros Svolos, a respected authority on constitutional law, as a major advocate—argued that the EAM/ELAS should not be left under the exclusive influence of the Communists. They argued that the presence of patriotic liberals and social democrats would have a restraining effect. The Communists skillfully played upon these expectations, knowing full well that power was to remain in their hands. Again they were hopeful that the liberation was fast approaching. The puppet regimes in the Balkans were tottering; the Red Army had already reached the Rumanian borders; in Bulgaria the Russophiles were becoming increasingly bold; and with the loss of North Africa, Germany had no use for Greece. Besides, the forces kept in the Balkans to maintain Nazi control were sorely needed along the hard-pressed eastern front. April seemed a likely time for a German withdrawal.

A confidential message from Cairo to the BMM in February had indicated that only a small Allied force would land in Greece to aid the Greek military forces coming from the Middle East. While the prospect of a small Allied force was welcome news to the Communist leadership, the idea of having to cope with the Greek military forces was not. True, these forces had many EAM sympathizers in their ranks, but soldiers were known to have obeyed their commanders even when the orders given were not entirely in keeping with their political beliefs. Rather than have to face them, a breakup of those units appeared as a safer alternative. Four days after the appearance of the PEEA, a group of soldiers' committees emerged in various units and took over actual command, declaring their allegiance to the PEEA. The rebellion spread like a raging forest fire throughout the Greek forces in the Middle East. Tsouderos had to resign; he was replaced by Venizelos, but the rebellion continued. Finally, on April 22, Churchill ordered the British commander in the Middle East "to fire against the rebel camp," if necessary. Faced with superior forces, the rebels surrendered. The KKE's Zachariades, speaking in 1945 on the breakup of these forces, implied that the mutiny had been deliberately provoked by the British to give them a pretext for eliminating those forces that were influenced by the EAM. He offered no evidence to support this allegation, which has been contradicted by secret papers made public recently by the British. These indicate that the British made every effort to avert rather than encourage the rebellion. That the demise of these forces did not actually serve the Communist aims in the end is true, but only because the country's liberation did not come in the spring of 1944 as they had expected.

The Lebanon Agreement

The British, who directed Greek affairs in those days, saw that a fresh start was needed. In the Middle East the Greek government no longer had any military forces; in Greece only Zervas' EDES remained as a serious rival to the ELAS. Psaros' EKKA had been eliminated in April following an ELAS attack; Psaros himself had been murdered. For all practical purposes, at the time of the German withdrawal the KKE and its EAM/ELAS faced no effective obstacle to a takeover. To block such an eventuality the British took two major steps. First, on the military side, they started the reconstruction of a Greek military force staffed with carefully selected officers. Second, on the political side, they initiated a bold diplomatic effort designed to bring the EAM/ELAS under control in the name of national unity. To a large extent, the plan followed the views of George Papandreou, who came to Egypt on April 15 from occupied Greece. In a talk with the British ambassador to the Greek government in Cairo he summed up his views epigrammatically: "one nation, one government, one army." He advised that a broad conference be convened soon, with delegates from all parties and resistance organizations, to set the foundations for a so-called Government of National Unity. Papandreou impressed Ambassador Leeper as a man "who knows what he wants and he does not hesitate to state it." With British backing, Papandreou replaced Venizelos as prime minister. On May 17 twenty-five individuals, representing seventeen political parties and resistance organizations, met in a broad conference in Lebanon. Under Papandreou's skillful diplomacy the conference reached a broad agreement within three days. The most important points provided for a Government of National Unity; the reorganization of the Greek armed forces in the Middle East; the unification of all guerrilla forces under the command of the Government of National Unity; the conditions of freedom and order after the liberation in order to permit the people to choose their own political and social institutions; an immediate end to terrorist activities; and the supply of food and medicine to Greece as soon as possible.

The Communist leadership in Greece received the news with mixed feelings. Some leaders argued that the agreement opened up the way for the KKE to infiltrate the new government. They explained that the Communists would necessarily have the only real levers of power because the government had no military forces while the ELAS in Greece was stronger than ever. Others, including some of the most powerful figures in the Communist leadership, expressed serious misgivings because, they suggested, the Government of National Unity would not be as powerless as anticipated. Gen. Constantine Ventiris, a tough professional soldier, had already been placed in command of the Greek general staff in Cairo and was busy organizing a new force. Besides, they argued, the Greek government could always "draw on the might of the British empire." On instructions from the guerrilla organizations in the mountains, the representatives of the PEEA, the EAM, and the KKE refused to accept the ministerial posts reserved for them in the new Government of National Unity, which was formed officially on May 24 with Papandreou as prime minister. A few days later, some of those representatives left Cairo for occupied Greece.

The British knew that they could spare only a limited force to support Papandreou's government should the Communists decide to repudiate the Lebanon Agreement. Convinced as they were that the KKE was an instrument of the Soviet Union, they sought to strike an understanding with Moscow. Already in April the British had discussed with the Russians the idea of placing Rumania under Soviet control and Greece under British control. In late May the American secretary of state, Cordell Hull, expressed serious reservations about what he considered a "division of Europe into spheres of influence." However, after a series of communications between Churchill and Roosevelt, the American president bypassed the state department and gave his sanction to the proposed agreement "on a three-month trial basis." The understanding did not take its final form until October, when Churchill met with Stalin in Moscow, but it had progressed sufficiently by mid-summer to have an impact on the attitudes of the KKE.

The Communist leaders continued to procrastinate about the Government of National Unity until July 25, when a Soviet military mission under Col. Gregory Popov arrived unexpectedly at the ELAS headquarters in the mountains. On August 2 the leaders of the PEEA and the EAM/ELAS retracted their previous objections and asked only that Papandreou be removed from the premiership. This demand was rejected by the other members of the cabinet. Without pressing the point further, six representatives of the PEEA-EAM-KKE camp joined the Government of National Unity on September 2. The danger of a Communist takeover was not completely eliminated, however. As Bartzotas, the secretary of the Athens Communist organization (KOA), revealed in 1952, "the KOA dealt, in early August, with the practical aspects of seizing power. We transferred all the party cadres to the ELAS, and the KOA decided on armed insurrection in two meetings at the beginning of September." Intelligence reports from occupied Greece indicating that the Communists were still planning to seize power by force were obviously valid.

To frustrate such designs and in keeping with one of the provisions of the Lebanon Agreement, Papandreou, with British backing, invited the leaders of the EDES and the ELAS to meet with government representatives and British military authorities to discuss steps for the unfication of all guerrilla forces. The meeting took place in Caserta, Italy, where it was agreed that all guerrilla forces would be placed under the command of Lt. Gen. R. M. Scobie, the British commander of the Allied troops that were to land in Greece. Incidentally, the British war council had decided in August to send a force of ten thousand men, but they planned to say nothing to the Russians about the size of the expeditionary force. In the end, a much smaller force accompanied the Government of National Unity when it came to Greece.

The Communist uprising

On October 18 the Government of National Unity arrived in Athens in the midst of great jubilation. The nightmare of Nazi occupation was over. Ten days earlier the Germans had begun to evacuate Greece. By October 12 Athens was free. The ELAS forces, in keeping with Moscow's instructions, made no attempt to seize power. In the words of Communist leader Bartzotas, "the First Army Corps of the ELAS alone (that is, the 20,000 elasites of Athens and Piraeus) . . . could have easily seized power . . . [but] instead of going ahead, instead of organizing the struggle for power, instead of seizing power, we capitulated and kept order!"

For the next two months Papandreou struggled with two enormous problems: first, relief for the destitute population and second, an end to the legacies of war and occupation, above all the presence of armed guerrillas with partisan loyalties. The royal issue had been somewhat muted because the king had not come to Greece at the time of liberation.

After long and painstaking discussions in the cabinet, an agreement was reached to form a national army composed initially of two brigades of equal strength, one with men from the Middle East forces and a unit of the EDES, and the other with men from the ELAS. Before this decision could be carried out, the KKE leadership reneged and opted instead for a forcible takeover. No doubt deep-seated suspicions on both sides played a part in escalating the conflict. In retrospect, it seems clear that the confrontation was inevitable. The pro-Communist forces in the country would have turned Greece into the type of "people's democracy" that was later imposed on eastern Europe. The British, determined to keep Greece on their side, were not going to sit by idly and let this happen. The Greek middle class and a considerable part of the peasantry hoped that the British would indeed step in at the crucial moment.

The Communists decided to move when they realized that the British forces in Greece were much weaker than expected. They were probably encouraged in this by Tito, who had his own grandiose plans for the Balkans. Very likely they did not ask for Soviet advice or permission. By December 1 ELAS units ordered by George Siantos of the KKE were already on the march, converging on Athens. Then, on December 3, a Communist-organized demonstration designed to show the EAM's popular strength ended with several persons dead or wounded under circumstances that still remain obscure. Any pretense of national unity was shattered. The so-called December revolution was on. Within a few days the ELAS forces placed most parts of the capital under their control; the Papandreou government appeared doomed. But the Communist high command made several tactical mistakes. Instead of storming the capital, they wasted precious time attacking isolated police stations on the periphery, executing civilians, taking hostages, and diverting considerable forces in an effort to eliminate the EDES in remote Epirus.

The British reacted vigorously and within two weeks a strong force reached the Greek capital and forced its way through the ELAS strongholds. Churchill, determined to keep Greece out of Communist control, came to Athens with Anthony Eden at Christmas and presided over a broad conference. At the meeting the representatives of the EAM/ELAS and the KKE posed impossible conditions and no agreement was reached.

In an effort to broaden the government's popular base, the British pressed the king, who was still in London, to appoint Archbishop Damaskinos as regent and to replace Papandreou with Nikolaos Plastiras, the aging liberal. The British had brought the old man to Athens from his home in France in the hope that his republican reputation would attract those who sympathized with the EAM out of antiroyalist convictions. By the time Plastiras took the oath of office on January 3, 1945, the battle had been decided in favor of the British. A week later, a truce was signed to take effect one minute after midnight on January 15.

With the Yalta Conference approaching, the British were understandably anxious to have a final settlement in Greece. This may explain the moderation shown by their spokesmen in the talks that took place at Varkiza, near Athens, late in January. The agreement that was signed on February 12 fully restored the Communist party and the EAM as legitimate political organizations, but ordered the disarming of the ELAS and all other guerrilla forces.

The "Third Round"

The December uprising and the atrocities committed by the Communists during those thirty-three days of fighting caused a dramatic shift in public attitudes. In April the KKE's former partners in the EAM and the PEEA broke away. The king, who previously seemed to have few supporters, emerged as a symbol of national resistance to communism. With the return of peace, the more traditional values of the peasantry and of the recovering middle class reinforced this anti-Communist wave.

The British, who were obviously the dominant factor in Greek politics, did not immediately grasp the extent of the change. In the last months of 1944 even Churchill had come to the conclusion that the pro-Western republican politicians were just as reliable an ally as King George. For several months throughout 1945 they supported a series of cabinets controlled by republican politicians in the hope that stability and tranquil conditions could be restored in the country by virtue of the more moderate attitude of these leaders toward the Communists and their more progressive social and economic views. These cabinets, however, failed to stem the anti-Communist tide or to reverse the growing feeling in favor of the king's return. Their inability to cope with the grave problems of inflation further discredited the idea of a republic while strengthening the Right, with its anti-Communist, royalist credo. The growing anticommunism was evident in other ways as well; for example, many ELAS men accused of common crimes were hunted down not only by security agencies but also by self-appointed vigilantes. The amnesty issued under the Varkiza Agreement had covered only the political leadership, not the rank-and-file who had actually committed the crimes. The heroes of yesterday were now the villains, and a new round of persecution began.

The Communist party was now under the direction of its secretary general, Nikos Zakhariades, who had been brought back to Greece from a concentration camp in Dachau in May by the British. He was as militant as ever. Aware that another uprising in Athens was impossible under the circumstances, he turned his attention to the possibility of a guerrilla operation assisted by Greece's northern neighbors. Those in the party who, like Siantos, favored a more moderate policy soon found themselves isolated. In spite of continuing economic hardships, spiraling prices, and limited opportunities for employment, the KKE found it impossible to regain its former political prominence. Conservatives, moderates, and even liberals kept the Communists politically at arm's length. At the same time, the state structure was being restored, however slowly.

By the end of the year, the Greek army had been increased to seventy-five thousand men. Political parties had reappeared, the villages were returning to normal after years of suffering, and life in the towns was resuming its customary rhythm. Most public services were restored, business enterprises were back in operation, and the small pleasures of daily life again were within reach. The election of a Vouli was to take place in March 1946, and a plebiscite on the king's return was to follow within six months. The bands of anti-Communist vigilantes were gradually being dispersed.

These hopeful signs of recovery failed to impress the Communist party. The Soviet Union, already at work in Eastern Europe establishing a zone of Communist-controlled states that would serve as a barrier against a resurgence of German militarism, seized upon the complaints of the Greek Communists that they were being persecuted by "monarcho-fascist thugs." In January the Soviet Union brought charges against the British before the security council of the United Nations. The Soviet government, to be sure, did not favor an armed operation in Greece; all they wanted was to balance Western accusations concerning Soviet activities in Eastern Europe with their own charges with regard to Greece. The Greek Communists, however, with Tito's encouragement, decided to try to seize power by force.

This decision was soon translated into action. On the eve of the first postwar election, on March 31, 1946, a Communist-led guerrilla band attached Litokhoron, a village in Thessalia. A few days earlier, against Soviet advice, the Greek Communist party and the EAM had decided to abstain from the election and called on their followers to boycott the voting. This was done even though the presence of international observers assured that the election would be conducted fairly. Scores of parties contested for the Vouli's 354 seats, under a version of proportional representation. The proroyalist parties won 206 seats. This result was especially noteworthy because the government at the time was headed by veteran republican Themistocles Sofoulis, who had been called to the premiership after a series of cabinet changes. The EAM was gravely disappointed because according to the Allied Mission for Observing the Greek Elections (AMFOGE), less than 10 percent of the electorate had responded to the call to boycott the election.

The election results confirmed the shift in favor of the king's return and foreshadowed the outcome of the plebiscite. On September 1, 70 percent cast their ballots in favor of the monarchy. The prorepublic leaders immediately accepted the verdict and the thorny issue was at last put to rest.

While the political system was being gradually reconstructed, economic conditions remained difficult, with rising prices, food and clothing shortages, and extensive unemployment. Many reasons could have been found for public discontent. Still, anti-Communism was equated with patriotism, and unless an individual was either deeply committed to Communist ideology or forced by circumstances to join the bands, he was not likely to take to the mountains. In this regard, the KKE's political designs were unwittingly assisted by the persecution of many ELAS men accused of criminal acts during the occupation and the December uprising. Moreover, many ELAS partisans and EAM followers, who found employment opportunities closed to them, were pushed by desperation to join the pro-Communist forces.

Throughout the summer of 1946, small guerrilla bands conducted hit-and-run attacks against gendarmerie stations in the countryside. Clean-up operations by government forces trying to destroy the bands had little effect. The guerrillas avoided clashes with the regular troops and easily slipped through army lines to the safety of their mountain hideouts. Terrified villagers refused to give information to the army since those few individuals who unwisely did so were soon found with their throats cut. Without enough forces to carry out sustained operations, the army had to resort to a strategy of static defense, which prevented one army unit from going to the assistance of another facing attack. Most of the guerrilla action was concentrated in the central and northern parts of the country, leaving many areas still unaffected.

In October the Communists instructed Markos Vafiades, a veteran party member from Macedonia, to go to the mountains and take over as the commander in chief of the Democratic Army of Greece (DSE), as the bands were now calling themselves. At first, the signs appeared to be favorable for the new Communist offensive. Yugoslavia was providing material assistance and had even established a training camp for Greek guerrillas at Boulkes; thousands of former ELAS men who had escaped to Greece's northern neighbors after the December uprising were available to join the bands; in the United Nations the Soviet Union was making a not entirely unsuccessful effort to portray the situation in Greece as the result of "fascist-like" persecution of innocent citizens by an oppressive regime. Probably the most encouraging sign of all for the Communists was that by the end of 1946 Britain, in the face of serious economic difficulties, was considering withdrawal from Greece. In February 1947 the British informed Washington that they could no longer carry the burden. Secretary of State Dean Acheson convinced President Truman that the United States should take over in order to prevent a Soviet advance to the Mediterranean. On March 12 Truman declared in a message to Congress: "The very existence of the Greek State is today threatened by the terrorist activities of several thousand armed men, led by Communists, who defy the Government's authority . . . Greece must have assistance if it is to become a self-supporting and self-respecting democracy. . . . The United States must supply that assistance." Although not immediately obvious, Truman's decision was a turning point not only for Greece but also for America's international role in the postwar period.

The effects of the Truman Doctrine, as the president's policy became known, were wide-ranging. During 1947 and 1948 the Greek army received extensive material assistance and developed the skills needed to improve its training and understanding of the peculiarities of guerrilla warfare. In time these advances made it possible for the army to abandon the ineffectual tactics of static defense. In the United Nations, Greece, with American encouragement and assistance, mounted a diplomatic counteroffensive and accused her northern neighbors of flagrant interference in the internal affairs of the country. A United Nations committee of inquiry reported in May 1947 that Albania, Yugoslavia, and Bulgaria had been actively supporting the Communist guerrillas in Greece.

In February 1948 Stalin, who was apparently worried by the American presence in Greece, summoned representatives of the Yugoslav leadership and insisted that they stop their support of the DSE. When they failed to show signs of unquestioning obedience, Stalin took more drastic steps. Between March and June 1948 he mounted a drive to have Tito removed from the leadership of Yugoslav communism. Tito, himself a veteran of Communist tactics, successfully beat Stalin at his own game. On June 28 the secret rivalry between Stalin and Tito came out into the open to the utter astonishment of most people who had long been accustomed to believing in the monolithic character of Communist unity under Soviet direction.

The Stalin-Tito rift added to the woes of the DSE. With the overwhelming majority of the Greek people opposing the Communist campaign, few individuals went to the mountains to reinforce the bands. At the same time, no army personnel or military units crossed over to the DSE lines. Zakhariades, who had joined Markos in the mountains late in 1947, insisted that the DSE should abandon its hit-and-run tactics and adopt a more conventional form of warfare. Zakhariades believed that this change would enable them to capture and hold some territory. He wanted to gain soon at least one town that would be suitable as the administrative seat of the "Temporary Democratic Government (PDK)," which Markos, on Zakhariades' instigation, had established in late December 1947. Markos objected to this change in strategy and tactics because he realized that by following a conventional form of warfare, the DSE was bound to lose the advantages of mobility and surprise, which are the essential features of the guerrilla type of fighting. The fact of the matter is that neither the conventional nor the guerrilla strategy could have served the DSE at this stage. Hit-and-run tactics would have made sense only if time were on the side of the DSE. But time was favoring the Greek army which, with growing strength and firepower, was able by the spring of 1948 to pass from the ineffective tactics of search-and-destroy to a well-planned strategy of cease-and-hold.

With the controversy over the monarchy no longer dividing the country's leadership, opposition to the DSE was virtually universal among the nation's politicians. Since September 1947 a coalition government led by Sofoulis and including representatives from all major parties had given dramatic proof of the nation's unity against the Communist offensive. Then, in January 1949, General Papagos was recalled to active duty, appointed commander in chief, and given very broad powers. By that time most of the Peloponnisos and Central Greece had been cleared of Communist bands. Local security was entrusted to village militia under regular officers, thus freeing additional forces for the final push against the remaining Communist strongholds in the north.

On the Communist side, Zakhariades ousted Markos in January 1949 and made a desperate attempt to shift to conventional warfare in the vain hope of being able to capture and retain inhabited territories. A series of major attacks on several towns in western Macedonia proved disastrous for the DSE. In conventional warfare the advantage was on the side of the regular army, which had much greater firepower.

In late July Communist guerrillas who had crossed into Yugoslavia to escape the pursuit of army units were disarmed and placed in custody. This was a major psychological blow for the Communists. Tito, who had been their principal mentor all these years, now turned against them. Although the Yugoslav decision to close the border had little effect militarily, it totally shattered the morale of the guerrillas. Then, on August 1, the Greek army launched its Operation Torch against the DSE's last strongholds along the Albanian border, in Grammos and Vitsi. With a heavy concentration of artillery, air power, and armor, the Greek army smashed through the Communist positions. First they hit with a deceptive maneuver in the direction of Grammos, and then they turned against the fortifications of the Vitsi mountain complex. With swift and deep penetrations, pincer movements, and frontal attacks, the Communist positions were blasted open. Of six guerrilla brigades, only one managed to escape toward Grammos. The remnants of the others sought refuge in Albania. Ten days later the Greek army opened its final drive against Grammos. After a few days of fierce fighting the Greek forces broke through the Communist positions and on August 30, the last Communist stronghold on Kamenik fell. The "Third Round," as the Communists had called their guerrilla campaign, was over. The losses in human life and material wealth were considerable. Thousands of villagers had been left homeless, while thousands of others had been living in refugee camps for months. A staggering need for rehabilitation and reconstruction lay ahead.

chapter 6
Reconstruction and Development

The advent of peace

Nine years of war had finally come to an end. The country was scarred. Over two thousand villages had been destroyed, half a million people had died of hunger, violence, and disease. Early efforts in 1945–46 to restore economic stability had foundered in a new upsurge of inflation. The drachma, which in December 1944 was set at a ratio of 150 drachmas to the dollar, had reached 15,000 drachmas to the dollar by 1949. Even this official rate of exchange did not represent the full extent of the decline of the drachma. In the black market a single dollar could command up to 25,000 drachmas. Farm production was severely hurt after so many years of almost interminable warfare. The resulting shortages, coupled with the dislocation of thousands of villagers and the reckless killing of draft and meat animals, forced the country to depend heavily on

222

supplies brought in by the United Nations relief agencies (UNRRA) and various Allied organizations. Industry, which was located at the time mostly in the Athens-Piraeus area, had not suffered from guerrilla attacks during the 1946–49 conflict, but the damaging effects of German occupation were still visible.

A cynical psychology, left from the days of occupation, undermined every effort to restore stability. People—from industrialists to housewives—put any surplus money they could set aside into gold sovereigns. Hardly anyone had savings on deposit in the banks. Kyriakos Varvaressos, a noted Greek economist, blamed the country's difficulties "not on the inadequacy of material means . . . but on the habits and the way of thinking acquired at the time of the occupation and retained in the postwar years . . . [These habits] combine greed with indifference for the public needs and fear and pessimism for the future of the country . . ." The assessment was accurate, but one might venture to say that after three decades of severe buffeting matters could have been even worse. The country had barely begun to recover from the Asia Minor disaster when it faced the effects of world economic depression. Then, after a short period of tranquility, the country went through the long nightmare of war, occupation, and civil strife. Now, at long last, a new era was about to begin.

In 1951 the Communist party, grudgingly admitting that the armed struggle was over, shifted to a policy of clandestine operations of espionage and sabotage. For the next three years groups of KKE agents slipped into Greece carrying explosives, wireless equipment, and weapons. They were discovered one after another, and several key Communists were arrested, tried, and sentenced to death. With anticommunism being a badge of national loyalty, the police authorities set up a pernicious system of classification, keeping files on almost everyone. To obtain something as simple and innocuous as a vendor's permit, a person first had to present a "certificate of social beliefs." Even the children could be tainted by a parent's past association with the EAM or the Communist party (outlawed since 1947). This fear of communism was to permeate national life for a generation—and it continues to play a key role even today. Concern with security dominated life in the villages. Many of those who had collaborated with the EAM/ELAS or the DSE had either to keep very quiet or leave the village and start life over again in the city. Most village adults were pressed into the units of local militia,

Traditional Life

Life in the villages retains old traditions; a woman at the loom. Copyright V. Papaioannou, Athens

(above) Tobacco, Greece's major export for decades. Courtesy, Greek Embassy, Press Office, Washington, D.C.

(below) Fishermen mending their nets. Courtesy, Greek Embassy, Press Office, Washington, D.C.

serving after hours on a rotation basis under regular officers. Their duties involved patrolling the vicinity or guarding at night the approaches to their village.

Yet, there were also hopeful signs. Most villagers who had been forced from their homes during the rebellion were now returning to their villages. Many, of course, found their cottages in ruins, but with government help reconstruction was soon underway; no such easy remedy could be found for the problem of the twenty-eight thousand children who were taken away into Eastern Europe by the Communists during the last months of the conflict. With the return of peace, travel to the countryside was no longer a hazardous adventure. In fact, many remote villages could now be reached for the first time by car over dirt roads opened up by the army for military purposes during the campaign.

In spite of all that had transpired in the previous decade, the villager's attachment to certain traditional values remained strong. Family ties continued to be vital and extensive; whatever other roles a man might play in his community, duty to his family always took precedence. Although the younger generation enjoyed more relaxed relationships between the sexes, marriages could still be arranged by the parents. To be sure, a dowry continued to be a matter of honor for the father of the bride and a practical necessity for the new couple, and insults to a husband's or a brother's honor could still be settled in blood. Religion, often inseparably mixed with superstition, remained a key aspect of rural life. With over 90 percent of the people being Greek Orthodox, the village priest was a central figure in the life of the community. He was typically a man of limited education who could not overpower the villagers with his earthy knowledge but rather evoked their respect with the mystique of his religious calling. This remains true even today. A sermon is still an unusual and extraordinary occurrence in a village church. Ritual is what dominates village life, with religious feasts being the principal communal events. Throughout the year these activities effectively break the monotony of daily routine.

At the same time, villagers who had been exposed to new ideas by contact with the EAM/ELAS or the DSE, or as soldiers in the army, or even as refugees in the towns, were no longer content with the kind of life they had known for generations. Imperceptibly, the traditional resistance of the villager to change had weakened; in time this would ease the government's efforts to consolidate scattered family plots into larger, more efficient units. This, in turn, would permit a shift to new crops or better methods of farming and the organization of cooperatives for canning or marketing farm products. In the following years, through support prices and other forms of assistance, the farmers gained a measure of financial security while their incomes rose. Better rewards stimulated production, and the gains were soon to be felt throughout the economy.

The most striking change appeared in the position of women, who traditionally were shackled to their position in society by a restrictive code of ethics and social conduct. Their new freedom from social taboos was more evident in the towns and cities, where an increasing number of women, especially younger ones, began to move into professional fields. With a measure of financial independence they became more assertive and self-confident. The change in public attitudes was reflected in the decision of the political leadership in 1951 to extend to women the right to vote in parliamentary elections.

With the return to normalcy, politics, which had maintained a rather low profile during the Communist rebellion, reemerged with renewed force. But, again, important changes could be detected. The controversy over the monarchy, which had divided the nation for almost four decades, was gone. King Paul—who had succeeded to the throne when his brother died on April 1, 1947—was a moderate and likable man. During the guerrilla war he and his wife, Queen Frederika, had shown courage and genuine concern, thereby winning the affection of the people. The throne now appeared to be securely anchored on a national consensus. Party politics no longer split the nation into hostile camps revolving mostly around personalities, economic policies, and minor disagreements over methods and objectives. As in years past, relations between politicians and voters—especially in the countryside—rested on kinship and personal ties nurtured by past favors or by expectations of future help. Still, there was an undercurrent of pressure for modernization of the political system and development of the economy.

These subtle pressures were already present during the election of 1950. As it often happens in politics, one personality came to personify the quest for change. General Papagos, who had been elevated to the rank of field marshal in recognition of his services to the nation, was a man of unassailable military prestige. Now many throughout the country were beginning to turn to him for leadership in the political arena as well. His lifelong devotion to the crown ought to have made the rise of his political star a most welcome sight for the royal couple. But, strange as it may seem, the opposite was true. King Paul did not want to alienate the liberal center by showing favor to Papagos. Queen Frederika, on her part, was more concerned with the warnings of palace officials that the strong-willed field marshal would brook no interference if he ever became prime minister. Her opposition to Papagos was shared—for different reasons—by most of the nation's political leaders, who dreaded the possibility of having to compete with this man. Only Spyros Markezinis, one of the most brilliant and ambitious politicians to emerge in the postwar years, was actively trying to convince the taciturn field marshal to enter politics. Papagos came very close to doing just that in January 1950 but he changed his mind when he saw that the coming election would again be held under a form of proportional representation. He was afraid that this system would very likely result in the fragmentation of voting support among several parties and force him to engage in the familiar gyrations of kaleidoscopic coalitions, thus dissipating his prestige and influence.

In the elections of March 5 candidates from ten different parties gained seats in the Vouli. The reappearance of Plastiras at the head of a new political party, the National Progressive Center Union (EPEK), was the only new element of note. The aging general was in favor of a policy of conciliation with the Left, but in the psychological climate of those days such a policy was bound to clash with the prevailing spirit of anticommunism.

For more than a year, one coalition cabinet followed another. These continuing changes at a time when the country needed a strong, stable government with the will and ability to tackle the immense problems of reconstruction and development, added momentum to the popular current supporting Papagos. Yet, the field marshal continued to serve as commander in chief of the armed forces and to remain outside the political arena. Suddenly on May 30, 1951, Papagos resigned. During the night a small group of officers who were zealously devoted to him erroneously concluded that their idol had been forced out by the government. In retaliation they seized a few state buildings and called on Papagos to take over as a military dictator. He came down to the headquarters of the rebellious officers and with a few stern words put an end to the affair.

King Paul and the new American ambassador, John Peurifoy,

agreed that the proportional system in the form used at the time was disastrous for the country. But this system was the only barrier against Papagos' participation. In the end, it was Plastiras who forced a change in the electoral system. Confident that his party was gaining ground, he refused to take part in another coalition government and pressed instead for an election with a reinforced version of proportional representation, designed to give more seats to parties gaining larger percentages of votes at the polls. Grudgingly the other leaders—with the exception of Papandreou, who continued to insist on the pure proportional system—shifted in favor of a change. On July 30 a new electoral law was enacted and a general election set for September 9. Although Papagos had assured the king that he had no intention of entering politics, he now issued a statement saying, "Cognizant of the gravity of the moment . . . and after weighing carefully my responsibilities to history, I have decided to participate in the electoral contest." He justified this aboutface by pointing to the need for a strong government.

The need was much too obvious. Reconstruction continued to move at a snails pace, while the international situation called for a clearcut foreign policy. The key problem in those days was Greece's participation in NATO. As long as the country was in the throes of a Communist rebellion, Britain and several other NATO members opposed admission for fear that they might be drawn into an unwanted conflict. Only the Americans openly favored the entry of Greece and Turkey into the alliance. British objections were finally removed when efforts to forge a Middle East Command linking Egypt with NATO failed and the Egyptians demanded instead the evacuation of the British forces from the Suez Canal. The assassination of pro-British King Abdullah in Jordan, the Anglo-Iranian dispute over the nationalization of the oil industry, and the Arab-Israeli dispute, finally convinced Britain that other steps should be taken to shore up the Western position in the eastern Mediterranean. On October 22, 1951, a protocol was signed for the admission of Greece and Turkey. The process was completed on February 18, 1952, when the two countries officially became members of NATO.

Six days after announcing his intention to enter politics, Papagos set up a new political party, the Greek Rally. In a different political system, a party created only a month before election day would have scant chance of making a respectable showing at the polls. But political parties in Greece have been traditionally of the "personalista" variety, that is, they are closely tied to the fortunes of one particular political figure. In spite of all that had passed, the parties still consisted of a narrow elite at the top and hardly any local organization reaching to the grass roots of the electorate. Local politicians with a personal following had no trouble shifting from one leading personality to another, forming new party ties and casting old ones to oblivion.

Within days the Greek Rally began to take shape as politicians from the other parties rushed to declare their allegiance to the new political organization. Papagos was actually attracting a broad spectrum of supporters. The middle class, recovering from the disastrous blows of the previous decade, wanted stability and a vigorous program of economic expansion. Reconstruction and stability were also the objectives of the peasants, who craved tranquility and a chance to till their land and harvest their crops in peace. Papagos promised the country a strong, stable government. The people who instinctively turned to Papagos, however, were also the people who were emotionally closer to the throne. As a result of the cool, almost unfriendly attitude of the palace toward Papagos, the Greek Rally gained only 114 seats out of 258 in the election of September 9. Plastiras' EPEK emerged as the second party with 74, followed by the Liberal party with 57. The new element was the rise of the United Democratic Left (EDA), a substitute for the outlawed Communist party. It won 10 seats. The Populists won 2 and Papandreou none.

When Papagos refused to form a coalition government with either Venizelos or Plastiras, the king turned to the leaders of the other two parties. Plastiras emerged as the new prime minister; the Plastiras-Venizelos coalition cabinet had a slim majority of only 2 votes. Plastiras favored a policy of reconciliation and moderation. The legacy of the guerrilla war weighed heavily on his mind. Whatever Plastiras' personal views, however, the security agencies went ahead with their efforts to uncover the KKE's operating agents. The clandestine activities of the Communists were largely ineffective and wasteful, but they kept the specter of a so-called Communist threat alive.

Because of the highly personalized character of Greek politics, illness and death have played a fateful role many times. In mid-November, only three weeks after he had become prime minister, Plastiras suffered a severe heart attack. Venizelos, as deputy premier, took over most of the responsibilities of leadership. The prime minister's illness made the king apprehensive for he knew that probably sooner rather than later he would have to face the prospect of another election. Papagos in the meantime was playing the role of the leader of the opposition with almost British propriety. Only on one occasion did he choose to show drastic disagreement. The political leaders had agreed in July to revise the constitution without actually going through the amendment procedure. When the Vouli decided in December to vote for the new draft, Papagos and the Greek Rally deputies left the chamber in a show of protest. Then, a resolution to approve the draft constitution was put to a vote, and of course it received overwhelming support. Ten days later, King Paul sent the document for publication and on January 1, 1952, Greece had a new constitution. Strictly speaking, it was hardly new; most of its provisions were identical with those of the 1911 constitution. In spite of his disagreement over the manner of its enactment, Papagos never spoke in public against the 1952 constitution.

For the next eight months, Plastiras lingered on, while Papagos patiently waited for his moment. A stroke in March ruled out any hope that Plastiras would soon recover. But since his resignation would revive the pressures for another election, he stayed on as prime minister although he was unable to perform any of his official duties. Finally, on November 16, 1952, an election was held under the plurality system. The Greek Rally received 49.6 percent of the total vote, a coalition of liberals won 36.6 percent, and the pro-Communist EDA got 10.5 percent. The remainder went to various independent candidates. Compared to the election of September 1951, the Greek Rally had increased its votes by 155,000 while the center-liberal coalition had lost 152,000. The EDA's support had remained unchanged. Under the winner-take-all plurality system, Papagos received 247 seats in the 300-seat Vouli. Markezinis, the real architect of the Greek Rally, could say with confidence the day after the results were in: "Our side will govern for twelve years." His prediction was to prove true, although he himself would soon be out of the picture.

Papagos moved in many directions with his characteristic thoroughness. With Greece already a NATO partner, he joined Turkey in an alliance with Yugoslavia. Less than five years had passed since Tito had supported the Communist insurgency in Greece, but his rift with Stalin had profoundly changed the international climate in the Balkans. Tito needed the cooperation of the West. Greece and Turkey, always concerned with Bulgarian intentions, responded to Tito's overtures, and an agreement of cooperation was signed by the three governments in Ankara in February 1953. Stalin's death a few days afterward, on March 5, did not immediately alter the picture.

With Markezinis as minister of coordination, Papagos turned his attention to the economic sector. American economic aid had become a major source of capital since 1948. It had helped the reconstruction and expansion of the country's network of roads, the repair of railway lines and bridges that had been destroyed in war, the improvement of port facilities, and the clearing up of the Corinth Canal, which had been blocked by the retreating Germans. American aid was also used to set the foundation for the country's electrification. Prior to 1950 very few villages had electricity and, with the exception of the major cities, almost everywhere else conditions remained rather primitive. By the time Papagos came to power, three hydroelectric plants and one thermoelectric plant were in the final stages of planning and some preliminary construction had already begun. In spite of these modest beginnings, the economy was suffering from basic structural defects and the consequences of the war years. The per capita income remained one of the lowest in Europe. Reliance on imports was high, and the export of agricultural commodities was subject to fluctuations in the world market. Deficits in the balance of trade were constantly increasing and confidence in the drachma was practically nil. Until 1952 American aid had helped to cover at least in part the trade deficits. But by the end of 1952 this vital source of economic support was being reduced in volume. Papagos and Markezinis moved to tackle the thorny economic problems.

On April 9, 1953, the government announced a drastic devaluation of the drachma. The official exchange rate at the time was $1 to 15,000 drachmas while dollars sold for 28,000 drachmas in the black market. Obviously the official rate was completely unrealistic. Instead of a minor readjustment, Markezinis changed the rate to 1:30,000, thereby outstripping even the black market. At first glance, this move appeared to be a dangerous gamble. Either the drastic devaluation would stimulate exports, tourism, and remittances from emigrants and shipping crews or it would lead to an even more dramatic erosion of public confidence in the drachma and throw the economy into a tailspin. The opposition made dire predictions, but

Markezinis was confident. On April 29 he left for Washington, carrying in his briefcase a four-year plan for economic development. Officials in the United States saw with obvious interest and satisfaction that a serious plan had been worked out by the Greek government. The basic lines of the plan had been initially drawn as early as 1950, but implementation called for a strong government. There were a number of reasons for this: first, a significant part of the plan had to be financed by private investment both domestic and foreign; second, a more efficient taxation system had to be devised; and third, a more realistic monetary and banking policy had to be followed. Markezinis was able to convince his foreign listeners that the Papagos government was able and willing to take whatever steps were needed.

Already by the summer of 1953 the ordinary citizen could feel in his own pocketbook the effects of economic stability and growing business activity. With his anticommunism beyond doubt, Papagos felt no qualms in opening up trade relations with the Eastern bloc. The government's popularity was on the rise while the liberal center received a serious blow in the death of Plastiras on July 26.

The Cypriot entanglement

The quest for an end to British colonial rule over Cyprus, which was never entirely silenced, was again emerging as a troublesome issue. The island had come under British control in 1878 but it remained nominally an Ottoman possession until 1915, when Turkey entered the war on the side of Germany and Britain formally annexed it. The Treaty of Lausanne in 1924 confirmed this annexation, and one year later Cyprus became a Crown Colony. Ever since the arrival of the British, the Greek majority comprising over 80 percent of the islanders raised the demand for enosis with Greece. The opportunity to bring about union was passed up by Greece in 1915, when the Zaimis government turned down a British offer to transfer Cyprus to Greece on the condition of her entering the war on the side of the Allies.

In the late 1940s, hopes that Britain, exhausted after the Second World War and with a Labour government in power, might be more willing to consider enosis, encouraged the Greek Cypriots to renew their pressure. Following tradition, the church played a leading role.

In 1950, a thirty-eight-year-old bishop was elected to the throne of the church of Cyprus as Makarios III. He had already gained prominence in January of that year by organizing a plebiscite in which over 90 percent of Greek Cypriots signed a declaration for enosis. The gesture appeared more symbolic than real at the time, but in fact it was the opening scene in a political drama that has yet to end. In 1951 Makarios met with George Grivas, a retired Greek army officer born in Cyprus, who proposed a campaign of violence to force the British out. Makarios was reluctant to approve such a scheme but he did not entirely discourage the diminutive, fiery colonel.

When Papagos came to power, the Cypriots felt that their cause had found a champion. He had apparently given Makarios some assurances that Greece would actively support the quest for enosis. In September 1953 Papagos took advantage of a private visit to Athens by British Foreign Minister Anthony Eden and raised the subject. He was rebuffed rudely. Still, public sentiment for enosis was rising and could not be ignored. In February 1954 Makarios arrived in Athens for a four-week visit. His idea was to bring the matter before the United Nations, generate world interest, and, by using moral pressure, force the British to free the island. Papagos reluctantly agreed to the Makarios plan but he felt that before undertaking such a campaign Greece should first make a last effort to reach an understanding with the British. London remained unmoved. Even a personal letter to Churchill from Queen Frederika failed to elicit a more friendly response. The British prime minister closed the door with cold finality: ". . . this is not the time, in the interests of either Greece, Great Britain, or, wider still, of NATO, for discussions about changes in the government of Cyprus. The island is of vital importance to the defense of the Middle East and of the Mediterranean . . ."

In August 1954 Athens witnessed the first public demonstration for Cypriot freedom. More than eighty thousand people gathered in the center of the city to hear fiery speeches by the advocates of enosis. When this huge crowd began to move in the direction of the British Embassy, the police tried to stop the demonstrators and violence broke out. That very same day, the Greek delegate to the United Nations submitted an official appeal for Cypriot self-determination. This was the beginning of a misguided diplomatic offensive. Greece wanted enosis under the guise of self-determination; and she hoped to reach this goal by enlisting the support of the anticolonial forces in the United Nations—including, of course, the members of the Soviet bloc and the Arab countries. This strategy suffered from a serious contradiction. Greece was a NATO member; self-determination—which, as everyone knew, really meant union with Greece—would merely expand NATO control to Cyprus. The very countries on whose support the Greek diplomatic effort so heavily relied had no genuine interest in promoting self-determination for Cyprus. They were only interested in using the Cypriot issue as a means of embarrassing Britain and the United States. Enosis made sense only in the context of NATO. Yet, from the very beginning, Greek diplomacy conducted the battle for Cyprus not only without the support of NATO but in opposition to its principal partners. Yet, it is very likely that the prospect of an arrangement that would have spread NATO's mantle to Cyprus without jeopardizing British defense interests in the area might have won NATO support. In any event, the United Nations was the wrong forum in which to pursue enosis because the international organization had no authority to force an end to British colonial rule on Cyprus.

Grivas, not particularly hopeful or impressed by the efforts of the diplomats, left secretly in November for his native island. Makarios, who was initially reluctant to endorse a campaign of violence, had by now changed his mind. In October, while passing through Athens, the archbishop had reportedly urged Grivas to move ahead with his plans. As soon as Grivas reached the island, he secretly began to recruit young Cypriots in a clandestine organization, the National Organization of Cypriot Fighters (EOKA).

The handling of the Cyprus issue was bound to disorient public loyalties. Greece's closest allies were now on the other side of the argument. A first sign of the resulting confusion came in the November municipal elections when leftist candidates scored unexpected gains.

The death of Papagos

At a time when the Cypriot entanglement and the problems of economic development required strong leadership, the country was to face the unsettling complication of having a seriously ill prime minister. For the period between March, when he fell ill, and October 1955, when he died, Papagos was prime minister only in name. Most of his official duties were taken over by the two deputy premiers, Panagiotis Kanellopoulos and Stefanos Stefanopoulos. A year earlier the government had lost its most dynamic personality when Markezinis resigned. He did so in a rage because Papagos rejected his demands for greater authority in the economic sector.

Papagos' illness, in spite of the medieval secrecy surrounding his actual condition, had an immediate impact on the political scene. Markezinis, who regarded himself as the legitimate heir to the leadership of the Greek Rally he had once helped to create, formed a party of his own in early February. It was his hope that eventually he could attract to its ranks most of the Greek Rally deputies. Venizelos, who had become discouraged after Papagos' rise to power, had given up the leadership of the Liberal party and had transferred the post to George Papandreou. With the onset of Papagos' illness, Venizelos' hopes were renewed, for now he could see approaching an end to the field marshal's domination of the political scene. Venizelos returned to Greece and asked Papandreou to step aside. He refused, and Venizelos created a new party of his own, the Liberal Democratic Union (FDE). Papagos' illness acted also as a green light to Grivas. On April 1 a series of explosions in several Cypriot towns marked the beginning of the EOKA's fight for enosis.

During the summer of 1955 Papagos remained in seclusion at his home in a fashionable suburb near Athens and not even the king knew how ill he was. But while Greece remained virtually without a prime minister, events of grave importance were taking place. In May, Khrushchev visited Belgrade in an effort to placate Tito. Although the Russian leader did not bring Yugoslavia back to the Soviet camp, relations did improve to the point where the agreements signed with Greece and Turkey in 1953 and in 1954 could silently be cast into oblivion. In June the British government invited not only Greece but also Turkey to a three-party conference to discuss the future of Cyprus. The introduction of Turkey as a third party to the dispute was to have far-reaching consequences. Followers of the Moslem faith amounted to 18 percent of the population on the island. These people, who regarded themselves as Turk-Cypriots, were the descendants of the soldiers and administrators who had ruled Cyprus in the name of the sultan since the island came under Ottoman rule in the fifteenth century. Turkey had given up any claim on Cyprus under the Treaty of Lausanne in 1924. Now, with a mere stroke of the pen, the British had brought Turkey back as a third party having an equal voice in the matter. In this way Britain created a more serious disruption in the area's security and stability than any change in the status of Cyprus might have caused. This became dramatically clear as soon as the conference opened on August 28. The Turkish delegation raised a wall of opposition to any thought of self-determination and insisted that if British rule was ever to be terminated, the island would have to be partitioned between Greece and Turkey. The British now had one more voice to counter the Greek aspirations.

On September 5 Turkish Foreign Minister Zorlou announced that as far as Turkey was concerned the conference was hopelessly deadlocked. That same night, the city of Salonika, which was enjoying the festive atmosphere of its annual international trade fair, was jolted shortly after midnight by a loud explosion. A time bomb had caused considerable damage to the Turkish consulate, which was located next to Mustafa Kemal's paternal home, a historic site preserved as such by the Greek government. The bomb had been brought into Greece a few days earlier by Mehmet Deni Kalp, the Turkish consul, in his diplomatic luggage. Although the explosion did not cause any damage to Kemal's old home, it was used to provoke the Turkish populace in Constantinople. The next day several Turkish newspapers carried lurid accounts and even faked pictures of the destruction presumably caused to Kemal's home. Within hours, as dusk fell over the city, thousands of enraged citizens lashed out against the churches, the shops, and the homes of Greeks. In Smyrna, the Greek pavilion in the city's trade fair was put to the torch by a throng of demonstrators. The effect of these events on the always tenuous Greek-Turkish friendship was devastating.

Early in October King Paul returned from a visit to Tito, where he had gone hoping to drum up support for the Cypriot cause. The king felt that under the circumstances of deteriorating relations with Turkey, Greece should not continue without an effective prime minister. In a letter he asked Papagos to name a successor. Afraid that an outright resignation might spell the end of the Greek Rally—which was in reality simply a cluster of politicians around Papagos—the two deputy premiers suggested that an acting prime minister be appointed. The king, disappointed and apprehensive, accepted the suggestion but was quick to point out that he saw it as only a temporary expedient. He could not foresee how temporary this was going to be; the next day, October 4, Papagos died.

Karamanlis moves to the foreground

The day before Papagos' funeral, King Paul invited Constantine Karamanlis to the palace and offered him the mandate to form a cabinet. He also gave him the authority to dissolve the Vouli and hold a new election. Karamanlis accepted without hesitation, although he indicated that he had no intention of using the threat of a new election to keep the Greek Rally together.

The king had decided to bypass the two deputy premiers and call to the helm a younger and more dynamic man. After his recent experiences with Plastiras and Papagos, when the country had been left for months without a prime minister, his choice was understandable. At forty-eight, Karamanlis was one of the most popular members of the Papagos cabinet. As minister of public works he had dazzled the public with his tough-minded determination to get things done, cutting through bureaucratic red tape, pushing through by sheer willpower projects that had been gathering dust for years. By temperament he was not a back-slapping politician, but he had a special talent for winning respect and cooperation among his colleagues. An uncommonly handsome man with a commanding presence, he wasted few words, preferring action and practical achievement to rhetorical pyrotechnics.

Of the two deputy premiers, only Kanellopoulos, whose niece was married to Karamanlis, agreed to help. Stefanopoulos denounced the king's choice and bolted the party, but only twenty-nine Greek Rally deputies followed him. Karamanlis had passed his first test successfully. Still, his sudden elevation inevitably opened the way to every type of insidious gossip. The most damaging charge was that he had been chosen by the palace, the Americans, and, of course, the ubiquitous British, to settle the Cypriot issue by burying the quest for enosis. Karamanlis, true, was more concerned with the country's economic development than he was with the expansion of Greek control over Cyprus. He shared the national desire to see Cyprus free but he was not burning with the emotional fire that seemed to consume so many Greeks at the time.

Actually, Karamanlis had no choice. To survive, he had to be firm

Constantine Karamanlis. United
Press International Photo

George Papandreou. United Press
International Photo

on the Cyprus issue and press in every appropriate forum for a just solution to the question. With Turkey seeking the island's partition, he had to fight back by constantly pointing out that the Moslem inhabitants were scattered all over the island, with Greeks and Turks often living side by side. Partition was not only impractical but also unfair since the Moslem minority did not exceed 18 percent of the island's population. Still, he knew that rational arguments do not always carry the day in diplomatic confrontations. To deal with the Cyprus issue effectively, he realized that he needed the prestige and authority that only the expression of popular support at the polls could confer. This was needed no less for the country's economic development. With direct economic aid from the United States reduced to a trickle, Greece needed to attract substantial amounts of foreign capital. Only a strong, stable government could have overcome the understandable reluctance of foreign investors or lending institutions.

Following a familiar tradition in Greek politics, Karamanlis announced on January 4 the end of the Greek Rally and the creation of a new party, which was to be known as the National Radical Union (ERE). Its title notwithstanding, the new party was not radical. Anti-Communist in its ideology, loyal to NATO, reasonably nationalistic, the party was concerned primarily with the country's economic development. To attract foreign capital, it made every effort to maintain price stability, construct the necessary facilities for industrialization, and provide investment incentives. All this was done on the premise that only increased production could raise the standard of living and benefit all segments of the population. By necessity, the party had to impose some restraints on consumption and welfare, but on the whole the economic gains were spread throughout the various social groups both in the urban areas and in the countryside.

In creating a new political party Karamanlis wanted to emphasize that he was initiating a new period—not as the successor of Papagos but as a leader in his own right. Most of the Greek Rally deputies shifted to Karamanlis. The ERE gained also the allegiance of several liberal politicians, among them Evangelos Averoff, who was later to play a decisive role on the Cypriot issue as Greece's foreign minister. With many indications of popular support, Karamanlis decided to take the country to a parliamentary election. The opposition parties insisted on another change in the electoral system—this time from plurality to proportional—threatening otherwise to join with the pro-Communist EDA in an electoral coalition. Karamanlis, afraid that a purely proportional system would once again break up the political forces and usher in another period of unstable cabinets, opted for a combination of plurality with proportional representation for the larger constituencies.

In the election of February 16 the ERE received 47.3 percent of the total vote and 165 out of 300 seats. The Democratic Union, which was a popular front electoral coalition that included the EDA, won 135 seats, 18 of which went to EDA candidates. Although the Democratic Union had failed to defeat the ERE, it had succeeded in ending the EDA's political isolation. With women voting for the first time in a parliamentary election, some of Karamanlis' detractors hastened to suggest that his handsome appearance had swayed many female votes.

With a solid majority in the Vouli, Karamanlis was now able to tackle more effectively the country's two most pressing problems: Cyprus and economic development. The dispute over Cyprus had now entered a more acute phase. After the breakdown of the London Conference during the previous summer, the British appointed Gen. John Harding to be governor of Cyprus. His stern measures against the EOKA showed that Britain was ready to go to any lengths to keep control of the island. At the same time, the international publicity generated by Harding's actions caused a great deal of embarrassment to Britain. Some way had to be found to reach at least an interim accommodation. Harding opened talks with Makarios over the possibility of self-government for the island. To an outsider, self-government appeared to be a reasonable way out of the impasse, but to the Greek Cypriots anything short of enosis was at the time a betrayal of a sacred cause. Makarios showed no interest in a compromise, and in March he was arrested and taken to the Seychelles islands in the Indian Ocean. Apparently the British hoped that by removing him from the scene, agitation for enosis would die out. Greek relations with Britain reached a new low. George Papandreou, now coleader with Sophocles Venizelos in a reconstituted Liberal party, called for a policy of "equal friendship" to East and West. Karamanlis, realizing that Greece could not afford a neutralist policy, insisted on the more moderate course of maintaining Greece's close ties with the West and NATO. Still, he had no choice but to press for Cypriot self-determination at the United

Nations. Another appeal in the fall of 1956 failed to produce any tangible results—except more ill feeling between Greece on the one side and Britain and Turkey on the other, with the United States leaning in the direction of Britain and Turkey.

Domestically, Karamanlis now had to face the subtle opposition of Queen Frederika. She had initially supported the king's choice, hoping that Karamanlis would always depend on the favor of the throne for his political survival. But she found rather early that Karamanlis, once he had his own parliamentary majority, had every intention of being his own man. During 1957 the Queen carried on a largely clandestine campaign to undermine Karamanlis. She had found in Venizelos a willing ally. They both favored some form of a coalition government between the ERE and moderate liberals under Venizelos' premiership. Frederika expected that with such an unstable arrangement, her chances of influencing the political process would grow. But with a solid ERE majority in the Vouli, such unorthodox solutions would only throw the crown into the cauldron of partisan politics. King Paul, in spite of his tendency to follow the queen's advice on many issues, carefully avoided the kind of entanglement that in the past had brought only misery to the occupants of the throne.

Throughout this period, Karamanlis was preoccupied with the country's economic development. The Public Power Corporation (DEI), which had been initially established with American economic and technical assistance, was given more extensive responsibilities through legislation. The construction of thermoelectric and hydro-electric plants was expanded. A dramatic increase in savings deposits opened new possibilities for the financing of industrial enterprises. A building boom was changing the face of Athens. The construction of new roads, the improvement of port facilities, the mechanization of agricultural techniques, the tapping of water resources for irrigation, the pursuit of serious efforts to develop industries for the processing of local mineral resources, and a growing tourist traffic, all helped Karamanlis win public acclaim.

At the same time, constant disagreements between the coleaders of the Liberal party—Venizelos and Papandreou—weakened the opposition's pressure. The first serious challenge came, oddly enough, from within the ERE in February 1958. In an effort to improve the political climate, Karamanlis authorized one of his associates, a former Liberal and now interior minister, Dimitrios

Makris, to discuss with Papandreou a revision of the electoral law that might be acceptable to all sides. They agreed on a version of proportional representation that offered certain advantages in the way of a bonus of seats to the party that came in second at the polls. It was accepted as a given that either the ERE or the Liberal party would win first or second spot. An increased number of seats for the second party would actually mean fewer seats for the party that came in third, which would most likely be the EDA. Karamanlis favored the emergence of what he called two nationally minded (that is, bourgeois) parties capable of alternating in power. The only requirement, in his view, was that neither party should ever try to improve its electoral chances by forming a coalition with the pro-Communist Left. Karamanlis also wanted to end the constant changes in the electoral law by establishing, permanently, the plurality system. With plurality, the EDA candidates would have no chance of winning except in a handful of constituencies. With the two parties alternating in power, the country could look forward to a long period of governmental stability.

When the Papandreou-Makris plan was presented to the cabinet, two ministers resigned in protest because in their view it unduly favored the Liberals. The next day fifteen other ERE deputies left the party. Karamanlis no longer had a majority in the Vouli.

The crisis, long in preparation behind the scenes, was directed exclusively against Karamanlis. We have already noted the secret campaign being conducted by Queen Frederika to undermine him. In addition, it is very likely that some Americans in the embassy— and of course, the British—were displeased by his continuing support of enosis for Cyprus. Within the ERE itself, certain key personalities from old, established political families resented Karamanlis' rise from humble beginnings and his rather gruff manner in dealing with sensitive colleagues.

All these disparate forces converged in February to unseat Karamanlis. He reacted with his characteristic boldness. Confident of public support, he advised the king to appoint a caretaker government and hold an election under the system that Papandreou and Makris had worked out. Venizelos, Queen Frederika, and apparently some members of the American embassy wanted the king to appoint a new government under another ERE personality, scuttling Karamanlis. They argued that a large number of the ERE's deputies would support the king's choice for prime minister and vote for him in the Vouli. The balance of votes needed for a majority would be provided by Liberal deputies. King Paul resisted these suggestions.*

The election was held on May 11. The attempt to jettison Karamanlis backfired in two ways. The ERE won 171 seats in the 300-seat Vouli; and the Liberal party, which was expected to win the second spot, came in a poor third with only 36 seats. To almost everyone's surprise, it was the pro-Communist EDA that emerged as the major opposition party with 79 seats and 25 percent of the total vote. The balance went to a group of centrist parties and the remnants of the once powerful Populist party. The emergence of the EDA as the country's major opposition party caused second thoughts in many quarters. With the economy moving at a brisk pace, employment high, prices stable, and signs of increasing prosperity visible everywhere, the doubling of the Left's electoral support within two years could only be attributed to public disillusionment with the West over the Cyprus issue.

The Zurich agreements

The replacement of British Prime Minister Anthony Eden with Harold Macmillan after the Suez affair resulted in a somewhat more flexible attitude on the part of the British toward Cyprus. Makarios was released from the Seychelles in April 1957, and Harding was replaced later in the year by Sir Hugh Foot, a man of liberal views. But by now the most difficult aspect of the problem was no longer the conflict between Greece and Britain but the irreconcilable demands of the Turks for partition and of the Greeks for enosis.

In June 1958 Macmillan came up with what appeared to be a compromise solution. Essentially, it was designed to shelve the issue at least for a while. The plan called for a three-way partnership. For seven years the island would be governed by a council consisting of a British governor, representatives of Greece and Turkey, and six Cypriot delegates (four Greek, two Turk) who would be elected by separate assemblies drawn from the two ethnic groups. The Greek

---

* In 1965 his son Constantine followed similar suggestions, which were at that time directed against the liberal center, with disastrous consequences for the political system.

government as well as Makarios rejected the plan as a clever design to impose partition through the back door. Brushing aside the Greek objections, Britain and Turkey went ahead with their contribution to the council. This caused a new flare-up of violence on the island, with Greek and Turk Cypriots now fighting against each other. In Greece, a Communist-sponsored, anti-NATO, peace movement, which was actually part of an international campaign under Soviet auspices directed against Western defense policies, was gaining ground. Even people who were ordinarily pro-Western spoke out in opposition to a proposed installation of missile bases in Greece. Washington now became concerned over the effect Cyprus was beginning to have on NATO cohesion. Karamanlis was no less apprehensive, but he had no alternative other than to go once again through the annual ritual of fruitless jousting at the United Nations.

In September 1958 Foreign Minister Evangelos Averoff went again before the world organization for another verbal bout with the British and the Turks. His arsenal of arguments was probably unassailable in moral terms, but diplomatically it was full of blunted arrows. Already Makarios had indicated that the aim of the Cypriots was no longer enosis but independence. Makarios had finally understood that enosis had little appeal to those whose help he needed most, but he made the statement about independence for Cyprus without first consulting the Greek government. Greece was inadvertently made to appear as an expansionist state interested in territorial aggrandizement. Under these circumstances the issue of Cypriot self-determination seemed a mere guise.

With the real conflict now emerging as being one between Greece and Turkey, Averoff tried to block any resolution at the United Nations that might give international recognition to Turkey's involvement in the dispute. Considering that Turkey had staked her claim since 1955, Greece was, in effect, seeking to impose a political fiction on the world organization. Political fictions may survive for some time but only when those who benefit by them have the power to make others accept them as real. Greece had no such power.

Shortly before the beginning of the debate, Averoff paid a visit to British Foreign Minister Selwyn Lloyd. Pointing to the damaging effect the Cyprus dispute had on NATO, Averoff proposed to withdraw the Greek appeal to the United Nations and place the whole matter in cold storage until a more opportune time when Britain would be able to decide on the island's future. He asked that in return an innocuous resolution be passed that would not mention Turkey. Given the state of public sentiment in Greece and Cyprus, this proposal amounted to a virtual betrayal of a cherished national cause. Still, it was an eminently sensible suggestion from the standpoint of national interest. If accepted, it might have removed Turkey from the center of the dispute and let the conflict subside. Then at some later time, perhaps as Britain's colonial empire was being liquidated, Cyprus would be freed in the normal course of events. Besides, in a less heated atmosphere, Greece and Turkey might be able to come to a mutually acceptable formula. Averoff had reasons to hope that his proposal might find ready response with the British. Each time the Cypriot issue came before the United Nations, Britain found herself in the uncomfortable role of a villain accused before public opinion for oppressing the freedom-loving people of Cyprus. A freezing of the dispute would end this annual parade of accusations, while restoring Britain's undisputed control over the island, with its obvious strategic and political advantages.

Selwyn Lloyd listened attentively to Averoff's proposal but then he pointed out that even if he accepted, the EOKA might not agree. The Greek foreign minister assured him that Grivas would cooperate. Selwyn Lloyd pressed on. Even assuming that Grivas would agree there was no assurance that the Turkish EOKA (that is, the Turk Cypriots armed by Turkey) would accept the freezing of the issue. "I am afraid you have come too late," Lloyd concluded. With the door to a graceful exit closed, Averoff went on with a brilliant but ineffectual effort to use high principle as a counterforce to political realism. In the end, the United Nations agreed on a resolution that, in spite of its otherwise innocuous content, recognized Turkey's interest. The wish was expressed in the resolution that the "three interested parties" will find an equitable solution.

Shortly after the end of the debate, Averoff encountered Turkish Foreign Minister Zorlou in the corridor. To his diplomatic congratulations, Averoff replied: "Both of us spoke well. But we are wasting our energies in petty politics, indulging in sterile acrimony over an issue that does not matter as much as the other major problems we face." "I fully agree," Zorlou replied, "we must find a solution." "But how can we find a solution when you insist that 20 percent of the people account as much as 80 percent," Averoff asked, referring to the relative strength of the two ethnic groups. "I would be less than serious if I claimed that 20 is equal to 80, but you refuse to accept that there are two communities on the island." Zorlou wanted to replace the term "minority" with the term "community" because "minority" implied a relationship of inferiority to the dominant majority.

Averoff could see that there was no way to impose a relationship implying inferior status on the Turk Cypriots, regardless of the term used. "If that is the problem," he said, "I agree that there are two communities, but we must also agree that one is much larger than the other." "In that case," Zorlou replied, "I think we have a basis for discussion." The next day, Averoff was invited to attend a broad meeting with the British, the Americans, and a few other key delegates. Here it developed that Britain and Turkey were willing to forego an assured victory in the General Assembly and accept instead a resolution that would not even contain a reference to the "three interested parties." Before the end of the meeting Averoff and Zorlou agreed to get together the following morning for a private talk.

It was a quiet Saturday morning, with the corridors of the United Nations virtually deserted, as the two foreign ministers met to search for ways out of the impasse. Zorlou spoke of a federal state with a 60 to 40 percent participation for the two communities, and a possible provision for military bases for Britain, Greece, and Turkey. Averoff replied that it would be difficult to accept a federal structure considering the dispersion of the Turk Cypriots throughout the island, but that he would support an independent Cyprus with participation of the two communities more or less in the proportions suggested by Zorlou. It was a relaxed, candid discussion without bitterness or acrimony. In the course of that morning, the seeds for the Zurich agreements were planted.

Averoff and Zorlou had set the wheels of diplomacy in motion. Early in February Karamanlis met in Zurich with Turkish Prime Minister Adnan Menderes and discussed the details of a constitutional setup for an independent Cyprus. The formula they developed excluded both enosis and partition and granted Britain sovereign rights over an airbase at Akrotiri and a military base at Dhikaia. Greece and Turkey were to have small military contingents on the island. The new sovereign republic of Cyprus would have a Greek Cypriot president and a Turk Cypriot vice-president. Each would have veto powers on matters of foreign relations, defense, and security. A House of Representatives would have fifty members, thirty-five of them elected by the Greek Cypriots and fifteen by the Turk Cypriots for a four-year term. In addition, the two communities would elect separate communal assemblies to deal with religious, educational, judicial, and other local matters. Personnel for the civil service would be drawn in the following ratio: 70 percent from the Greek community and 30 percent from the Turkish. The republic would also have an army of two thousand men, with 60 percent coming from the Greek community and 40 percent from the Turkish community. Britain, Greece, and Turkey assumed the responsibility of guaranteeing the faithful application of the constitution, the key provisions of which could not be changed.

The recognition of extensive rights to the Turkish community angered many Greek Cypriots, and in the London conference that followed, Makarios raised serious objections although he had initially approved the Zurich arrangements. In the end he was persuaded to abide by the agreements, and the papers were signed on February 19, 1959. In December 1959 Archbishop Makarios was elected president and Dr. Fazil Kücük vice-president of the forthcoming new state. A joint constitutional commission completed its work in April 1960, and on August 16 Cyprus officially became an independent and sovereign republic. Many gave a sigh of relief hoping that this issue, which had for years poisoned relations within NATO, was forever settled. But to those who had dreamed of enosis, the Zurich-London compromise was merely a sugarcoated surrender to Anglo-American pressures.

chapter 7
Conflict and Instability

The European Economic Community

The solution to the Cypriot dispute brought Karamanlis no immediate political benefits since it excluded enosis; still, the end of violence on the island promised that there would be a change in the public mood as time went on. For now, Karamanlis was free to tackle other problems that he considered more pressing. In an effort to tap new resources for the country's economic development in the face of dwindling American assistance, the Greek government decided to apply in July 1959 for membership to the European Economic Community. Greece, being far behind the six EEC partners in terms of economic development, could not hope or even wish for full participation. Her objective was to gain associate status, which would allow for a long period of adjustment. During the

248

crucial years of transition to full membership, Greek industry and agriculture would be given special treatment.

Public feelings on this major initiative were somewhat mixed. For generations the Greek people did not regard their country as being part of Europe. Greeks would speak of "going to Europe," and to them this meant trips to fascinating cities like Vienna, Paris, and Berlin. Until the Americans came during the postwar years, the elite in almost every area of endeavor in Greece had had the benefit of higher studies in Europe, primarily France and Germany. Members of the shipowning community had traditionally been associated with England. The idea of joining the EEC had a strong emotional appeal to many because it symbolized the country's advance from Balkan backwardness to European sophistication. And to those who still held a grudge against the British and Americans over Cyprus, membership in the EEC promised the country's emancipation from the monopoly of Anglo-American influence. Voices of misgivings and opposition to EEC participation were not absent, of course. Many industrialists who had long ago grown accustomed to the protective shield of tariffs and quotas, could not easily shift to the more competitive conditions prevailing within the EEC.

For almost two years arguments for and against membership were explored in different forums. Notably, at no point did disagreement follow a conservative/liberal dichotomy. Only the EDA as a political party opposed, for obvious reasons, any ties with the European Economic Community. In the end the advocates of participation won out. No less important, of course, was the attitude of the EEC countries; they supported the admission of Greece—and Turkey, which had also applied for associate status—because they welcomed the opportunity to explore new commercial ventures in an area which, since the end of the war, had been dominated by Anglo-American interests. The treaty granting associate membership was signed in Athens on July 10, 1961. Karamanlis had added another major achievement to his record.

The "relentless struggle"

The moment for consummating the EEC agreement appeared well-chosen. The term of the 1958 Vouli was to expire in

May 1962. But Karamanlis was not planning to wait till then. He was contemplating the calling of an election some time in the fall of 1961. Already in May, the government had submitted to the Vouli a new electoral law that provided for a reinforced version of proportional representation with modifications designed to prevent the EDA from repeating its 1958 electoral success. Venizelos made every effort to delay a confrontation at the polls because the liberal opposition continued to remain fragmented and ineffectual. His attempt to use Grivas—who had returned to Greece after the Zurich-London agreements on Cyprus—as a unifying element for the liberal center turned into a pitiful fiasco. Grivas, an ultrarightist at heart, was the last person to lead the centrist, liberal forces. Worse, Grivas proved that he was most effective when in hiding. In public he cut a rather unconvincing figure as a political leader. The failure of the Grivas experiment hurt Venizelos while, by contrast, it buoyed the prestige of George Papandreou, whose arguments that all liberal forces should unite into a single party capable of defeating the ERE gained ground.

During this period Karamanlis continued to have difficulties with Queen Frederika. On one issue after another he had to fight both against the opposition's claim that he was the product of palace favoritism, and against the queen's complaints that he was uncooperative and even hostile to the wishes of the palace. In early January 1961 Karamanlis had a meeting with King Paul and stated delicately but with firmness that unless the queen stopped interfering with the work of his government he would have no alternative but to resign in protest. King Paul, a moderate and prudent man, spoke to his wife, who agreed to be less aggressive in the future. Of course the incident merely fanned the queen's resentment.

In mid-September Karamanlis advised the king to form a caretaker cabinet, dissolve the Vouli, and call a new election. Four days later, September 19, the several centrist, liberal parties formed the Center Union party with George Papandreou as its leader and an eight-member executive committee. The following day the king appointed Gen. Constantine Dovas, the chief of his military household, as prime minister. The election was set for October 29.

Papandreou was extremely confident as election day approached. Venizelos was less certain. But even the pessimists in the Center Union agreed that at the very least Karamanlis would fail to win an independent majority and thus the ERE would have to seek some form of coalition. The results came as a shattering surprise to the CU. The ERE won 50.57 percent of the total vote and 176 seats. The CU, together with Markezinis' Progressive party, gained 33.69 percent and 100 seats. The Pandemocratic Front (PAME), which included the EDA, garnered 15.50 percent and 24 seats. The failure of the Center Union should not have come as such a shock to its leadership. The CU had been created only five weeks before election day. True, Greek parties have rarely relied on a broad and well-structured organization, but even so the Center Union did not even have enough time to convince large segments of uncommitted voters that it could indeed provide a viable alternative to the ERE. More important, the record of the Karamanlis government, especially in the economic sector, was quite impressive. Karamanlis' well-planned effort to develop the economy had begun to bear substantial and tangible fruits. Indeed, for the first time in the history of modern Greece, the economy was moving toward the take-off stage for sustained growth. In less than seven years, the gross national product had increased by almost 45 percent, with an average growth rate of over 6 percent annually, in constant prices.

The leadership of the Center Union did not accept defeat gracefully. Two days after the election, Papandreou denounced the result as "the product of violence and fraud." The initial suggestion to pursue this line of attack came from Venizelos. He thought that by applying sustained pressure the Center Union would eventually force the crown to push Karamanlis aside and seek to improve its relations with the liberal center by promoting some form of a coalition government. Papandreou eagerly embraced Venizelos' suggestion, and for the next two years he kept on what he called a "relentless struggle against Karamanlis' illegal government." This in itself introduced a distinctly unsettling element into the political system. To make matters worse, Papandreou accused the leadership of the army of being accomplices to "the orgy of fraud," which presumably had been organized by the "ERE's police state." Ever since the end of the war, the nation's leadership had kept the armed forces out of politics. It appeared that the lessons of the past had had a salutary effect and that in the future the politicians would be careful not to allow or provoke the politicization of the army. Papandreou, disregarding past experience, made the grave error of identifying the military leadership with one political party.

The charges of fraud and violence were never conclusively proven.

A simple cross guards this tiny spring garden atop a dark rock pinnacle, the site of an inaccessible medieval monastery or meteora ("hanging monastery").

Photographs on pp. 252–57 taken by David O. Johnson in April 1973. Converted from color to black and white.

In Ios: an ancient evergreen tree silhouetted by late afternoon light; a stately church overlooking the rocky entrance to the harbor.

A Greek woman near Mycenae spins thread of goat's wool as her ancestors did by twisting loose woolen fibers on the distaff in her left hand to the spindle in her right hand. (*right*) A harborside shrine at Nauplia on the Gulf of Argolis.

(*left*) Bright sunlight is the bleach for the town laundry on Mykonos.

(*top*) Clean lines typify one of the countless cubistic white chapels on Mykonos.

(*bottom*) Young Greek dancers help celebrate April 21 on Thira.

Sunset over the mountains of the
Peloponnisos in the harbor of Nauplia.

As a matter of fact, Karamanlis, who wanted to prevent another EDA success like the one in 1958, had on several occasions during the campaign advised his listeners to vote for the Center Union if they did not wish to vote for the ERE. It is important to remember here that these were the years of the Cold War. The phobia of communism was still a strong factor in Greek politics. Many lesser officials throughout the state apparatus, especially the police and the gendarmerie, were pro-ERE in their political sympathies. More important, they were strongly anti-Communist. Many of them considered the liberal center as being soft on communism. Some excesses undoubtedly took place during the voting, but they were not the result of a deliberate, centrally planned effort. The election was conducted by a caretaker government that was anything but friendly to Karamanlis. Most likely, the result would have been about the same even without the excessive zeal of the ERE stalwarts in the administration and in the army.

The relentless struggle, which was pursued by Papandreou with unusual tenacity and consistency, seriously undermined the political system. Inevitably, the throne, too, was brought into the controversy. Papandreou severed all relations with the palace, refusing to attend even such social events as the wedding of Princess Sophie to Juan Carlos of Bourbon in May 1962. Papandreou injected another explosive element into the conflict, when, during a speech in Salonika on May 27, he called on Greek youth "to terrorize the terrorists." The Karamanlis "regime" was portrayed as a police state bordering on fascism. The climate of moderation that had prevailed in the 1950s disappeared. In late 1962 Papandreou turned his pressure directly on the king, calling on him to intervene and remove Karamanlis' "illegal" government. In a private message to Papandreou, Karamanlis prophetically said, "it is unwise to involve the throne in a partisan controversy because those who advance such ideas today may come to regret it in the future." Papandreou would be the victim of precisely such an intervention in July 1965.

The weakening of political stability and national cohesion caused by the Papandreou-Karamanlis conflict was, strangely enough, taking place at a time of rising prosperity and unmistakable economic progress. It seemed to negate all theories tying political instability to economic difficulties. Yet, the relentless struggle would have remained merely a hollow slogan if it were not for the fact that there did exist a substantial undercurrent of resentment among those who did not share as much as they thought they should in the increasing national product. Karamanlis was determined to push economic development vigorously before undertaking any extensive measures to deal with the problems of social welfare. With a rising gross national product, the amenities of modern living were entering the Greek homes but not as rapidly or as widely as many wished. Unsatisfied expectations could easily be converted into political opposition. Yet, Karamanlis, committed as he was to a policy of economic development, could not match the Center Union's promises for social benefits.

Karamanlis had been considering for some time a revision of the 1952 constitution in the hopes of making it a more efficient instrument in the face of the new circumstances surrounding the rapidly developing socioeconomic system. He also hoped that since many of the changes he planned to propose would be attractive to Papandreou—especially those providing for the protection of social and economic rights as well as those designed to curb potential abuses of power by the palace—some degree of cooperation might be reached to blunt the destabilizing impact of the relentless struggle. In February 1962 Karamanlis proposed to the Vouli the revision of several articles of the 1952 constitution.

Papandreou, who was determined to pursue his fight to the end, dismissed the proposal as a clever ploy to prolong the life of the Karamanlis government and shift the attention of the legislature to a project which, by its very nature and magnitude, would keep the parliamentary wheels going for a long time. The Center Union and the EDA refused to participate in a thirty-member constitutional committee that was to include deputies from all the parties represented in the Vouli in proportion to each party's parliamentary strength. Although a truncated twenty-member committee with eighteen ERE and two Progressive party deputies did begin deliberations on March 13, the whole affair was soon forgotten in the midst of growing partisan controversy.

In 1963 relations between Queen Frederika and Karamanlis became increasingly strained. In January a serious dispute developed over the selection of Metropolitan Iakovos as archbishop. In Greece there is no separation of church and state; the Orthodox church is connected with the state through a complex network of legal and traditional ties. Iakovos had the strong support of Queen Frederika, and at the outset Karamanlis had no serious objections to his election by the synod. The crisis broke out when certain bishops accused Iakovos of immoral conduct. The charges were later dropped, but in the meantime the public outcry over the issue forced Iakovos to resign shortly after his election. The unsavory affair left a bitter aftertaste in many quarters and a residue of public disrespect for the integrity of the church hierarchy. Queen Frederika was infuriated because she felt Karamanlis had failed to stand up for Iakovos. Probably there was little that Karamanlis could have done once the charges of sodomy and lewd conduct began to fly. Nevertheless, the queen was not satisfied with the prime minister's explanations.

A pleasant interlude to the thickening political atmosphere came on January 28, 1963, when Diadohos Constantine became engaged to the beautiful Danish princess, Anna-Maria. But even on this happy occasion, Papandreou did not depart from his set policy of no relations with the palace. By contrast, Venizelos continued his friendly contacts with the royal couple, much to Papandreou's constant irritation. Frederika and Venizelos agreed on one point: a way had to be found to jettison Karamanlis. Papandreou had no quarrel with their objective, but he disagreed strongly on the question of an appropriate method. Venizelos favored a transitional coalition government supported by elements of the ERE and the Center Union. He believed that he was the right man to head such a government. Papandreou was very suspicious of such a scheme because he feared it would inevitably undermine his own position as the leader of the CU. Furthermore, a transitional coalition government was hardly in keeping with his relentless struggle against Karamanlis.

A stepped-up campaign against Karamanlis' so-called police state was soon joined by liberal and leftist circles abroad. Major newspapers in the West were not only carrying stories of police oppression, but they were painting a picture of a regime that was purportedly being held in power by royal favor, American support, and a parliamentary majority manufactured through fraud and violence. The climax came on May 22, when an EDA deputy, Grigoris Lambrakis was killed in Salonika. An athlete of international renown in his youth, Lambrakis had become a prominent physician, a member of the legislature, and one of the EDA's most charismatic leaders. He had gone to Salonika to address one of those peace rallies directed against nuclear weapons and American imperialism.

After the meeting, Lambrakis decided to walk back to his hotel, rejecting an offer of police protection against anti-Communist demonstrators who were apparently waiting outside. As Lambrakis and a small group of his associates were crossing the small square in front of the meeting hall, a tricycle motorcart appeared from an adjacent street. Racing through the square at top speed, it brushed past the group and knocked Lambrakis violently to the ground. He remained in a deep coma for almost five days and then, in spite of all medical effort, died on May 27.*

The killing of Lambrakis became immediately an explosive political issue. Not only the EDA, but also Papandreou saw in it an opportunity to give fresh impetus to the relentless struggle and deliver a telling blow to Karamanlis. Although the Greek government had nothing to gain from this brutal act, Papandreou publicly accused Karamanlis of being an "accomplice" and an "instigator" to the killing. He called on King Paul "to dismiss the illegal, criminal government of the ERE and to conduct honest and free elections."

In Britain fifteen members of Parliament signed a letter to Karamanlis, denouncing the Lambrakis affair as a "political crime." Reports from London indicated that the impending state visit of King Paul and Queen Frederika would be used as an opportunity to unleash vicious demonstrations aimed at embarrassing the Greek government. On Saturday, June 8, Karamanlis had a meeting with King Paul and advised that the visit be postponed. The king seemed to find the arguments of his prime minister convincing. Still, with the British government officially taking the position that the visit was most desirable, King Paul was concerned that a refusal from the Greek side might offend Queen Elizabeth and thereby damage relations between the two governments. Karamanlis and the king agreed to meet again after the weekend for a final decision. The prime minister had already told the king that he would resign if the monarch insisted on going. The king was visibly unhappy when he met again with Karamanlis on June 11 and flatly announced his intention to go ahead with the visit. Karamanlis replied that he had no choice but to submit his resignation. With this, his eight years in power came to an end.

* A dramatization of this incident, based on a novel by a Communist writer, was presented in the film Z by Costa-Gavras.

The rise and fall of the Center Union

In his capacity as the outgoing prime minister, Karamanlis advised the king to dissolve the Vouli and proclaim a new election under the plurality electoral system, which had been approved as the country's permanent system in 1961. Aware of Papandreou's strong opposition to the plurality system, King Paul decided on a different course of action. He appointed a new government under Panagiotis Pipinelis, an ERE personality and a member of Karamanlis' last cabinet. Karamanlis had named Pipinelis himself because he felt he was the man least likely to usurp ERE leadership. Shortly thereafter Karamanlis left for Switzerland on an extended "vacation." He was deeply discouraged by the secret war conducted against him by the palace, and by the relentless struggle that had been poisoning politics for almost two years. Feeling disheartened by the ugly turn of events following the Lambrakis killing and fatigued after eight years of struggling with enormous domestic problems and foreign conflicts, Karamanlis was leaning toward the idea of withdrawing entirely from active politics. Still, he wanted to give one more, final battle.

Initially the king wanted to postpone an electoral confrontation until tempers had cooled off on all sides. The royal trip to London had not turned out to be the disaster Karamanlis feared, but neither was it an unmitigated success. Leftist groups had staged their demonstrations, some newspapers had published unfriendly editorials, but on the whole it passed without any serious disruption in British-Greek relations. The replacement of Karamanlis with Pipinelis had taken some of the heat out of the relentless struggle. Karamanlis, however, saw a long postponement of the election as a threat to the cohesion of the ERE. Papandreou was also anxious to go to the polls because he wanted to take advantage of the fact that the ERE was still suffering from the impact of its recent setbacks. The king eventually agreed to dissolve the Vouli and call a new election. But Papandreou did not want, as he said, "merely to have an election," instead he was insisting on "an honest and fair election." Threatening to boycott the election, he forced the king to replace the Pipinelis cabinet with a caretaker government headed by a prominent jurist. The Vouli had already accepted another of Papandreou's demands and had replaced the plurality electoral system with one that was similar to the 1961 proportional version. The election was set for November 3.

Karamanlis, who had returned to Greece to lead the ERE's electoral campaign, was mildly optimistic. Venizelos was uncertain. Only Papandreou was confident that the Center Union would emerge victorious. When the votes were counted, the CU came out with 42.04 percent of the total and 138 seats—a plurality of 6 votes over the ERE's 132—but without an independent majority of its own. The balance was actually held by the EDA which, with 14.34 percent of the vote, had received 28 seats. Markezinis' Progressive party had only 3.33 percent and 2 seats. Karamanlis advised King Paul to keep the caretaker cabinet in office until the new Vouli had opened and a new presidium had been selected. He hoped that some conservative elements of the Center Union might shift to the ERE, thus giving it a majority.

With Queen Frederika and Diadohos Constantine arguing strongly in favor of a Papandreou government, the king gave the mandate to the leader of the Center Union. His action was constitutionally proper since Papandreou had relatively the largest bloc of votes in the Vouli. Karamanlis, however, saw this as another indication of royal disfavor. Instead of staying on to lead the opposition, he left the country on December 9, announcing his decision to end his political career. He appointed Kanellopoulos as the new leader of the ERE. In a letter addressed to the members of his party he let his feelings of frustration and foreboding show through the carefully chosen words. He could not continue in politics, he intimated, without coming into serious conflict with the throne and thereby risk throwing the country into chaos. He chose to leave the political arena instead. In retrospect, his departure from the stage, however justified it may have been in his own mind, deprived the country of a leader whose prestige and influence could have averted many of the upheavals that in the end destroyed the political system.

Ten days after Karamanlis' departure, the added support of the EDA deputies gave Papandreou a clear majority in the Vouli. Unwilling to stay in power with the aid of what he called the Communist votes, he asked the king to dissolve the Vouli and call a new election. Speaking to the legislature, Papandreou announced a series of social measures and promised to introduce many more in the future if his party were given a clear majority in the next election. Some efforts behind the scenes to form a coalition government failed and another caretaker government was formed to hold another parliamentary election on February 16, 1964.

While the country was going through the motions of an electoral campaign, peace on the island of Cyprus was shattered by a new flare-up of violence. For many months the island had been embroiled in serious disputes over the implementation of key constitutional provisions. Dissatisfied with some of the actions of the Makarios government, the representatives of the Turk Cypriots had used their veto powers over taxation, causing a serious disruption in the government's operations. Makarios, who had long favored several revisions of the constitution, presented the Turk Cypriot leaders with a list of thirteen proposals on November 30, 1963. With Karamanlis out of power, Makarios felt freer to pursue changes in the Zurich-London agreements. The Turkish government, however, rejected the proposed changes as being totally unacceptable. Bloody clashes between Cypriot Turks and Cypriot Greeks erupted in Nicosia and elsewhere on the island. On December 26 Makarios appealed to the Security Council of the United Nations, accusing Turkey of planning to invade Cyprus. With British intervention the fighting stopped temporarily, but the situation remained tense and a threat of renewed violence was ominously hovering over the island. The Greek-Turkish conflict over Cyprus had entered a new chapter.

Kanellopoulos, in his new role as the leader of the ERE, launched a vigorous electoral campaign, but the party, without the magic of Karamanlis, had no chance of success. Besides, the country was moving into a new and different period. For more than a decade, the so-called Right had been in power. Now the time had come for the Center to take over. Labels of Right and Center do not necessarily mean, in the Greek context, that a real division exists between a conservative or reactionary philosophy on the one side and a liberal or progressive credo on the other. Both camps have close connections with the big business segments of the economic community and both espouse populist and socially-minded policies favoring lower income groups. The differences are mostly in the emphasis each camp usually attaches to each of these two elements of policy. Nonetheless, Papandreou and the Center Union did represent in 1964 a shift to a more socially-minded economic policy, a greater moderation toward the Left, and, of course, the gradual dismantling of the Karamanlis state.

Many who viewed with apprehension the forthcoming changes placed their hopes for a more moderate approach on Venizelos, who was expected to exert a restraining influence on Papandreou's more aggressive liberalism. But Venizelos died suddenly on February 7 of a heart attack. With his passing, Papandreou appeared to be the unchallenged leader of the Center Union. Yet, in less than fifteen months, internal conflicts would bring about Papandreou's downfall and the disintegration of the Center Union. A first sign of the impending trouble came as soon as the new Vouli convened to elect its president. Thirty-three CU deputies voted against George Novas, who was Papandreou's choice. This opposition came from the left wing of the party, which was led by Elias Tsirimokos and Savas Papapolitis. During the second round of voting these two leaders, having already made their point, voted for Novas, and he was elected. The incident reminded political observers that the Center Union was actually a loose coalition of centrist-liberal groups ranging from moderate right to moderate left.

King Paul, though ill with terminal cancer, presided over the swearing-in ceremony for Papandreou's new government on February 19. The monarch died less than a month later. Twenty-three-year-old Constantine appeared before the Vouli accompanied by Papandreou and took the royal oath. The young monarch standing next to the crusty old Papandreou seemed to symbolize a new era of good feeling. Appearances, however, were to prove deceptive.

Strange as it may seem, Papandreou's son Andreas added to his many problems. For more than twenty years Andreas Papandreou had lived in the United States, where he was a distinguished professor of econometrics at the University of California, Berkeley. He returned to Greece in 1961. Karamanlis had invited him to come home as a friendly gesture to the aging Papandreou, who longed to be close to his grandchildren. Andreas remained aloof from Greek politics until the election of February 1964, when he ran for office for the first time. Not surprisingly, he won handily. After the election his attitude changed drastically and within a few months he emerged as the leader of the left-of-center forces in the Center Union and a major contender to succeed his father. His appointment as minister of the prime minister's office did not cause much of a stir at first, although it was rather unusual for a newcomer to politics to rise so rapidly to cabinet status.

The trouble started when Andreas Papandreou moved in June to a higher post as alternate minister of coordination. From this enormously influential post he tried not only to bring the banking system under his control but also to force a renegotiation of major contracts with foreign concerns. He failed in these efforts when the more moderate elements in the Center Union led by Constantine Mitsotakis, who was then minister of finance and a chief aspirant for the succession to the party leadership, raised strong objections. The moderates won because the elder Papandreou realized that an open conflict with big business might break up the party, which included many personalities with strongly "capitalist" convictions. He also realized that uncertainty over contractual obligations was bound to discourage foreign investors, and the government's economic policies had made the need for foreign capital more pressing than ever. To live up to preelection promises, the government had approved wage and salary increases, higher payments to the farmers for staple products, and larger outlays for education and welfare. These policies had stimulated the demand for imports and thus played havoc with the balance of trade, increasing the deficit from $57 million in 1963 to $172 million in 1964. At the same time, the rate of inflation had almost doubled in a year. With inflation pushing the costs up and with funds being channelled into socially-oriented expenditures, the volume of public investments declined. Still, the economy had enough momentum to move on; the gross national product continued to rise at a high rate although the level declined from 9.1 in 1962–63 to 8.7 in 1964 and 7.3 in 1965.

While the effects of Papandreou's economic policies were mixed at best, the most serious challenge to the government lay elsewhere. Violence on Cyprus had subsided after the arrival of a United Nations peacekeeping force that took up the thankless task of trying to keep Greeks and Turks apart. But the tension remained, and a UN-appointed mediator found his task extremely frustrating. In June 1964 President Johnson made an effort to bring Greece and Turkey together, but Papandreou would agree only to a separate meeting with the American president. The talks that were held in Washington failed to produce any positive results, however, because Papandreou, in full agreement with Makarios, insisted that a solution to the issue of Cyprus be sought exclusively in the context of the United Nations.

The failure of these talks led to a series of measures on both sides of the conflict. Makarios introduced conscription and an economic blockade of the Turkish enclaves that had been formed on the island by Turk Cypriots fleeing their villages after the clashes of the previous December. Soldiers from Greece were secretly brought in to bolster the Makarios government. According to some accounts, these troops were also to be used to help Greece and Cyprus declare enosis unilaterally at an opportune moment and thus create the impression of a fait accompli. On the other side of the conflict, the Turks were busy sending arms and "volunteers" in preparation for a possible invasion. In August a Greek Cypriot attack on the village of Kokkinou, where the Turks unloaded supplies, was countered with bombing strikes by Turkish aircraft and a threat of invasion. War seemed imminent. Makarios appealed to Greece for air cover but Papandreou refused to send it, reasoning that because of the considerable distance between Cyprus and the Greek mainland the air force could not be used effectively. At this critical moment, the Soviet government came out in support of Makarios and Cypriot independence, while President Johnson appealed to Turkey not to carry out its threat to invade the island. Turkey complied with the American request and the danger of war temporarily passed. Nevertheless, Washington remained unhappy with this protracted conflict that had for so long affected two NATO partners. In mid-August, representatives from both sides met in Geneva under the auspices of the United Nations to discuss an American plan—initially suggested by Dean Acheson—which provided for the island's union with Greece and the transfer of a large parcel of land to Turkey for a military base. Makarios rejected this scheme of "double enosis" as a guise for partition. Andreas Papandreou, who had already become a very influential figure on matters relating to Cyprus, sided strongly with Makarios. The Geneva talks collapsed.

Although elated with Andreas' support, Makarios was not entirely happy with the rest of the Greek government. In spite of past promises to follow an independent foreign policy, George Papandreou could not treat lightly the country's ties with NATO. In contrast, Makarios, who favored an independent Cyprus without any NATO involvement, had no difficulty in forging closer relations with the Soviet Union or the neutralist camp. Although he certainly had no intention of "turning Cyprus into a Mediterranean Cuba," as some American officials feared, he could not afford to ignore Moscow's offer of support. In late 1964 Makarios' decision to buy weapons from Czechoslovakia seemed to indicate a further drift to the Left.

George Papandreou was facing a serious dilemma not only over Cyprus but over his domestic policies as well. His campaign promises had raised high hopes that could not possibly be fulfilled all at once, and for the first four months of his premiership he had tried to steer a rather moderate course. Inevitably his moderate policies alienated many of those who had been at the forefront of the relentless struggle, hoping that a Papandreou victory would move the country to the Left. But a clearcut shift to the Left was opposed by some of the most influential elements of the Center Union. This dilemma was underscored by the results of the municipal elections in July, when the EDA candidates received unprecedented support. In Athens the EDA slate won a plurality with 30 percent of the total compared to 25 percent for the candidates associated with the Center Union. Similar EDA successes were repeated in several other cities and towns.

Very likely, the shift of many voters to the Left was at least partly inspired by the events in Cyprus and the widespread disaffection with Western policies on this matter. Whatever the reason, the elder Papandreou saw in the EDA's successes a strong reason for paying greater heed to the demands of the left-of-center forces in the party, who consisted mostly of dissatisfied intellectuals, some old EAM followers, Plastiras republicans, and workers. In the past this element of the party was represented by Elias Tsirimokos and Savas Papapolitis, but by the fall of 1964, those who favored radical solutions and were not totally committed to the EDA turned increasingly to Andreas Papandreou. Already in February he had pointedly demonstrated his independence by ordering the state-controlled radio network to stop relaying Voice of America broadcasts because they appeared to have a pro-Turkish slant. This move was widely praised at the time, even by many of those who had not voted for the Center Union. During the talks on the Cypriot problem in Washington in June, he appeared to be more influential than the foreign minister, Stavros Costopoulos.

The forces of the Right quickly recognized the fact that Andreas

Papandreou was rapidly rising as a dynamic and attractive leader of the leftist movement in the country. Moreover, many of the moderate leaders in the Center Union viewed his skyrocket to power with suspicion. Newspapers associated with the ERE or with the moderate forces in the Center Union opened a barrage of accusations against Andreas, who unwisely had done certain favors for personal friends in his capacity as alternate minister of coordination. In November Andreas submitted his resignation. This drastic step was not without advantage for him. He was already engaged in a serious effort to build a broad political base for himself, and his cabinet membership stood in the way. Once he had resigned he was free to attack the establishment, which in his definition included the palace, the Americans, the so-called economic oligarchy, and a rather unspecified junta in the army. Now he could indulge in his provocative rhetoric without embarrassing the government.

Andreas Papandreou's advance to national prominence was highlighted during a four-day visit to Cyprus. Although he was only a deputy in the Vouli at the time, he had been personally invited by Makarios and then given a highly significant and impressive welcome. When he returned to Athens, Andreas found his influence among the center-left groups immensely strengthened. In their view the Americans had forced him to resign because he had blocked a solution to the Cyprus problem along the lines of the Acheson plan. This allegation reflected the fact that the Cypriot problem had now become entangled in the Cold War. Elements from the pro-NATO side of the controversy favored some form of enosis to end the conflict, while left-oriented groups insisted on independence and neutrality. George Papandreou was caught somewhere in the middle. In a discussion of the problem with Makarios, the elder Papandreou made it clear that if the archbishop made "any sort of political commitment to Moscow . . . the Greek Government would find itself in the difficult position of having to denounce [Makarios] and cancel its commitment to defend Cyprus." Makarios did not sign any agreements with Moscow, but still he continued to rely on the Soviet Union and the neutralist camp for support.

In late February 1965 Kanellopoulos offered to give the ERE's support to another Center Union cabinet if Papandreou were removed from the premiership. The ERE leader was aware that several important personalities in the Center Union were disillusioned with the prime minister. Those who opposed a shift to the left in the country's social and political orientation had much to object to in Papandreou's administration. With serious concern and apprehension they noted Papandreou's support of an EDA move to bring charges of corruption against Karamanlis; his appointment of Tsirimokos, who was still remembered as a leader of the EAM, to the sensitive ministry of interior which controlled the security agencies; and his acceptance in March of an invitation to visit Moscow. Papandreou had to postpone his trip to the Soviet Union, and the charges against Karamanlis were eventually dropped, but the growing mistrust of Papandreou persisted.

In April the premier's opponents were apparently spurred to take more determined action against him after he reappointed Andreas to the same post he had previously held in the cabinet. Andreas himself would later acknowledge that this was a "strategic error." A coalition representing varied interests and a shared suspicion of the government's apparent shift to the Left, began to congeal beneath the surface. It included dedicated anti-Communists, right-of-center personalities in the Center Union, business groups dissatisfied with the government's economic policies, palace officials, newspaper publishers, and military officers at various levels who found both Papandreous rather lukewarm toward NATO and even neutralist. It mattered little that the elder Papandreou was certainly not anti-NATO, for this group saw Andreas as the prime mover behind the scenes. His role was probably a great deal less decisive than what his detractors believed, but nonetheless the fact remained that he was indeed exerting considerable influence over the shape of government policies. Partly by virtue of the force of events and partly by design, Andreas was actually forging a political alliance with the Left, hoping to win over most of the EDA followers with the exception of hardcore Communists. His opponents, recalling similar unsuccessful attempts by the liberals who joined the EAM or the PEEA, predicted that the approach followed by Andreas would merely open the gates of power to the pro-Communist Left. Significantly, the Communist leaders of the EDA viewed their cooperation with Andreas as a step toward achieving their own rise to power.

The anti-Papandreou forces shifted into high gear during the spring of 1965, when the Papandreou government took certain steps that seemed to foreshadow a wide purge of the officer corps. The government had found a document which purportedly outlined the role of the armed forces in preventing the success of "Communists, fellow travelers, and neutrals" in the election of November 1961. The plan was identified under the code name "Pericles." George Papandreou seized on this document as the final vindication of his charges against the Karamanlis government. An investigation into the affair implicated several officers, including the army chief of staff, General Genimatas. For good measure, Papandreou revived allegations concerning a clandestine organization of officers, known as the IDEA, even though this organization was largely inoperative during the sixties. It had been established in the late forties during the guerrilla campaign, and it had looked to Papagos as its natural leader. The only time this organization had actually attempted to interfere openly with the political process was in June 1951 at the time of Papagos' resignation, but the affair was terminated quickly by Papagos himself. Both the Pericles plan and the IDEA organization had historical rather than political significance in 1965, but by reviving these old issues Papandreou gave the impression that he was, without cause for such action, merely trying to eliminate "unfriendly" officers and bring the military establishment under partisan control. A confrontation between the government and anti-Papandreou forces became simply a matter of time.

It all started in a rather oblique way. George Grivas, who was at the time commander of the Greek Cypriot military forces, sent a secret report to Petros Garoufalias, the defense minister in the Papandreou cabinet. In his report Grivas claimed to have uncovered the existence of a clandestine organization of leftist officers, known as ASPIDA, with cells both in Cyprus and in Greece. Almost as an afterthought, Grivas dropped a hint that Andreas Papandreou appeared to be involved. A copy of the report was forwarded to King Constantine. No hard evidence exists to this day that Andreas was actively involved. Probably, the officers of ASPIDA looked to him as the political personality whose views they were most closely aligned with. The ASPIDA affair could have been easily cleared up, without it ever having had to reach the proportions of a major crisis, but the alleged involvement of Andreas Papandreou added a sinister element to the issue that refused to let it die. Opponents of the younger Papandreou quickly interpreted the affair as an attempt on his part to mobilize leftist elements in the armed forces and use them "to dismantle the structure of special privilege," which in his view "impeded the economic, social, and political development of the country." Andreas, of course, saw the ASPIDA affair as a nefarious plot to eliminate him from the political stage.

The controversy escalated in late May when George Papandreou decided to take over the ministry of defense personally, replacing his old friend Petros Garoufalias. The king suggested that some other person of Papandreou's choice be appointed so as to avoid charges that an investigation into the ASPIDA affair would be used to whitewash Andreas. The elder Papandreou thought that the king's suggestion cast doubt on his integrity and moral courage. He retorted by saying: "If I am not trusted as the minister of defense how can I be trusted as the prime minister?" It was in this frame of mind that the king and Papandreou came to a showdown on the evening of July 15, 1965. King Constantine insisted that the prime minister should appoint to the ministry of defense anyone except himself. Papandreou argued that with his integrity being questioned he had no place remaining on as prime minister. Each man appeared to be convinced that his stand was morally unassailable. In the end Papandreou offered to resign and the king immediately accepted, fearing that if he delayed the prime minister might use the authority of his office during the night to try and rally support. Some of the king's advisers even predicted that Papandreou might try to establish a dictatorship with the help of the Left and possibly even try to turn Greece into a republic. In retrospect, it could be said that such fears were highly exaggerated, but they doubtless appeared quite real at the time.

In any event, the king and Papandreou both mishandled a relatively minor disagreement, allowing themselves to become entangled in the intrigues and machinations of self-seeking politicians, newspaper publishers, and ambitious state officials. Worse, an election, which ordinarily would have been the only proper solution to the impasse, was seen by both principals and the public as a contest between the king and the Papandreous. Thus, a parliamentary election had been distorted into a constitutional referendum with the future of the throne at stake. Even before the evening of July 15, the king had apparently been convinced that an early election would only benefit the Papandreous and bring humiliation to the throne. To his surprise, the outgoing prime minister failed to recommend elections before leaving the palace; he probably planned to do so the following day. In any event, the king was relieved because he would have found it difficult to refuse.

Less than an hour after Papandreou's departure from the palace, King Constantine swore into office a new cabinet headed by the president of the Vouli, George Novas. Technically, this was another Center Union government; in reality, however, this new government actually reflected an attempt to split the party and, if possible, isolate the Papandreous.

Novas failed to win a majority in the Vouli and the king had to resort to other combinations. All kinds of pressures and inducements were used to convince enough CU deputies to desert the Papandreou camp. Eventually a cabinet under Stefanopoulos received the votes of forty Center Union deputies and those of the ERE and was confirmed in office. In the meantime, however, the throne had become totally entangled in a partisan conflict.

Papandreou began to press for a general election from the first day after his resignation. His "second relentless struggle" and his vehement attacks against what he called the "palace coup" found warm support from the Communist Left, which mobilized mass demonstrations and strikes in his behalf. The KKE central committee prepared a statement entitled, "With a Nationwide, All-Democratic Call to Arms, the Plans of the Palace, the Junta, and the Foreigners Can be Thwarted." It was broadcast over Voice of Truth radio from Eastern Europe and called "on all democrats, everyone who wants democratic order and normality, to mass mobilizations, meetings, and strikes—to a nationwide, all-democratic rally."

While some of the apostates of the Center Union, who shifted their support to the Stefanopoulos government, may have had questionable motives, the most prominent among them sincerely believed that in aligning themselves with the throne they were serving the country at great political cost to themselves. They wanted to restore stability and prepare the country for a parliamentary election that would have no constitutional overtones. Whatever their motives, they could not play the role of a disinterested broker. Quite simply, they were *not* neutral in the dispute, nor for that matter were they unrelated to the principals. Instead, they had become one of the major issues in the quarrel. Besides, regardless of the efforts of the apostates, an election would still be seen as a contest between the king and the Papandreous as long as the latter continued their attacks on the palace.

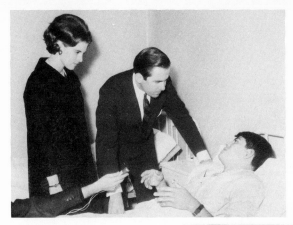

(above) The last royal couple, King Constantine and Queen Anna-Maria. Courtesy, Greek Embassy, Press Office, Washington, D.C.

Tanks in the streets of Athens, 1967. United Press International Photo

The end of parliamentary democracy

The Stefanopoulos government survived until December 1966. Although it rested on a slender margin of only four votes in the Vouli, it did take unexpectedly bold measures to check the country's movement toward a serious economic downturn. Nevertheless, it received little credit for its rather successful economic performance. Papandreou's vociferous campaign against the palace went on unabatedly. It was punctuated by numerous strikes brought on by the rising cost of living, for which, in fact, Papandreou's own policies were largely responsible. The foes identified by the Papandreous, especially by Andreas, were the same villains the EDA and the pro-Communist Left had long been attacking: the palace, the junta, the economic oligarchy, and the American CIA. Communist activists were prominent in the strikes and demonstrations, and they often provoked violent incidents with the police. A so-called popular front from below seemed to emerge behind the rhetoric of constitutional propriety and political liberty, with the pro-Communist Left taking advantage of the political disarray to promote its own drive for power. On May 25, 1966, Manolis Glezos, a Communist of long standing and one of the principal leaders of the EDA, outlined in a closed meeting of the party's executive committee the strategy to be followed in the event of a parliamentary election. He proposed that the EDA engage in the same maneuver it had used in the 1964 election when it did not enter candidates in several constituencies. This was done to improve the chances of CU candidates at the expense of the ERE. Glezos went on to say that after a victory of the Papandreou forces in another election, the EDA should then apply the following four-step plan: "Phase One: We will support the government [formed by Papandreou]; Phase Two: We will partici-pate in the government; Phase Three: We will be the government and they will be the participants; Phase Four: We alone will be the government." Although this particular plan was not made known publicly at the time, enough evidence was available to convince many quarters that an election could well open the way to the Communist Left. Andreas Papandreou, in an article in the *New York Times Magazine* of July 21, 1968, claimed that he expected the Center Union to receive 63 percent of the total vote. Obviously such a feat would have been nearly impossible without wholesale support from the EDA's followers.

Throughout 1966 public respect for the parliamentary institutions was undermined by almost daily allegations of corruption, opportunism, and cynicism in high places. Many would have agreed then that the political system was in urgent need of modernization. The most consistent and far-reaching pressure for radical systemic changes came from Andreas Papandreou and the Left. Strange as it may seem, pressure for change also came from the army. Many officers—with their professional penchant for order and efficiency—privately expressed contempt for the politicians and their petty intrigues and quarrels. Because these members of the military were also anti-Communist, they saw with genuine alarm the possibility of a Communist advance on the Papandreous' shoulders. By the end of 1966 the likelihood of a military coup was openly discussed in the cafés of Athens.

Eventually some moderate voices were raised in favor of a compromise: the Papandreous should cease their attacks on the throne, and the king should agree to an early election date. The Stefanopoulos government would have to be replaced, of course, by a nonpolitical cabinet composed of personalities acceptable to all concerned and charged specifically with the preparation of a parliamentary election. The king appeared receptive to this idea as early as August 1966, and by December, such an understanding was actually reached. A service cabinet was formed under John Paraskevopoulos, a banker, to hold an election within six months. The country appeared to enter a new period of political moderation as both George Papandreou, as the leader of the Center Union, and Panagiotis Kanellopoulos, as the leader of the ERE, endorsed the plan.

Optimism proved premature. The more extreme elements on both sides rejected the agreement, claiming either that it was a blunder or that it was an unholy compromise with the palace and the so-called economic oligarchy. Disregarding the endorsement of the compromise plan given by his father in December, Andreas continued his attacks on the throne. He was convinced that any compromise with the establishment would tarnish his image as the champion of the so-called progressive forces in the country. This, he felt, would disillusion those vocal elements that had been partly responsible for building up his image as the most controversial, and to some the most significant, political personality in Greece. While the elder Papandreou stood scrupulously by the agreement, Andreas deliberately set about removing the most essential requirement for holding an election, that is, the assurance that a Papandreou victory would not be interpreted as a repudiation of the throne. The elder Papandreou, who realized that only through an election could he transform his popularity into a mandate for reassuming the reins of power, was furious with his son.

Andreas was not the only foe of the December agreement. Many elements of the Right—in politics and, more importantly, in the army—opposed the agreement, fearing that the election it provided for would return the Papandreous to power. In their own way, these rightist elements also undermined the agreement.

Late in March 1967 the Paraskevopoulos caretaker government unwisely allowed the trial of the officers involved in the ASPIDA to take place. To make matters even worse, proceedings were started to bring to trial those civilians who were accused of masterminding the affair, with Andreas Papandreou the most prominent among them. Since Andreas was a deputy, the public prosecutor asked that his parliamentary immunity be lifted. The majority in the legislature rejected the request, but Andreas and his friends nevertheless interpreted the prosecutor's move as a ploy to eliminate him from the forthcoming electoral contest. Fearful that Andreas might be arrested once the Vouli was dissolved, at which time the immunity would not apply, the elder Papandreou introduced a proposal to extend parliamentary immunity to the period between elections. Kanellopoulos objected that the proposal was unconstitutional in that it amounted to amending the constitution by ordinary legislation. Technically he was right; politically, the objection struck a fatal blow to the December agreement.

On March 30 the Paraskevopoulos cabinet resigned. Two days later, the king invited George Papandreou to form a coalition government representing all political parties to conduct an honest and fair election. Papandreou responded by saying that the parties could hardly cooperate in the government while they were at the same time fighting out an electoral campaign. He advised that another caretaker government be formed. But with the political tempers again at a fever pitch, the king felt that a caretaker government would not have the ability to meet a serious challenge from the Left or the Papandreous. Already Andreas was threatening to have the new government of the Center Union take the oath of office in Constitution Square in a mass demonstration. To calm those who feared a Papandreou victory at the polls—and to forestall a forcible intervention from the Right and the military—the king asked Kanellopoulos to form a government and hold a parliamentary election on May 28. At this critical moment, Kanellopoulos wrote to Karamanlis in Paris and called him to return to Greece and lead the electoral campaign for the ERE. Karamanlis replied that the erosion of the political system had advanced to the point that he would either have to leave again in six months or resort to a dictatorship— and he had no intention of becoming a dictator.

The electoral campaign had hardly begun when, in the first week of April, demonstrations and riots in Athens and Salonika gave a foretaste of what was to follow. The senior commanders in the army seriously explored the question of taking over the reins of power until a more moderate political climate returned. They were thinking in terms of acting with the king's consent and even with the approval and cooperation of the Kanellopoulos cabinet. The latter had already discussed the matter and "had decided to invoke article 91 of the constitution and proclaim martial law" if the situation grew more ominous. Below the level of senior commanders, a group of lower-ranking officers were also thinking in terms of military intervention; but their objectives were far-reaching. They wanted much more than just to forestall a Papandreou victory, for they were at odds with the entire political system as practiced in Greece at the time. They opposed the rousfeti psychology, the oligarchic structure of political parties, the inefficiency and procrastination of an overbearing bureaucracy, and the petty intrigues and rivalries of the politicians. In their view all these abuses plus an assortment of other shortcomings threatened to deliver the country to the Communists. Strangely, some of their complaints were almost exact replicas of Andreas Papandreou's charges against the system. But to them, Andreas wanted to eliminate those shortcomings by turning the country over to the Communists. In contrast, they wanted to right the wrongs in what they called a "national" spirit. The political system was thus under attack from three different directions. Karamanlis considered it to be eroded beyond repair; Andreas and the Left wanted to change it along socialist lines; the officers wanted to bring about change by implementing national, anti-Communist principles.

The group of younger military officers had no title, no formal organization. Its guiding spirit was Col. George Papadopoulos, a man almost entirely unknown to the general public at the time. The group was relatively small in numbers, with its hard core not exceeding two or three dozen. However, given the psychology that was prevalent in the army during the spring of 1967, the group could easily count on the automatic support of hundreds of other officers who shared their feelings of apprehension and their desire for a more efficient and equitable political system. Without such support, which was actually generated by the disintegration of the political system, no group of officers, regardless of the ambition or the ability of its members, could have succeeded in forcibly taking over the government. But in the spring of 1967, partisan hysteria and the abandonment of seriousness and moderation had actually paved the way for such a military coup. Andreas Papandreou, in particular, with the EDA as a very energetic backer, intensified his attacks against the palace and the establishment. For the first time since the war years, a political alliance had been formed between one segment of the bourgeois democratic leadership and the partisans of the pro-Communist Left. And Andreas Papandreou was the leader. Now both sides talked openly about a military intervention. In assessing the possibility of a coup, Andreas and the Left assumed that the army was effectively controlled by the commanders at the top of the hierarchical pyramid. They also saw the army as an instrument of the palace, the establishment, and the Americans. They thought that if they could keep an eye on the king and the top military leaders they could safely anticipate the actions of the army; so they kept a close watch on those quarters.

But the blow came from an entirely unexpected direction. The Papadopoulos group that led the military coup in the early morning hours of April 21, 1967, acted completely on its own and as such surprised practically everyone. The insurgents succeeded with unbelievable ease because a large number of uninitiated officers responded to the orders, which had falsely been issued in the name of the king, in the belief that the future of the country was at stake. In retrospect, it could be said that the coup was made inevitable by the erosion of the democratic process, the breakdown of order, and above all the emerging alliance between a section of the Center and the pro-Communist Left. In spite of the fact that the military regime suspended most individual freedoms and arrested a considerable number of Leftist activists, a large majority of ordinary citizens, who were worried over the possibility of a violent conflict or a Commu-

nist takeover, welcomed the intervention of the military with a sigh
of relief.

In lieu of an epilogue . . .

Developments since the military coup of April 21, 1967,
are much too near and controversial to be treated as history. The
record is far from complete. For this reason, key events are presented
in the following pages only to carry the story to the present.

The Papadopoulos group did not represent the traditional Right.
True, most of the officers had supported Papagos and then
Karamanlis, and their rather diffuse and somewhat inarticulate
philosophy included an almost instinctive opposition to communism. But in the last few years before the coup they had become
increasingly critical of the parliamentary system as practiced in
Greece. Furthermore, they had become contemptuous of politicians,
who, in their view, played a corrupt game. They were supporters of
the throne but only to the extent that this institution served as a
safeguard of the nation. Since most of them came from poor rural
families, they showed a penchant for populist policies favoring the
lower income groups and especially the peasantry. Unlike their
senior commanders they had not been emotionally absorbed into
the establishment. Their socioeconomic views and their quest for
political modernization was not, in fact, far removed from those of
Andreas Papandreou. Primarily, the telling contrast was that their
goals were wrapped in a nationalist mantle. Characteristically, where
Andreas would have adopted the dimotiki linguistic idiom, they
adhered adamantly to a tortuous form of katharevousa.

When the Papadopoulos group came to power a host of problems
were waiting for them. Towering above all others were those
associated with the economic situation and the uncertainty over
Cyprus. The economy, in spite of some improvement, had not fully
regained its vigor after the slowdown of 1964–66. For a country that
depends heavily on foreign investments, tourism, and remittances
from shipping, emigrants, and workers employed in Europe, Greece
could ill-afford foreign opposition to the military regime. Yet, from
the outset, foreign reaction was generally negative, even hostile. At
the same time, the new rulers were fearful that public uncertainty
and lack of confidence in the government might set in motion an

inflationary spiral. They were prudent enough to enlist the services of competent economists, and by acting with moderation and restraint, they were able to preserve economic stability and set the stage for vigorous expansion. In fact, within a year the economy had improved to the point that they could raise salaries and wages and even write off the debts of farmers, which weighed heavily on agriculture.

The Cypriot problem proved more vexing. However, with a controlled press and a ban on demonstrations and expressions of public disagreement, government leaders were less handicapped by public opinion than their democratic predecessors had been. An effort in September 1967 to reach a compromise with the Turkish government along the lines of the Acheson plan failed. The Turks, who were no longer interested in a compromise, pressed for the full implementation of the Zurich agreements in a way that would have amounted to a virtual partition of the island between the two communities. Makarios was adamant against accepting any such agreement. In Cyprus tension mounted and in late October clashes broke out in several areas. Turkey again threatened to invade the island and demanded the immediate dismissal of Grivas, whom the Turks considered responsible for the incidents. Turkey also insisted on the recall of all Greek troops in excess of the 950 men allowed by the Zurich agreements. Since 1964 more than 9,000 Greek soldiers had slipped into the island and had actually been incorporated into the Greek Cypriot forces. The Turks were not unaware of their presence but they had remained silent, assuming that these forces would also act as a restraint on Makarios and prevent mistreatment of the Turk Cypriots. Now the Turkish government decided that these forces were not such a reliable shield after all. The military government in Athens recalled Grivas for "consultations." At the same time, Cyrus Vance, President Johnson's personal emissary, shuttled from Athens to Ankara to Nicosia and back in an effort to avert a war between Greece and Turkey. Most Greek forces were already poised along the Greek-Turkish frontier in Thrace. In the end, with the face-saving device of a United Nations resolution, Greece agreed to remove the 9,000 troops from Cyprus, and Turkey proceeded to dismantle her war preparations. The confrontation had ended in an obvious setback for Greece.

At this critical moment, King Constantine decided to act. From the outset, his relations with the military government had been strained. He had originally decided to go along with the regime only because he realized that under the circumstances he had no choice. Actually the king was biding his time, waiting for the opportune moment to topple the military regime from power. The events in Cyprus seemed to offer an opening; his most trusted advisers insisted that many officers had been disillusioned with the inept handling of the Cypriot crisis and the humiliating compromise that ensued. The key commanders of the forces that were assembled in Macedonia and Thrace during the Cyprus crisis were presumably ready to side with the king.

With hardly any preparation, King Constantine boarded his personal plane with his family on the morning of December 13 and flew to the northern town of Kavalla. He had chosen to start his move in Macedonia because, as he said, "most of the army was there." In so doing he had overlooked a basic lesson of Greek history, namely, whoever controls Athens is most likely to gain control over the entire country. Although the king's appearance was met with enthusiasm by the people in Kavalla, the rest of the country had no idea what Constantine was doing. Hardly anyone heard his recorded message to the people, which was being broadcast over a little-used radio station in Larisa. Early in the afternoon, the Papadopoulos group, which was in full control of the major broadcasting facilities in Athens and Salonika, began to tell the country its own version of the story. Worse, the high-ranking officers in command of the major military units in northern Greece were quickly neutralized by junior officers. The latter were in contact with Papadopoulos and had already been assigned to play precisely such a role in the event of a move by the king. Almost without a shot being fired, Constantine's amateurish effort collapsed. During the night he flew with his family to Rome and self-exile.

Gen. George Zoitakis was named regent and George Papadopoulos emerged as prime minister. Following admonitions from Washington, Papadopoulos assumed a very moderate stance toward the king. The constitutional system, he said, continued to be that of crowned democracy and the king remained as head of state, "temporarily unable to carry out his duties." A broad amnesty absolved not only those officers who had sided with the king on December 13, but also those involved in the ASPIDA affair. Andreas Papandreou, who had been arrested the night of the April coup, was released from prison. He soon left the country with his family and settled in Toronto, dividing his time between teaching and opposition activities against the Greek government.

Now that the need to oblige the palace had disappeared, Papadopoulos took steps to remove from active service those officers and civil servants whose loyalty to the regime was questionable. At the same time, the government, in keeping with a promise given a few days after the April coup, went ahead with the drafting of a new constitution. A committee of jurists was appointed in May and by the middle of December they came up with a document that was hopelessly flawed, clearly showing signs of uncertainty and confusion. The military rulers had left the committee without any instructions because they had in mind to write their own charter in due course. This they did in the months between March and August 1968.

The constitution produced by the military rulers retained the system of vasilevomeni dimokratia, although it did curtail somewhat the king's functions. This was done to minimize the chances of the throne's present and future involvement in politics. A council of the nation was set up to act as the king's formal adviser in times of political crisis. A Vouli elected by universal and secret ballot was to have all the functions and powers familiar to Western legislatures. To speed up the legislative process, the Vouli was to be divided into two sections, with the most important issues reserved for the plenary sessions. In addition to a comprehensive set of rules for the protection of human rights, the constitution provided, for the first time in Greek experience, for the protection of the citizen's economic and social rights. In the past, all Greek constitutions had failed to establish an independent organ with authority to settle disputes over the meaning of the various constitutional clauses, especially those defining the powers and functions of the throne, the cabinet, and the Vouli. This time, a constitutional court was to assume this crucial responsibility of authoritative interpretation. Most of the innovations contained in the new constitution could be traced to the proposals Karamanlis had made in 1963 and even to the suggestions of the 1948 and 1949 parliamentary committees. All in all the new constitution, which was approved in a referendum on September 29, 1968, was modern and democratic. But there was an important drawback: most of its key articles were to remain inoperative for an indefinite period of time. Since the voting had taken place under martial law, most of the former political leaders

Modern Greece

Athens today. Greek National Tourist Office

(left, above) The progress of industrialization, 1973: an oil refinery near Athens.
Courtesy, Greek Embassy, Press Office, Washington, D.C.

**(left, below) Piraeus: in 1833 a deserted inlet; today, a major Mediterranean
port.** "Union" News-Photos Agency, Athens

rejected the outcome. Yet, at that critical moment, it was still possible to have reached a compromise around the new constitution; but the king from his self-exile in Rome and the political leaders in Athens rejected such suggestions and the opportunity was passed.

In spite of a proliferation of resistance organizations in Greece and the activities of emigré groups abroad, the regime grew stronger with every passing day. Few Greeks were willing to resort to violence because the memories of civil conflict in recent years were still very vivid. Besides, as long as the majority of the officers in the army remained loyal to the Papadopoulos government, no physical force existed that was capable of bringing about a change in the regime. The opposition was fragmented, disorganized, and irreconcilably divided by internal quarrels, conflicting ambitions, and contrasting ideologies.

The government scored its greatest successes in the economic sector. Stability and favorable terms attracted foreign investors. Internal and foreign borrowing financed an extensive public works program, which carried a long step forward the development initiated by Karamanlis. Tourism surpassed the most optimistic projections of earlier years, and the enchanting countryside was dotted with numerous new hotels and other facilities. Many large and medium-sized plants were added to those industrial units established in the previous years. Most important, this expansion was accomplished without inflation. The drachma remained one of the most stable currencies in the world. Aware that the products of Greek industry could not easily compete in the international marketplace with those of advanced industrial nations, the government encouraged the production of commodities that could be sold domestically, thus reducing the need for importing similar items. Emigration to Western Europe, which had started in the late fifties and had reached a level of a quarter of a million workers, was gradually slowed down as more opportunities for industrial employment opened up in Greece. The benefits of a rising national income were rather fairly distributed and this played a decisive role in making the regime more tolerable in spite of its restrictive features. Within five years the per capita income in constant prices had gone up by more than 40 percent.

With increasing industrialization, the social changes that had already started in the late fifties went forward. New employment opportunities in industry, commerce, tourism, and services reduced the reliance of university and high-school graduates on government jobs; women entered the labor market in clerical and professional occupations at a rising rate, thus gaining greater freedom from family restraints; consumer tastes became more sophisticated and more demanding. Even in agriculture significant changes could be seen. Mechanization, irrigation, and electric power enabled farmers to shift to more profitable crops, such as fruits and vegetables, which could be exported to the markets of Europe thanks to the modern facilities of refrigeration.

The government's economic record was not matched by equal achievements in other sectors. Education remained in a state of confusion, vacillating between an excessive attachment to classical and religious matters and the realization that an industrial society calls for a more practical and secular form of instruction. The linguistic problem between katharevousa and demotiki remained as acute as ever, with students still going through the schizophrenic experience of learning the vernacular in primary school and then the pure linguistic form in high school. The obvious and simple solution of adopting the spoken idiom, which is well-developed and universally used, has been ignored or resisted by those who chart the course of education. On the positive side, an extensive network of vocational schools was established and now provides training for several thousand youngsters of both sexes. In other areas the record is equally mixed. The government introduced an extensive and long overdue program of decentralizing the administrative apparatus, which should free citizens from the need to trot to Athens for the most trifling matters. But even this unquestionable blessing has been marred by the reluctance of civil servants to show initiative or take responsibility for fear of incurring the displeasure of the regime.

The government relaxed gradually the restrictions imposed at the time of the April coup. All those arrested at the time were released from detention camps, the press was allowed some freedom of expression, and, with the exception of those personally involved in antigovernment activities, the ordinary citizen did not feel in his daily life that the country was actually under a dictatorial regime. Nonetheless, the government was subjected to many pressures from abroad—the American government had suspended some forms of military aid, the European Economic Community had slowed down the process of Greece's admission to full membership status, and the Council of Europe had forced Greece to withdraw in December

1969 under charges of police oppression and torture of prisoners. In the end the government managed to weather those pressures.

In the years after the approval of the 1968 constitution, the Papadopoulos government repeatedly declared its intention to move toward its full and genuine implementation. But the king's refusal to compromise with the regime, and the growing antimonarchical sentiments among younger officers as well as some of the key members of the ruling group made implementation difficult. A prime reason for the difficulty was that under the constitution the king had to return to his throne before or shortly after the first parliamentary election. By the end of 1972 Papadopoulos had shifted in favor of a drastic change—the abolition of the monarchy. Turning Greece into a republic was not an initial intention of the Papadopoulos group. The change of heart came only gradually, after several attempts to reach a compromise with Constantine failed. In mid-May 1973 a poorly prepared attempt by royalist officers in the navy to seize the fleet, blockade Piraeus, and force the government to resign—a rather naive plan under the circumstances—gave Papadopoulos the pretext to make his move. The would-be mutineers were accused of having acted in the name and with the knowledge of Constantine.

On June 1 Prime Minister Papadopoulos made a surprise announcement. The monarchy, he said, had been abolished by decree, and Greece had become a "presidential parliamentary republic." With this, several key clauses of the 1968 constitution became irrelevant. The new arrangements provided for a president and a vice-president elected for a seven-year term; a premier, who must have majority support in the legislature to stay in office; and an elected Vouli of no more than two hundred deputies with a five-year term. The new arrangements were approved by 76 percent referendum on July 29. The voters had a choice between approval and rejection; however, a negative vote, according to the government, would not restore the monarchy. In the referendum the voters also approved the elevation of Papadopoulos to the post of president, with Gen. Odysseus Angelis as vice-president. A new government under Spyros Markezinis, the noted historian and leader of the small Progressive party, was formed to hold elections in 1974. In the process, Papadopoulos pushed aside most of his colleagues who had been his "constituency" for more than six years; but his fatal mistake was not seeking to replace them with another "constituency." Since his objective was to move the country to a democratic form of government, support could have come primarily from those who had a genuine stake in the process, the professional politicians. Papadopoulos and Markezinis should have approached them with clear and unassailable guarantees that their efforts to democratize the country were sincere. Instead, they merely managed to alienate the politicians and foment their suspicions by keeping intact the extraordinary powers vested in the president under the hastily drafted constitutional act in June and by not opening an effective dialogue leading to a joint decision over the detailed steps to be taken in the process of democratization.

In November 1973, elements of the extreme Left—which viewed democratization as a clever ploy by Papadopoulos to perpetuate his own rule—and the hard-liners in the army—who watched the liberalization of the dictatorship with apprehension and who no longer had any love for Papadopoulos—moved from both sides to end the experiment. Student protests escalated into serious clashes in the center of Athens in mid-November. Papadopoulos summoned tanks to restore order, and martial law, which had been lifted in October, was imposed again. A week later, on November 25, forces commanded by military policy chief Brig. Dimitrios Ioannidis deposed Papadopoulos in a bloodless coup. Gen. Faedon Gizikis, a moderate officer, was placed in the post of president of the Republic. Adamantios Androutsopoulos, for more than five years a minister in the Papadopoulos government, took over as premier. For the second time in less than seven years the armed forces were being tied to a dictatorial regime. Many were now turning toward Karamanlis, still in Paris, the only man with the prestige and popular acceptance needed to pull the country without violence out of the quagmire of military rule. . . .

A Note on Biographical Resources

In preparing this volume I drew on numerous published sources as well as on my own familiarity with the country. I also benefited greatly from close ties with major public figures in Greece and access to papers and other materials that are not yet available to the general public. While most of the works cited in this note are in English, I had to rely extensively on important sources in Greek; several of these are mentioned here for the perusal of those who are able to read Greek. In addition to works in this essay, I consulted newspaper files, personal archives, and official documents published by the Greek government, the British government, the U.S. Department of State, the United Nations, and other authorities. Details on more recent events, made public here for the first time, are based on information and unpublished documents given the author by the protagonists.

To guide readers interested in specific periods of modern Greek history or certain aspects of Greek society and life, I have grouped the most useful sources accordingly.

For more detailed information on the Greek War of Independence, see N. Botzaris, *Visions balkaniques dans la révolution grecque, 1784–1821* (Paris, 1962); C. W. Crawley, *The Question of Greek Independence* (Cambridge, 1930); Douglas Dakin, *British Intelligence of Events in Greece, 1824–1827* (Athens, 1959); A. V. Daskalakis, *I Enarxis tis Ellinikis Epanastaseos tou 1821* (Athens, 1962); George Finlay, *History of Greece* (London, 1877); D. Makriyannis, *Memoirs*, translated and edited by H. A. Lidderdale (London, 1966); Lewis Sergeant, *Greece in the Nineteenth Century* (London, 1897); H. Temperley, *The Foreign Policy of Canning, 1822–1827* (London, 1925); G. Tertsetis, *Apomnimonevmata Agoniston tou 1821* (Athens, 1970 reissue); and C. M. Woodhouse, *The Greek War of Independence* (London, 1952).

For information on the period from 1830 to the end of the nineteenth century, see Edmond About, *La Grèce contemporaine* (Paris, 1860); D. Dontas, *Greece and the Great Powers, 1863–1875* (Thessaloniki, 1966); G. Finlay, *History of Greece* (London, 1877); Barbara Jelavich, *Russia and the Greek Revolution of 1843* (Munich, 1966); H. Korizis, *Die Politischen Parteien Griechenlands* (Nürnberg, 1966); J. Mavrogordato, *Modern Greece, 1800–1931* (London, 1931); John A. Petropoulos, *Politics and Statecraft in the Kingdom of Greece, 1833–1843* (Princeton, 1968); D. Pournaras, *Kharilaos Trikoupis*, 2 vols. (Athens, 1950); E. Prevelakis, *British Policy towards the Change of Dynasty in Greece* (Athens, 1953); and Lewis Sergeant, *Greece in the Nineteenth Century* (London, 1897).

For the early part of the twentieth century until the 1922 disaster in Asia Minor, the following are recommended: M. S. Anderson, *The Eastern Question* (London, 1966); D. Dakin, *The Greek Struggle in Macedonia, 1897–1913* (Thessaloniki, 1966); Foivos Grigoriadis, *Dihasmos—Mikra Asia* (Athens, 1971); E. C. Helmreich, *The Diplomacy of the Balkan Wars, 1912–13* (Cambridge, Mass., 1938); Spyros Melas, *I Epanastasi tou 1909* (Athens, 1957); A. A. Pallis, *Greece's Anatolian Venture and After* (London, 1937); Alan Palmer, *The Gardeners of Salonika: The Macedonian Cam-*

paign, 1915–1918 (London, 1965); G. Ventiris, *I Ellas tou 1910–1920*, 2 vols., 2nd ed. (Athens, 1970).

These works are useful for the period between 1922 till the outbreak of World War II: G. Dafnis, *I Ellas Metaxy thyo Polemon*, 2 vols. (Athens, 1955); Foivos Grigoriadis, *Elliniki Dimokratia* (Athens, 1971); Stelio Hourmouzios, *No Ordinary Crown* (London, 1972); D. G. Kousoulas, *Revolution and Defeat: The Story of the Greek Communist Party, 1918–1949* (London, 1965); A. A. Pallis, *Greece's Anatolian Venture and After* (London, 1937); D. Pentzopoulos, *The Balkan Exchange of Minorities and Its Impact on Greece* (Paris, 1962); C. M. Woodhouse, *The Story of Modern Greece* (London, 1968).

The best books about the war years and the Communist guerrilla campaign of 1946–49 are Elizabeth Barker, *Macedonia—Its Place in Balkan Power Politics* (London, 1950); Richard Capell, *Simiomata: A Greek Note Book, 1944–1945* (London, 1945); M. Cervi, *Storia della Guerra di Grecia* (Milano, 1965); T. A. Couloumbis, *Greek Political Reaction to America and NATO* (New Haven, 1966); John O. Iatrides, *Revolt in Athens: The Greek Communist "Second Round," 1944–1945* (Princeton, 1972); D. G. Kousoulas, *The Price of Freedom: Greece in World Affairs, 1939–1953* (Syracuse, 1953) and *Revolution and Defeat: The Story of the Greek Communist Party* (London, 1965); Sir Reginald Leeper, *When Greek Meets Greek* (London, 1950); W. H. McNeill, *The Greek Dilemma: War and Aftermath* (New York, 1947); E. C. W. Myers, *Greek Entanglement* (London, 1950); E. O'Ballance, *The Greek Civil War, 1944–1949* (London, 1966); George Papandreou, *I Apeleftherosis tis Ellados* (Athens, 1948); P. Philon, *The Question of Northern Epirus* (Washington, D.C., 1945); P. N. Pipinelis, *Europe and the Albanian Question* (Chicago, 1963); K. Pyromaglou, *I Ethniki Antistasis* (Athens, 1947); L. S. Stavrianos, *Greece: American Dilemma and Opportunity* (Chicago, 1952); E. Tsouderos, *Ellinikes Anomalies sti Mesi Anatoli* (Athens, 1945) and *Diplomatika Paraskinia, 1941–1944* (Athens, 1950); S. Xydis, *Greece and the Great Powers, 1944–47* (Thessaloniki, 1963); G. B. Zotiades, *The Macedonian Controversy* (Thessaloniki, 1954).

The postwar years are studied in Maurice Genevoix, *La Grèce de Caramanlis* (Paris, 1972), now also available in English; David Holden, *Greece without Columns* (Philadelphia, 1972); Stelio Hourmouzios, *No Ordinary Crown* (London, 1972); Keith Legg, *Politics in Modern Greece* (Stanford, 1969); Andreas Papandreou, *Democracy at Gunpoint: The Greek Front* (New York, 1970); Robert Stephens, *Cyprus: A Place of Arms* (London, 1966); Kenneth Young, *The Greek Passion* (London, 1968).

Students interested in works dealing with social, economic, and cultural matters may find the following titles useful: G. F. Breal and Ralph Turvey, *Studies in Greek Taxation* (Athens, 1964); J. K. Campbell, *Honour, Family and Patronage* (Oxford, 1964); J. K. Campbell and P. Sherrard, *Modern Greece* (New York, 1968); H. Ellis, *Industrial Capital in Greek Development* (Athens, 1964); David Holden, *Greece Without Columns* (Philadelphia, 1972); Bernard Kayser, *Social and Economic Atlas of Greece* (Athens, 1964); Edmund Keeley and P. Sherrard, *Six Poets of Modern Greece* (London, 1960); Keith Legg, *Politics in Modern Greece* (Stanford, 1969); George Seferis, *On the Greek Style* (London, 1967); C. Trypanis, *Medieval and Modern Greek Poetry* (Oxford, 1951); Timothy Ware, *The Orthodox Church* (Harmondsworth, 1963); Benjamin Ward, *Greek Regional Development* (Athens, 1963).

INDEX